D1481751

WITHDRAWN

*Mexicano* Resistance in the Southwest

# MEXICANO RESISTANCE IN THE SOUTHWEST

## "The Sacred Right of Self-Preservation"

BY ROBERT J. ROSENBAUM

UNIVERSITY OF TEXAS PRESS   AUSTIN AND LONDON

Requests for permission to reproduce material from
this work should be sent to Permissions, University
of Texas Press, Box 7819, Austin, Texas 78712.

Library of Congress Cataloging in Publication Data

Rosenbaum, Robert J   1943–
    *Mexicano* Resistance in the Southwest.
    (The Dan Danciger Publication series)

    Based on the author's thesis, University of Texas
at Austin.
    Bibliography: p.
    Includes index.
    1. Mexican Americans—Southwest, New—His-
tory.   2. Southwest, New—History—1848–
3. Southwest, New—Social conditions.   I. Title.
F790.M5R67     979'.0046872     80-18964
ISBN 0-292-77562-8

For Jim and Laura Louise

*To defend ourselves, and making use of the sacred right of self-preservation, we have assembled in a popular meeting with a view of discussing a means to put an end to our misfortunes.*

*Our personal enemies shall not possess our lands until they have fattened [them] with their own gore.*

Juan Nepomuceno Cortina
Rancho del Carmen
County of Cameron
September 30, 1859

# Contents

# MAPS

# ILLUSTRATIONS

# Preface

I began this study more than a decade ago as a dissertation in history at the University of Texas at Austin. My project involved an analysis of New Mexico politics during the territorial years that included the perspectives of all of the cultural groups active in the political arena. Early in my research, however, I came upon Las Gorras Blancas—the White Caps—of San Miguel County, an organization of poor *mexicanos* that did things conventional Anglo wisdom did not allow *los pobres* to do. In the first place, *los pobres* organized; in the second place, they attacked *americanos* and rich *mexicanos* who acted like Anglos.

The discovery of Las Gorras Blancas refocused my dissertation from an analysis of politics in a multicultural setting to an examination of *mexicano* resistance to *americano* encroachment in New Mexico Territory. This book represents a geographic, temporal, and conceptual expansion on the dissertation. I have included some discussion of resistance in Texas and California; I have added some thoughts about the impact of nineteenth-century activities on twentieth-century developments; and I have attempted to place my observations about *mexicano* resistance in the general contexts of popular rebellions on the one hand and pluralistic societies on the other.

## A Note on Method and Sources

The writing of a history that purports to emphasize what the author takes to be *mexicano* perspectives is a complicated undertaking. For one thing, *mexicanos* left few written records; for another, the chasms of time and cultural heritage separate the historian and the subjects. My attempt to write a bottom-up history about people of a cultural heritage other than my own involved examining a wide range of materials—contemporary accounts, government reports, statistical data, anthropological studies, folklore and oral history—and weighing the results in terms of theoretical approaches adapted from the social sciences.

Most traditional sources—letters, newspapers, testimony, memoirs, and scholarly literature—were generated by Anglos. These sources are valuable for finding out what happened from the Anglo point of view, of course, and they also reflect, with varying degrees of detail and accuracy, what went on in *mexicano* communities. The correspondence of Thomas Benton Catron, for example, who attended to New Mexico politics with the same attention to minutiae that Lord Newcastle applied to English politics of the mid-eighteenth century, reveals a great deal about the way that *políticos* worked on the county and precinct level. Land grant documents and testimony about land grants afford other glimpses of *mexicano* activities and perspectives, while newspapers like *La Voz del Pueblo* provide insights into the educated segments of *mexicano* communities.

Statistical data offer quantitative indications for a social framework in which to place impressions garnered from narrative sources. U.S. censuses, irregular enumerations like the Maxwell Land Grant Settlers Book, county assessment rolls, precinct-by-precinct election returns, and records of contracts with U.S. agencies allow demographic, economic, and political relationships between *americano* and *mexicano* to be outlined and compared.

The literature that addresses culture, peasants, and political violence suggests the means by which the evidence can be assessed. The footnotes make obvious my debts to Clifford Geertz, Eric Hobsbawm, and Eric Wolf in this regard. Anthropological and sociological studies of specific Hispanic communities also proved helpful, although a word of caution is appropriate. Studies like Margaret Mead's "The Spanish-Americans in New Mexico, U.S.A." in her *Cultural Patterns and Technical Change* are usually synchronic and deal with general cultural patterns. The historian concerned with specific events must treat such generalizations carefully. Authority in *mexicano* communities, for example, is presented as the pattern of obedience to the father in the family writ large. If this were literally true, Las Gorras Blancas would not have revolted.

In the absence of written records, the historian must turn to folklore and interviews in order to get a sense of the way *mexicanos* remember and interpret the past. The notes make quite evident my admiration for the works of Américo Paredes. I did not go into the field to interview until I had done extensive traditional research. I then collected stories about the events in question from individuals who remembered them or who knew the oral tradition about them, and who were willing to talk to me. I treated this information as critically as I treated information from any other source. On the whole, I found oral history extremely valuable: in many cases oral tradition directly confirmed my inferences, and in several instances informants contributed additional detail that enhanced my picture of *mexicano* resistance.

## A Note on Accent Marks and Names for Ethnic Groups

The use of accents in Spanish varies from writer to writer and with the formality of the medium. In addition, conventions change over time: for example, it was common in the nineteenth century to accent Santa Fé, whereas now the accent is generally omitted. This disparity prompted me to adopt the following guidelines for my use of accents. First, I reproduced quoted material as it appeared in the original; second, I followed current practice regarding the names of individuals except when those names appear in quoted passages; and third, I followed current usage for Spanish words and phrases except when a word struck me as sufficiently familiar to English speakers as to make the accent mark seem affected—thus, *rio* and *cañon*, not *río* and *cañón*.

No terms for the ethnic or cultural groups from either English or Spanish traditions enjoy universal acceptance. In general, I have tried to use the names employed in Spanish-language nineteenth-century U.S. sources. The most common were *mexicano* and *americano; nuevo mexicano, neo-mexicano, tejano, californio, norteamericano* (meaning Anglo), and *extranjero* (meaning stranger or foreigner) appear as well. For variety, I used Anglo and Hispano, and Anglo American and Mexican American (the latter referring to individuals of Mexican descent now living within the borders of the United States). I have avoided using Chicano, *la raza*, Latin American, or Spanish American except when used by people to name themselves or when the term is merely descriptive—referring to migrants from South American countries to the California gold fields as Latin Americans, for example—because twentieth-century usage of these terms implies political stances that are not applicable to the nineteenth century.

## Acknowledgments

In the course of my work, I have imposed upon the good will of a number of individuals and the good auspices of several institutions.

Dr. Myra Ellen Jenkins, State Historian of New Mexico, and her staff at the New Mexico State Archives and Records Center in Santa Fe, went well beyond the call of duty on my behalf. The staffs of the National Archives, the Coronado Room of the Zimmerman Library at the University of New Mexico, and the Barker History Center at the University of Texas provided welcome assistance and valuable suggestions.

Ricardo Griego and Tobías Durán of the University of New Mexico, Willie Sánchez and Cristóbal Trujillo of New Mexico Highlands University, and Tony Márquez and Dwight Durán of Las Vegas, New Mexico, took time from their busy schedules to help me obtain interviews from the people on the land grants who remembered the outbreaks. And without Don Miguel Gonzales of La Loma on the Antonchico Grant, who served as guide, interpreter, and host, the interviews would not have taken place.

I cannot pretend to thank everyone upon whom I inflicted portions of this manuscript, but prominent among those whose patience and good humor I tried to the limit are Robert W. Larson of the University of Northern Colorado, G. L. Seligmann, Jr., of North Texas State University, and Joseph Hawes of Kansas State University. Lawrence C. Goodwyn of Duke University first inspired me to use oral history. And special thanks go to two members of my dissertation committee, Richard Bauman of the Anthropology Department and John E. Sunder of the History Department at the University of Texas at Austin. They little imagined, when they consented to have me as a student, that they were taking on a task of some ten years' duration, but neither failed to respond to my cries for help with good grace and rigorous criticism.

I have yet to solve the mysteries of spelling, grammar, syntax, and typing. Barbara Brenizer transformed this work from a jumble of tablet paper to a polished typescript, never complaining when I missed my deadlines but, somehow, always meeting hers. My wife, Elizabeth Harris, took time from her professional obligations to help turn my convoluted verbiage into something approaching readable prose.

The people mentioned above, and many others, helped me avoid the most obvious pitfalls of writing history. Any failings in this work are mine.

*Mexicano* Resistance in the Southwest

# CHAPTER 1

# Conquered Citizens

It rained on August 18, 1846, and the road into Santa Fe was muddy. Stephen Watts Kearny led the Army of the West along the slippery road to the capital of the Department of New Mexico. When he reached the central plaza, Kearny greeted Lieutenant-Governor Juan Bautista Vigil y Alarid and raised the flag of the United States above the Palace of the Governors. In the words of Second Lieutenant George Rutledge Gibson, they entered Santa Fe "without facing the least resistance in any way . . ."[1] The mud had posed the biggest obstacle to the conquest of Mexico's oldest northern province. U.S. troops had not fired a shot.[2]

Kearny remained in Santa Fe until the end of September, sending patrols to neighboring villages and developing the framework for an interim government under the United States. He reported to Washington that New Mexican residents were contented with the change in government, appointed Charles Bent interim governor, and divided his command. Leaving most of the Army of the West behind to hold the department, subdue the Navajo, and, ultimately, march south toward Chihuahua, Kearny led some four hundred dragoons toward California. He entered Los Angeles on January 10, 1847, and brought to an end the official combat begun by the Bear Flag Rebellion and continued by the occupation of the seaports under Commodore John D. Sloat and later under Commodore Robert F. Stockton.[3]

U.S. victories in New Mexico and California concluded a military process begun eleven years earlier with the Battle of San Antonio. Anglo Americans held Mexico's far northern frontier by virtue of force. The campaign against Mexico City and the subsequent Treaty of Guadalupe Hidalgo sealed the conquest and extended United States sovereignty from the Sabine to the Pacific.

Speed dominates Anglo Americans' perception of their victory.

On one level, chronology supports this view. Kearny entered New Mexico in mid-August and departed for California in less than six weeks. John Charles Frémont began overt hostilities in March, 1846, and Kearny's occupation of Los Angeles the following January finished the military dimension of the conquest of California.[4] The first engagement of the Texas Revolution, the Battle of San Antonio, had occurred on December 5, 1835, and the Battle of San Jacinto in April, 1836, had secured Anglo control.[5] Zachary Taylor provoked the Rio Grande skirmish on April 25, 1846, that justified the U.S. declaration of war;[6] the fall of Mexico City less than eighteen months later, on September 14, 1847, brought combat to an end.

The above chronologies, however, are selective; they mark the time span of official or quasi-official hostilities, not the extent of violence between *mexicano* and *americano*. The official chronology of Texas, for example, gives no indication of the eleven years of guerrilla warfare after San Jacinto, of attack and counterattack along the disputed Texas-Mexico border. Confining attention to the six weeks of Kearny's "bloodless" conquest omits the Taos Revolt in January, 1847, which claimed the life of Governor Bent, and the uprisings in Mora, Santa Cruz, Las Vegas, and El Brazito that followed. Stressing the rapidity of official combat mutes the half-century of blandishments and intrigue that prepared the way for U.S. troops. Finally, the emphasis on U.S. military action leaves the internal political turmoil, which consumed most of Mexico's energies and resources, out of the picture of the "speedy" conquest.

Speed dominates the Anglo Americans' perception because it justifies the war and, by extension, U.S. expansion. The brevity of the war kept questions about the morality of the conflict to a minimum at the time, and such questions have hardly been burning issues since. Speed also allowed Anglo Americans to avoid looking too closely at what the conquest meant for the conquered, what acquisition meant for the acquired. Rapid victory implies little or no resistance. A belief in little or no resistance leads to several comfortable attitudes toward the defeated. The victors can assume that the conquered really wanted to be conquered. The victors can use their win as evidence that the losers are a benighted, backward people who will benefit by the change in the long run—a kind of parental "this hurts me more than it hurts you" rationalization. A third attitude takes the speed of conquest as proof that the defeated are a cowardly and inferior branch of humankind, patently unfit for self-determination and prosperity in God's chosen land. Anglos expressed all three, often simultaneously, to justify and explain U.S. expansion into the Southwest.

Anglo American beliefs to the contrary notwithstanding, Mexican Americans did resist, did try to protect themselves against the realities of United States rule, and they are still resisting. Included into the nation as an adjunct, almost an afterthought, of territorial expansion, Mexican Americans had to respond to an alien presence self-consciously hell-bent after Progress. Like the other ethnic groups that make up the pluralistic national society, Mexican Americans had to cope with life in the United States during the phenomenal growth of the nineteenth century. But the Mexican American way of coping derived from their unique position among the groups that add up to the whole of United States population.

## Mexican Americans

The Treaty of Guadalupe Hidalgo provided international legitimacy to the fact of the U.S. conquest. The treaty established two basic things for *mexicano* residents: first, it created nearly all of the present boundary between Mexico and the United States; second, it stipulated that all former citizens of Mexico who so chose could become U.S. citizens and that all property rights valid under Mexico would be honored by the new government. The treaty gave the U.S. a vast area of land, but placed encumbering restrictions upon a significant portion of it; and the treaty transformed enemies to compatriots. Both facts proved to be continual sources of confusion and friction.[7]

The population of the United States includes a myriad of ethnic affiliations and cultural traditions. In general terms, however, all but three groups can be called voluntary citizens or residents. The three exceptions—Afro Americans, Native Americans, and Mexican Americans—are involuntary Americans because their inclusion in the country resulted from Anglo American aggression.[8] Native Americans and Mexican Americans share the additional distinction of being territorial minorities. They came with the land. And of the three, only Mexican Americans received citizenship at the time of their inclusion.

Anglo Americans took an ambivalent view toward the territorially acquired citizens, particularly since they came through war. Some other *mexicano* characteristics compounded Anglo American ambivalence toward their new compatriots. Unlike either of the other involuntary minorities, Mexican Americans came from a European-derived tradition. Yet the marked infusion of Indian culture and genes pointed to a kind of difference and inferiority similar to that in the Anglo perception of Afro Americans and Native Americans. *Mexicanos* used a written European language, practiced a Christian religion, employed "civilized" political and legal systems, and engaged in recognizable economic enterprises. But the forms of these familiar social traits were a far cry from their shape in Anglo America. The language was Spanish, not English. The religion was Roman Catholic, not Protestant. The political system was hierarchical, oligarchical, and traditional, not democratic, representational, and ideological. Economic practices were preindustrial, monopolistic, elite, and mercantile, if not downright feudal; not individual, capitalistic, and competitive, in theory at least.

Indians who came with the land formed one category in the American scheme of things; Europeans made up another. *Mexicanos* combined elements from both, thereby embodying a contradiction that confused the issue of citizenship in Anglo minds. The presence of Mexico immediately to the south complicated matters. The Treaty of Guadalupe Hidalgo provided citizenship for the residents of the conquered land *at the time*; the treaty made no provision for later migrants. And migration to the former Mexican provinces and farther north continues unabated. The *mexicano* population grew over time and included people who shared language, religion, customs, physical appearance, and who were often actual blood relatives, but who were divided by the technicality of citizenship. Identification of citizen from alien was a difficult process and one which Anglo Americans were in no hurry to sort out—the alien dimension afforded a convenient justification for discrimination against all.

If Anglos found it convenient to label all *mexicanos* Mexican aliens, the majority of *mexicanos* showed little inclination to embrace the new regime. The new border took longer for the residents to recognize in practice than it took to establish in international law. This was especially true in the Lower Rio Grande Valley of Texas from Brownsville to the two Laredos, where the river that marked the international boundary had been the unifying artery for the community for a century. With the exception of some few *políticos* among the provincial elites, *mexicanos* did not identify with abstractions like colony or nation. Most *mexicanos* extended their traditional lack of concern to the new authority.

If anything, *mexicanos* held on to an identification with Mexico. Their lack of concern about questions of national sovereignty joined with their memory of historic unity with the peoples to the south. Migration reinforced the memory, and the obvious differences between the *americanos* and themselves honed it into a sense of community captured by the name *la raza*, the race. Modern Chicano militants who call for a nation of Aztlán located in northern Mexico and the southwestern United States are reminders that the tradition of unity—of the artificiality of the border—is far from dead.

Mexicanos are a conquered people who had the misfortune to be severed from their larger community; their situation is analogous to that of the Italian population in the Austrian Tyrol. The amputation caused relatively little pain at the moment of incision, but the surgery was not, and is not, complete. As the nineteenth century wore on, the conquerors made their presence increasingly felt and their domination ever more apparent. The central question of this study is, then: How did mexicanos respond to the increasing pressures brought by Anglo American domination?

## Culture and Conflict

The history of mexicano-americano coexistence in the southwestern United States is a history of the confrontation between cultures. What Anglo Americans did, or tried to do, and the ways that mexicanos responded, or tried to respond, came from the assumptions about what was possible and desirable that each group brought to the situation. Their experiences over the course of the nineteenth century modified what each group thought was possible and desirable, but experience did not lessen conflict; in fact, tensions mounted through the nineteenth century and into the twentieth.

There are probably as many definitions of culture as there are practicing social scientists. For the purposes of this study, culture refers to the ways that people of the same culture make sense of their situation, predict what is likely to happen, and, therefore, act in the world. Social life is the base, or source, of culture, and culture consists of the common meanings that members of a particular group attach to the various facets of life that they must, in some fashion, address together. In this way, culture may be thought of as analogous to, but not identical with, language. As anthropologist Clifford Geertz says, "Culture consists of the socially established structures of meanings in terms of which people do such things as signal conspiracies and join them or perceive insults and answer them." [9]

It comes as no surprise to anyone aware of the civil rights ferment during the 1960s that the articles in the Treaty of Guadalupe Hidalgo providing for full citizenship and property rights did not result in economic opportunity or social integration for mexicanos. Socially established structures of meaning about different peoples are not changed by the stroke of a pen. Conflict in one way or another marked the two groups' interaction, and cultural differences provided the contexts for their persistent conflicts.

Mexicano culture differed from americano culture in three major, but interrelated, ways. The two peoples differed in their views about the size of the communities to which they belonged, in their perceptions of the boundaries of the world in which it was possible and desirable to act. Put another way, the two differed in the degree to which nationalism provided a socially established structure of meaning. *Mexicanos* and *americanos* differed in the range of options and kind of assumptions they brought to dealing with material resources; that is, they differed in the degree of economic complexity they thought to be possible or desirable. And *mexicanos* differed from *americanos* in the specific social traits—language, religion, and the obvious physical characteristics like skin color that are called race—that each group used to identify its members and, consequently, to identify outsiders. In other words, *mexicanos* and *americanos* were self-determined ethnic groups.

Nationalism and economic complexity are often thought of as developmental categories. Historically, the rise of modern nations and the emergence of complex industrial societies occurred through processes of growth that were roughly parallel and mutually supportive although by no means exactly concurrent. Ethnicity can be called permanent because ethnic affiliation and hostility between ethnic groups bear no necessary correlation to political or economic development; the evidence suggests that ethnic distinctions are persistently maintained throughout changing circumstances and that, if anything, they are strengthened by frequent interaction between groups.

A cautionary word about the above categories, however, is appropriate. Human beings do not live their lives by referring to an orderly cultural storeroom and choosing the correct meaning for the situation at hand; frequently a particular action or trait cuts across a number of neat analytical categories. In life, the socially established structures of meaning form, if not a seamless fabric, at least a tangled web. The above classifications serve only as useful ways to approach the differences between *americano* and *mexicano* cultures that affected the history of conflict between the two peoples.

### *Nationalism*

Compared to *mexicano* residents in the conquered territory, *americanos* had a highly developed sense of nationalism.

The long history of resistance to the Crown by the individual English colonies that culminated in the joint action of the revolutionary era and, ultimately, in independence, provided the base for nationalistic sentiment. The ratification of the Constitution further heightened public awareness of and commitment to the new nation.

By the mid-nineteenth century, the War of Independence and the formation of the new republic had been raised to the level of myth, a myth that stressed democratic ideology with its emphasis on egalitarian participation, representative institutions, and the due process of law, along with the heroic stories of the Patriots and Founding Fathers.[10]

An equally long tradition of expansion, of believing that it was possible and desirable for Anglo American settlement to move into the western lands, joined with the myth to produce the mid-century push to the Pacific—of which the Mexican War was a part—that is called the era of Manifest Destiny.[11] And the communities built by westering Anglo Americans underscore the strength of nationalism: they mirrored, with minor exceptions, the forms of the eastern societies, and their founders expressed a universal desire for them to be admitted as states, as equal partners into the nation.

By the second quarter of the nineteenth century, the United States exhibited the characteristics of a modern nation. It was a rational bureaucracy governed by the rule of law and a depersonalized political system made legitimate by an ideology. Myth and mobility combined to make Anglo Americans loyal to the United States; the nation received an allegiance that transcended internal factions and unified against external powers. Mobility eroded regional attachments, while the myth provided the means for national identification to take their place.[12]

Mexicanos did not have a strong sense of nationalism, and this was especially true for the northern provinces. In the first place, Mexico did not become an independent nation until 1820, just at the time that americanos began making significant inroads into Texas, New Mexico, and California. Second, a century of internal turmoil and civil war followed Mexican independence so that there was neither a consistent government nor a consistent ideology that could command an overriding loyalty. And third, throughout their existence the northern provinces had served as isolated frontiers guarding the border for the benefit of the interior. As frontier outposts, the northern provinces were separated from the central government and from each other; in addition, they often found their self-interest—particularly in the realm of commerce—at odds with governmental policies. The highly stratified society, in which a few powerful families dealt with matters of government, law, and trade while the majority attended to the business of survival, further mitigated against nationalistic sentiment.

In the absence of nationalism, mexicano attachments formed around region, race, religion, language, and custom. Anthropologists give the name *primordial* to these kinds of bases for community spirit and point out that they are often more powerful unifying sentiments than loyalty to an abstract nation.[13] *Mexicanos* certainly formed strong unions around these factors, with a crucial difference of scale compared to the *americano* sense of community.

After family relationships, regional affiliations provided the first and strongest lines of association among *mexicanos*. Regional affiliations started with the village and moved out to the land grant, the province, and, in the face of increasing Anglo pressure, to the general area of northern Mexico now bisected by the international border, like the concentric circles made by a stone tossed into water. And, like the circles on the water's surface, the affiliations grew progressively weaker the farther they moved away from the center. The history of violent resistance demonstrates that *mexicano* unity was strong enough to support extreme measures for correcting, or trying to correct, their situation, but the unity rarely extended beyond the immediate locality. The myriad of intersecting concentric circles of regional affiliation never produced a union equal in scale to that formed by *americano* nationalism.

As Anglo pressure increased during the nineteenth and into the twentieth century, race, religion, language, and custom rose in importance as foci for social alliances. Race offered a quick device for distinguishing friend from foe, a device that was strengthened as experiences of Anglo discrimination became more numerous and widespread. Similarly, religion forged social bonds as Protestants railed against papist "superstitions" and "priest-dominated" schools; the growth of the lay brotherhood of Penitentes in New Mexico during the latter half of the nineteenth century is perhaps the most dramatic example of religion-based solidarity.[14] In a like manner, the Spanish language was a source of pride and group identification, and one that has persisted in the face of constant Anglo contempt and prohibition. And custom, the traditional way of doing things, proved to be another fount of friction and identification as *americanos* fumed about "backward" and "ignorant" *mexicanos*, while *mexicanos* saw gringos as ill-mannered and childlike, greedy and soulless.

*Mexicano* social attachments have lasted for more than one and a quarter centuries under United States sovereignty; the fact of longevity alone attests to their strength. From the perspective of understanding the conquest and subsequent response to defeat, the factor that must be constantly remembered is the difference in scale—of the size of the arena in which it was possible and desirable to act—between the Anglo and Hispanic world views. Of equal importance for an understanding of *mexicano* history in the nineteenth-century United States is an appreciation of the difference between Anglo and Hispanic economic orientations.

### Economic Complexity

The majority of *mexicanos* in the conquered territory functioned in terms of a peasant economy of long standing, while the *americano* newcomers brought with them an entrepreneurial tradition that was in the first flush of industrial development and clothed with the rhetoric of individualistic capitalism.

Most *mexicanos* engaged in subsistence agriculture solidly rooted in the traditions and social relationships of their village or land grant. They were concerned with survival and prosperity within the traditional community. Producing a surplus for market was very low on their list of priorities. They were more concerned with maintaining the traditional arrangements that guaranteed them access to land and to the aid of their relatives and neighbors. *Mexicanos* followed what economists call a "use value economy" rather than a "market value economy." As anthropologist Eric Wolf says, "The peasant does not operate an enterprise in the economic sense; he runs a household, not a business concern."[15]

*Mexicanos* ran households within the framework created by their traditional community arrangements. But within this framework *mexicanos* functioned autonomously. That is, they made independent decisions about what to plant, where to build, or when to irrigate; they were neither tenant farmers nor hired laborers.[16] Unlike other independent cultivators, such as the Pueblo Indians before the arrival of the Spanish, however, *mexicanos* were subject to the dictates of an overarching state with a government and a social elite that limited their freedom of action.[17] The tradition of autonomous control over local matters tempered by the occasional demands of distant authorities shaped, in large measure, the nature of nineteenth-century resistance to Anglo American domination.

Attitudes toward land—what it is possible and desirable to do with this basic resource—form one of the major distinctions between a peasant economy and one with a capitalistic orientation. For peasants, land is one of the givens of the world. Like family, religion, or seasonal change, land is part of the total environment that sustains the community and gives it its focus and direction. Bourgeois society, as historian Eric Hobsbawm points out, requires a transformation of land tenure and ownership: "land [has] to be turned into a commodity, possessed by private owners and freely purchasable and saleable by them."[18]

Anglo Americans arrived in the conquered region with a long tradition of viewing land as a commodity that could be bought and sold by individuals. Besides being a commodity itself, land was seen as producing commodities; crops, livestock, minerals, or timber were all items to be sold. Along with this strong sense of agrarian and extractive capitalism, Anglo Americans brought with them an eagerness for technological innovation—railroads and manufacturing—and a body of financial institutions—banks and corporations of stockholders—that were alien to the *mexicano* world. Finally, Anglos brought a network of social connections that extended to the commercial centers of Europe. From one point of view, the conflict between *americano* and *mexicano* was a struggle between expectant capitalist and established peasant.

The capitalist-peasant dichotomy caused the conflict; it helped shape the form of the struggle as well. The tradition of autonomy provided *mexicanos* with the disposition to resist and an organizational structure with which to try. They were used to making their own decisions and experienced in dealing with threats to their communities. In this sense, the peasant tradition provided the springboard for resistance. But, to refer to Eric Hobsbawm again, peasants have only two frameworks for action: "the universe ... always bounded by what they know or have heard of; [and] their locality ... which is more or less limited to the world in which their social, economic, and other activities take place." [19] Thus, the *mexicano* world view, discussed above in terms of relative nationalism, limited resistance and prevented effective opposition to Anglo American control during the nineteenth century.

Nationalism and economic complexity develop in relationship to each other. As societies increase their control over the natural environment, they increase the amount and varieties of the resources they can use or misuse.[20] The number, variety, and size of social networks within societies also increase. The interaction between nationalism and economic complexity has produced the complex societies of modern industrial nations. In general terms, then, the conflict between *americano* and *mexicano* can be seen as a struggle between peoples from a complex world who imposed their forms, for their benefit, upon a more traditional society. But the conflict was also between ethnic groups, and, as the recent past amply demonstrates, ethnic hostilities bear no necessary correlation to relative development.

### *Ethnic Hostility*

*Mexicanos* could identify other *mexicanos*, *americanos* could identify other *americanos*, and each group could identify the other.

Primordial relationships like race, custom, religion, or language form the basis for ethnic identification. As the histories of the new third world nations suggest, attachments formed around one or more primordial themes are often strong enough to override nationalism. But attachments of this kind usually predate nationalistic sentiment, and they frequently continue even after the emergence of a coherent nation.[21]

Ethnic identification serves the purposes of incorporation and exclusion. It is a means of separating friend from foe, good people from bad. Ethnicity, then, is both a form of self-identification and a way to categorize outsiders. The evidence indicates that interaction between ethnic groups heightens distinctions between peoples rather than erodes them, even when the characteristics of their cultures have become similar through the same process of interaction.[22] Certainly as the incidences of interaction between *mexicano* and *americano* rose, *mexicanos* increasingly relied upon ethnic criteria for community spirit.

Since ethnic distinctions are used to distinguish insiders from outsiders, they usually imply hostility—often latent, but frequently, as the history of the United States reveals, actively violent. The forms that ethnic hostility takes—slurs and assertions of inborn inferiority, economic and political discrimination, lynching and riots—are distressingly familiar. And the persistence of ethnic hostility throughout American history forms the other side of Anglo American nationalism, a constant threat of disunity that remains unsolved. Since their inclusion in the nation, Mexican Americans have been caught in the tensions created between ethnic identification and national unity.

The United States is an ethnically and culturally diverse nation. Yet the dominant traditions in the country come directly from those of England: political and economic organization, language, religion, law, even the ideal citizen, the famous WASP. Anglo Americans founded their intense nationalism on the twin beliefs that the country possessed the world's most productive society and that it enjoyed the best of all possible forms of government. Anglo Americans linked democracy and material abundance to the innate characteristics of Anglo Saxons, a direct connection of political and economic organization with ethnicity. Thus, the optimism so characteristic of Anglo nationalism, particularly during the nineteenth century, carries the pessimistic strain that fears the effect that non–Anglo Saxon peoples might have on the country.

The optimistic attitude toward non–Anglo Saxons praised diversity.[23] Most frequently using the metaphor of the melting pot, those who believed in the vitality of American institutions and in the opportunities for self-improvement inherent in egalitarian de-mocracy argued that education would enable the newcomers to shed their inferior traits and "melt" into the American mainstream. But the melting pot concept did not allow for a true mixture of all con-tributing peoples; rather it assumed that "impurities" would be boiled away and that the newcomers would be shaped into good Americans, that is, Anglo Americans.[24] The optimistic response was ethnocentric, but it was not racist; it assumed that all peoples were potentially capable of learning to be Anglo Americans, and the pro-cedures of naturalization with their emphasis on English literacy and American history testify to this. *Mexicanos*, however, were cit-izens by right of treaty; they had not been melted first.

Pessimists expressed their fears in nativist movements that tried to curb or eliminate the threat of contamination posed by non–Anglo Saxons. Historically, nativism has perceived three basic dangers to the nation: a biological danger from inferior races that would pollute the American population; a Catholic threat that grew out of general Protestant fervor and the specific belief that Catholics' loyalty to the Pope, a foreign power, would supersede their loyalty to the nation; and a fear of political "radicals" who, shaped in the corruption of nondemocratic regimes, would not realize that the only "true" revo-lution had already occurred.[25] The Know Nothing Party, the several Ku Klux Klans, and the immigration restrictions of 1924 based on quotas according to national origin stand out as landmarks to the nativist strain that has always been present in the country.

To nineteenth-century nativist eyes, *mexicanos* clearly embod-ied the racial and papist threats, and as time went on they were seen as a political threat as well. And the optimists despaired of what they saw as *mexicanos'* stubborn and misguided refusal to copy An-glo Americans.

## *Mexicano* Response

*Mexicanos* responded to the combination of attitudes and institutions brought by swelling numbers of Anglo Americans with four basic tac-tics: withdrawal, accommodation, assimilation, and resistance.

Withdrawal—ignoring the fact of conquest as much as possi-ble—was the preferred tactic for the majority. Buffers of unsettled land between Anglo and Hispanic communities in Texas and New Mexico allowed *mexicanos* to ignore *americanos* in the rhythms of day-to-day and season-to-season life, so that physical separation per-mitted withdrawal to work with relative success during the bulk of the nineteenth century. Accommodation—interaction accompanied by jousting for position and advantage—was used by the elite and upwardly mobile, particularly in New Mexico, where they had something with which to bargain, with some success. It was an approach, however, that often fragmented mexicanos, who frequently found themselves allied with Anglos against other combinations of mexicanos and americanos. And some few among the elite assimilated, of whom Miguel A. Otero, Jr., who served for nine years as territorial governor of New Mexico, is an outstanding example.[26]

The general pattern of response to Anglo America consisted of a social pyramid with an accommodating-assimilating elite at the top and at its base las masas de los hombres pobres—literally, the masses of poor men—who tried to ignore the newcomers or withdraw from them as much as possible. But friction occurred between the two groups, and it frequently erupted in outbreaks of violence.

### Violent Resistance

When seen as a whole, the nineteenth century landscape of the Southwest appears dotted with brushfire conflicts between mexicanos and americanos. Some flared sharply and threatened to engulf whole towns and the surrounding countryside; isolated flashes of outrage, of just having had enough, left scorched spots like those along railroad tracks started by the hotboxes from passing trains. And in some places, violence smoldered constantly, leaving a perpetual atmospheric haze like the smog over Los Angeles.

Violence is not new to human societies; in fact, it seems to be a constant of the human condition. As political scientist Ted Robert Gurr observes, European states and empires through the past twenty-four centuries have averaged one year of violent disturbance in five, counting "important" disturbances only, and since 1945 violent attempts to overthrow governments have been more frequent than elections throughout the world.[27]

The fact that mexicanos violently resisted Anglo American domination may come as a surprise. Resistance does not fit the myth of the speedy conquest; neither does it square with the stereotype of cowardly and inferior "meskins" nor the comforting belief in the benevolence and general attractiveness of the American way of life.

Equally important, however, in accounting for the omission of mexicano resistance from Anglo American historic consciousness is the fact that uprisings never fundamentally threatened Anglo American control; they never achieved a sufficient size or posed a severe enough threat to be recognized as revolutions.

Most of the literature about civil disorder and internal violence focuses on revolutions, the large-scale attempt to overthrow government, and either ignores urban riots and rural uprisings or dismisses them as insignificant expressions of frustration by the oppressed.[28] Only recently have historians, anthropologists, and political scientists begun to examine these expressions of popular discontent as political activity—attempts by social groups to influence and determine matters that affect their common welfare.[29]

During the course of the nineteenth century, *mexicanos* employed violence as one means for retaining some measure of self-determination in the face of an increasingly oppressive new regime. All incidents of political violence fall within the general category that Hobsbawm terms "peasant" or "primitive" rebellions, although several cases carried hints of other possibilities.[30] The outbreaks divide into five types within Hobsbawm's "peasant" framework: Border Warfare, where the locale provided a unifying theme to all of the resistance even though each of the other types appeared; Social Banditry, the most basic and constant expression of hostility that was carried out by individuals who refused to submit and who enjoyed the support of their general communities; Community Upheavals, when tensions became sufficiently high and widespread to precipitate a "spontaneous" outbreak; Long-Term Skirmishing, where violent set-tos occurred at a low level of intensity but over a long period of time; and Coordinated Rebellions.

### Law and Land

Friction between *mexicano* and *americano* involved race, language, religion, food, sex, and almost every other conceivable cultural distinction. But the points where friction usually provoked violent resistance were law and land.

Anglo Americans brought their version of the English common law to the conquered territory. *Mexicanos*, particularly *los pobres*, accustomed to the more personalized and traditional procedures of the alcaldes, found Anglo law confusing. It was in English, in itself a problem, and the fact that Anglos blatantly manipulated legal codes and court procedures added to the *mexicanos'* resentment. Law enforcement contributed a more pronounced level of anger. *Mexicanos* perceived their treatment by Anglo peace officers as capricious and unjust; the number of unpunished lynchings and killings of *mexicanos* by *americanos* gave stark evidence for the accuracy of this perception.

Land provided the other major stimulus for violence. Both Anglo and Hispanic competed for it. Fundamental differences in practices of land tenure and conceptions about proper land use, particularly the tensions inherent in the transformation of land into a saleable commodity, complicated the fundamental competition. And the terms of the Treaty of Guadalupe Hidalgo, guaranteeing property rights but not specifying how traditional Hispanic forms of land ownership were to be translated into modes compatible with American law, added to the confusion and increased distrust and hostility.

Thus, the confrontation between *mexicano* and *americano* is a history of conflict. The conflict was between cultures, and it occurred on two levels: often conflict grew out of misunderstanding, as neither group understood the other's socially established structures of meaning; at least as often, however, conflict was between meanings—each understood the other well enough and that was precisely the problem. They didn't want the same things.

Western expansion and the frontier experience is often cited as the most distinctive feature about the United States and the source of the qualities that are identified as uniquely American.[31] How accurate that interpretation is, is a matter of debate. But the history of the *mexicano* peoples in the Southwest leads to a somewhat different characterization. Because *mexicanos* followed an essentially peasant culture in their traditional homelands and were but recently severed from their mother country, the conflict between *mexicano* and *americano* emerges as the most European occurrence in the history of the trans–Mississippi West. And an understanding of the conflict begins with the Spanish settlement of the Borderlands.

CHAPTER 2

# The Northern Outposts

Less than thirty years after winning independence from Spain, Mexico lost half of its territory through the Texas Revolution and the Mexican War.[1] The lost territory had been part of Mexico for some two and a half centuries: Coronado had penetrated the Great Plains as far as present-day Kansas by the early 1540s; Spanish settlement along the upper Rio Grande began in 1598, nine years before the Virginia Company planted Jamestown.[2] But the region proved harsh and unattractive—settlers did not rush northward—and colonial administrators soon cast it in the role of a buffer protecting the more populous and richer interior.

The settlements guarding imperial Spain's northern perimeter clustered in three regions in what are now parts of Texas, New Mexico, and California, irregular dots on a boundary that arced from the Sabine River to the Pacific Ocean.[3] The northern provinces remained frontier communities well into the nineteenth century, and they were frontiers both in the New World sense of outposts of European "civilization" in the "wilderness" and in the Old World sense of the boundary between one national power and another.

The northern settlements were isolated from the interior and the central authorities. They were also isolated from each other, making them like, in the words of historian Howard Lamar, "an attenuated island chain awash in a sea of hostiles."[4] The isolation left them vulnerable to attack and prone to economic hardships. In all three areas there developed traditional peasant societies dependent upon subsistence agriculture and supporting a few powerful families who administered local government and chafed at the restrictions imposed by the colonial regime. The aspirations of the provincial elites were often at odds with the policies of the central government, and this internal tension complicated the problems posed by the Anglo American advance, undermining the outposts' role as defenders of the frontier.

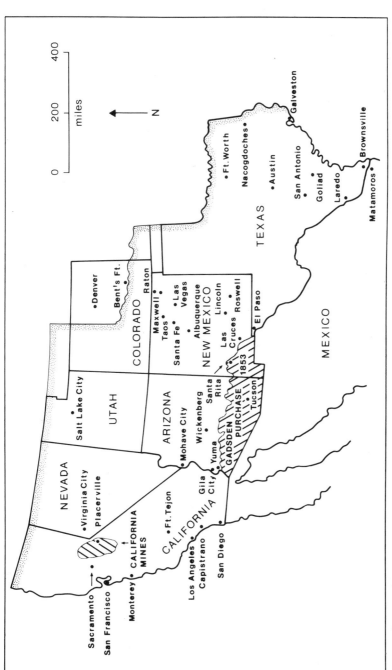

Map 1. The Southwest

The northern outposts shared general characteristics. There were, however, significant differences in their pre-Anglo histories and in the nature of Anglo American encroachment when it ultimately happened. The differences both in the nature of the *americano* impact and in the historic base upon which to draw produced regional variations in the ways *mexicanos* responded to Anglo American sovereignty in the nineteenth century. New Mexico was the oldest northern province and the one where *mexicano* influence lasted the longest. It is a fitting place to begin.

## New Mexico

Unlike Texas or California, New Mexico did not attract large numbers of Anglo migrants—Hispanic-surnamed residents did not drop below fifty percent of the population until after 1940.[5] Moreover, unlike its eastern and western counterparts, New Mexico did not immediately become a state. A long period of territorial organization severely limited the range of options the *mexicanos* could choose from within the Anglo American political system. Nonetheless, numerical superiority, representational government after a fashion, and the terms of the Treaty of Guadalupe Hidalgo protecting the property of the conquered people and stipulating that they would enjoy "all the rights of the citizens of the United States" raised the possibility that *nuevos mexicanos* could continue to control their native land.[6]

They did not. In New Mexico, however, Anglo domination came about through a process of attrition that is not yet complete. Anglo erosion of native New Mexican society was punctuated by violent confrontations rooted in a culture of some 250 years' standing.

### The Settling of New Mexico

Spanish settlement of New Mexico went through three phases. The first lasted eighty-two years and marked the effort to secure the upper Rio Grande del Norte. A revolt of the Pueblo Indians in 1680 drove the Spanish out for twelve years. Reoccupation began in 1692, initiating the second phase. During the eighteenth century, New Mexicans worked out patterns of life that persisted into the American period. The third phase, characterized by significant geographic and commercial expansion, began late in the eighteenth century and continued well into the American territorial years.[7]

In August, 1598, a caravan of settlers, soldiers, servants, and Franciscan missionaries, led by Don Juan de Oñate, reached the upper Rio Grande. Charged with the tasks of erecting permanent settlements, searching for gold and silver, and converting the Indians, the settlers found New Mexico nearly devoid of precious metals, grudging in agricultural bounty, and fruitful only in the souls available for conversion. Colonial authorities quickly came to regard New Mexico as a mission field and a military buffer; a long era of isolation broken infrequently by directives from Mexico City began.

The colonists maintained a tenuous hold on the province as they sought to wrest a living from the land without succumbing to natural disaster or Pueblo wrath. By 1609 settlements stretched north to Taos and downriver to Qualaca as the settlers imposed their presence on the Pueblo Indians. For the Franciscans, the sedentary Pueblo Indians were convenient targets for conversion; for the settlers, the Indians offered a labor supply. Pueblo land appealed to the Spanish for the same reasons that it had attracted the Indians—it was fertile, bordered the only dependable water in the region, and was fairly safe from attack by nomadic Indians. Missionaries probed as far west as Zuñi country and east to the Pecos Pueblo, but the secular population clung to the Rio Grande and its immediate tributaries. There it remained for the better part of two centuries, interrupted only by the Pueblo Revolt in 1680.

Don Diego de Vargas reoccupied the northern river villages in 1692. Using seventeenth-century foundations, the Spanish reclaimed and intensified settlement along the Rio Grande, but they did not expand the boundaries of the area under Hispanic control. Surrounded by hostile Indians, New Mexico remained a frugal oasis no larger than that subjugated by Oñate in 1598.

As the eighteenth century faded into the nineteenth, a "spontaneous unspectacular folk movement" developed that helped stamp the Southwest with *mexicano* characteristics which still exist.[8] Ironically, when New Mexicans finally started to branch out, they quickly ran into the vanguards of Anglo American expansion.

The governor awarded the San Miguel del Bado Grant on the upper Pecos River in 1794. From this base in the eastern foothills of the Sangre de Cristo Mountains, *mexicanos* moved across the eastern plains in an irregular fan that reached the areas that are now Colorado, the Texas Panhandle, and the lower Pecos Valley. Settlers also followed the Rio Grande past Taos, and the Chama River into the San Luis Valley. Westward they roamed deep into Navajo and Apache country, while to the south they began to fill the Mesilla Valley.

Anglos entered a community just breaking out of a long static era. A well-entrenched New Mexican society occupied the productive lands along the Rio Grande, and New Mexicans were expanding in all directions from the river and mountain center. The first Anglo

arrivals settled along the Rio Grande and tried to work within Hispanic society. As *americanos* strengthened their grip on the region,
demographic patterns changed. Ranchers and homesteaders, particularly those moving west after the Civil War, settled on the cir-
cumference of Hispanic New Mexico, filling the four corners of the
territory and exerting increasing pressure toward the Rio Grande.

Land was the basic resource of the territory, the object of both
settling peoples, and caused the greatest friction between Anglo and
native New Mexican. They competed directly for possession of the
land, but of equal importance, *mexicano* and *americano* differed in
their conceptions of proper land use and valid title.

### *Land*

New Mexicans acquired land by grant upon petition to the governor.
Three types of grants prevailed: the community grant, given to a
group of at least ten households; the proprietary town grant or villa,
awarded to a *patrón* who promised to settle at least thirty families,
construct the plaza and church, and support a priest; and the *sitio*—
hacienda or ranch—a large tract given to a proprietor with no stip-
ulations about settlement.[9]

The grants were often quite large, and all were of specific tracts;
landmarks described the external boundaries of each. As part of the
ceremony of formal possession, grantees rode the boundaries and
erected cornerstones in the presence of a government official.

Recipients of a community grant distributed homesites and
farming land by drawing lots, with fields marked out in equitable
strips along waterways and the remainder of the grant land held
in common, free to all for pasture, timber, firewood, and watering
holes. The proprietor of a villa apportioned land at his discretion,
while a *hacendado* or ranchero—the owner of a *sitio*—had no reg-
ulations governing use of the land. But large rancheros needed labor,
usually acquired through a system of permanent debt, and their *peones* built villages on ranch land and cultivated gardens for food.[10]

All grants rested on Spanish, and later Mexican, law and had
distinguishing features of purpose, makeup, rights, and obligations.
Often, grant documents did not spell out these distinctions clearly,
but assumed a knowledge of the customs of the country. Boundaries
were vague, with grants frequently overlapping, and many ranchers
roamed crown land or over each others' ranges without opposition.
Distinctions tended to blur. On some community grants, powerful
families who employed many grant residents came to regard parts of
the common land as theirs alone, while *peones* on *sitios* farmed the
*patrón's* land and grazed their few head of stock on the *patrón's* pas-

ture, regarding such privileges as their right. Although documents outlined general patterns of ownership and distinguished between types of grants, in practice it was tradition, not registered title, that determined land ownership and use.

The Treaty of Guadalupe Hidalgo and the fact of *mexicano* numerical superiority in New Mexico made Anglo Americans conscious of Spanish and Mexican grants. U.S. land law was the law of the territory, but the treaty stipulated that property rights valid under Mexico must be honored. U.S. officials somehow had to bring New Mexican land tenure patterns into line with Anglo American policies. Anglo speculators, who saw in the tangled situation a chance to create large landed estates, compounded a difficult problem.

American land policy featured precise measurement and documentation, assumed individual ownership, and came out of a tradition that expected western land to be open for settlement.[11] It stood in stark contrast to the New Mexican system couched in Spanish documents, general landmarks, vague terminology, and an assumed shared tradition. Land speculation in New Mexico took on wondrous forms. Lawyers and investors (often identical) had a field day using fees, intimidation, bribery, and fraud to realize great profit and enormous power. Stormy controversy grew out of the web of titles that they did little to clarify.

Fraud and corruption permeated the New Mexican land grant situation, but even persons of honest intentions found it difficult to reconcile *mexicano* and *americano* traditions. The idea of community-owned common land—vague in limits and owned by an imperfectly defined corporate entity—and the time-honored privileges of *peones* on *sitios* proved particularly hard for Anglo Americans to comprehend or tolerate.

The newcomers also brought to the territory an economic system that expected individuals to realize profit-making surpluses. A few wealthy or ambitious native New Mexicans welcomed the new ways, but for the vast majority of *mexicanos* the Anglo American economic system made no sense. They ignored it when they could; when it affected them directly, especially when it threatened their land, they resisted violently.

### The Traditional Economy

Subsistence agriculture and grazing supported New Mexicans for two and a half centuries. Sheep raising was the only industry that created a surplus; from the seventeenth to the twentieth centuries, sheep were the most important product of the province.[12] North of Santa Fe, the rough Rio Arriba country sheltered small communities of poor farmers, but south of the capital, the open, rolling terrain of the Rio Abajo allowed concentrated sheep raising. Here the great homes of the *ricos* were only a few miles apart; here lived the elite who looked for greater opportunities.[13]

Bound to the products of the land, New Mexicans had long tried to reach distant markets for manufactured goods.[14] In 1609 the Crown initiated, funded, and conducted a triennial supply train connecting the remote north with Chihuahua and Durango. Begun to provision the missions, the caravan soon served the secular community as well. In the eighteenth century, *ricos* sent annual trains to the Chihuahua fair held every January. But New Mexicans always suffered from transportation problems, high prices, and low profits. In their search for more favorable commercial relationships, New Mexicans developed some commerce with merchants in Sonora and flirted with French traders moving west from the Mississippi Valley.

In eighteenth-century New Mexico, a wealthy minority pushed to enrich the province and decrease its isolation, while most people concentrated on day-to-day survival. By the nineteenth century, commercial growth began to follow in the wake of geographic expansion. With Mexican independence, trade barriers came down. In 1821, William Becknell, an Indian trader from Missouri, chanced upon a patrol of New Mexican soldiers who escorted him to Santa Fe, where he found a market eager for his wares. Becknell and his successors strengthened the trade network between Missouri and New Mexico, essentially a northeastern extension of the Santa Fe–Chihuahua route, and provided more and cheaper goods than New Mexicans previously had been able to obtain.[15]

The Santa Fe trade was a harbinger of Kearny's occupation. Anglo merchants worked with, and began to modify, existing New Mexican economic relationships. Allying with segments of the native elite—sometimes marrying into prominent families and becoming naturalized citizens—the *americanos extranjeros*, or American foreigners, functioned as fur traders, freighters, merchants, and ultimately land owners, thus intensifying and modifying the role of the *rico* who doubled as a caravan entrepreneur and retail merchant. The Santa Fe trade supported a number of *mexicanos* whose interests began to point to the north and east and many capitalists in St. Louis who looked to the south and west for profit.

A powerful foreign community in alliance with influential native New Mexicans produced an "American Party" that increased tensions between government officials and ambitious merchants. Mexico welcomed Anglo traders but tolerated subversion no more than Spain had done. By 1830 Mexico began to place restrictions on foreign merchants and naturalized citizens.[16] But the American Party's influence continued unabated, and the alliance continued into the transitional era following Kearny's entrance.

### Politics and Economics: The Territorial Years

Mexican independence left New Mexican government relatively undisturbed. Under Mexican sovereignty, governors were usually native-born and tended to serve shorter terms than they had under colonial administration. But the governor remained the supreme civil and military authority in the province, with only pro forma assistance from a lieutenant governor and an *asemblea*. Local government fell to *juezes de paz*, alcaldes, and prefects—combination police and judicial officers who maintained order through custom, common sense, and a minimum of statute law.[17] No codified legal system defined due process, a lack *americanos* found shocking.[18] The governor reigned supreme in New Mexico, although paradoxically he did not interfere very much in local affairs. Opponents of the governor had to appeal to his superior in Mexico or revolt. Both tactics were used; a revolt in 1837 claimed the life of the incumbent, Albino Pérez.[19]

Immediately after taking Santa Fe, Kearny, acting under instructions from President Polk, promulgated a civil government that combined both New Mexican and Anglo American institutions.[20] The Taos Revolt of January 1847 terminated this experiment in blending from the two traditions, and the Army administered the province until territorial organization became a fact in 1851.[21] The short-lived government erected by Kearny, however, indicates two things: that even before the treaty, the United States intended to offer citizenship to the conquered people, and that the mixture of *americano* and *mexicano* forms anticipated the problems inherent in the transition.

The Organic Act creating the Territory of New Mexico as part of the Compromise of 1850 did not reflect Kearny's sensitivity to New Mexico's cultural dualism. Territorial organization imposed appointive offices like governor, solicitor general, district judges, and U.S. marshals. It established upper and lower houses of a representative legislature and required that local government be organized in counties complete with probate judges, sheriffs, county commissioners, and assessors.

The change in organization and nomenclature did not necessarily inaugurate a change in practices. Powerful families still held sway in their bailiwicks, and probate judges, sheriffs, and county commissioners often behaved like prefects and alcaldes of old. Complained one federal judge in 1858: ". . . the District Courts have been *cur*-tailed of much of their jurisdiction, which have been *dove*-tailed into the Probate Courts by [the] Legislative Assembly. I would not be surprised if the next Assembly should pass an act repealing the Organic Act and establishing a Monarchy."[22]

New Mexico's political system comprised an uneasy mixture of *americanos* and *mexicanos*. The offices of first rank in the territory were filled by appointment in Washington and thus became part of national patronage. Many important local offices were filled by the governor. Anglos held these positions. *Mexicanos*, however, made their presence felt in electoral politics. The only territory-wide elective office was delegate-in-Congress; *mexicanos* held it for thirty-seven of the territory's sixty-one years. Between 1865 and 1912, the percentage of native New Mexicans in the territorial Council ranged from a high of 100 percent to a low of 25 percent; in the territorial House from a high of 95 percent to a low of 42 percent. Twenty times the Council elected a *mexicano* as its president, and the House had a native as its Speaker for fourteen sessions. *Mexicano* office holding was even more striking in county politics.[23]

These yardsticks demonstrate that Anglos did not overwhelm the territory. The existence of elective offices, requiring majorities of the overwhelmingly *mexicano* electorate, insured the inclusion of the active New Mexican elite in the decision-making process. *Mexicanos* never again controlled their homeland, but *americanos* needed support from the native community, and this support did not come without concessions.

Economic life mirrored political patterns, although here Anglos gained more quickly. Many *mexicano* ranchers and merchants increased their wealth, especially those who dated their or their families' connection with *americanos* to the early days of the Santa Fe trade and the American Party. Successful Anglos were usually lawyers and merchants from the Northeast or Midwest who had the ability to work within New Mexican culture with a minimum of friction, frequently marrying into prominent local families.[24]

Merchant and pastoral interests intertwined in what one historian called "mercantile capitalism."[25] Through barter, contracting for crops, dealing in livestock or hides, or grazing sheep on a *partido* basis—a kind of sharecropping wherein the shepherd received a portion of the lamb crop for guarding the flock—the merchant occupied a pivotal role.

The grazier-merchant connection extended traditional New Mexican economic patterns with the new participants exerting a subtle influence toward change. Other aspects of the Anglo regime caused more immediate alterations: federal salaries and contracts provided a major source of income; capital ventures like mines, railroads, and banks required entrée to Eastern and foreign investment circles. Native New Mexicans rarely engaged in such enterprises.[26]

A small group dominated the economic and political upper circles. A surprisingly stable association of lawyers, politicians, and speculators known as the Santa Fe Ring was the most powerful clique. According to Governor Edmund G. Ross, the Ring formed around Stephen B. Elkins and Thomas B. Catron, two lawyers who adopted "the language and habits of the country in order to accomplish the objects of their ambition."[27] The two began by dealing in land grants and moved from this base to other enterprises "till the affairs of the Territory came to be run almost exclusively" in their interests.[28]

A flexible alliance, the Santa Fe Ring included mexicano politicians who used their influence with the electorate in an agile attempt to work within both cultures and thereby retain their positions as leaders of society. The territorial magnates perched at the top of a shifting mexicano network of interrelationships and spheres of influence. Precinct, county, and regional groupings held active and alert factions attuned to their self-interest; both native jefes políticos (political bosses) and Anglo bosses had to work very hard and almost continuously to win and maintain factional support.[29]

Isolation and low economic productivity molded distinct patterns in New Mexico which American acquisition did not change very quickly. Isolation had prevented earlier in New Mexico a sense of identification with either New Spain or Mexico. This characteristic continued under the United States; local problems dominated the New Mexican consciousness, and the New Mexicans remained apathetic about distant governments. The land-based, peasant economy supported a traditional, stratified society that did not lead to strong loyalties to New Mexico as a political community. Allegiance went to family, locality, or class, not to the province. Fragmentation prevented organized opposition to the conquerors and allowed americanos to make ever-larger inroads into New Mexico. But numerical superiority allowed mexicanos to impede abrupt, dislocative change.

In contrast, Anglo American control of Texas and California came with great rapidity. Hispanic settlement in neither province was as old, as numerous, nor as developed as in New Mexico; the history of Anglo American encroachment differed in each, and both differed from the New Mexican experience. Mexicano resistance in Texas and California, therefore, followed distinct forms.

## California

Anglo America won New Mexico in 1846, but it took the remainder of the century for the victors to solidify their hold on the practical matters of political and economic life. Anglo American forces lost the only serious battle of the war in California, but within two years of the Treaty of Guadalupe Hidalgo, *americanos* had nullified the influence of *californios* in their homeland.

The Gold Rush was the primary reason for the difference between New Mexico and California. Some 10,000 *californios* lived in the province in 1846. An estimated 100,000 argonauts arrived in 1849 alone, and by 1852 the newcomers numbered some 250,000. The combination of population growth and national, even international, excitement helped get California admitted to the Union as a state by September 9, 1850.[30]

Had New Mexico received a similar influx of population, it is doubtful that even the well-entrenched *nuevos mexicanos* could have held out for very long. But California was not New Mexico. At the time of the war, *californios* were second- or at most third-generation colonists. In contrast to the stable, richly textured traditions of New Mexican village life, California was in the throes of political and economic turmoil when the war began.[31]

California's young, small, and rapidly changing society made the province vulnerable to foreign domination, and the Forty-Niners did it in gold. Even without the Gold Rush, however, it was likely that California's qualities would have attracted large numbers of Anglos very quickly. New Mexico was a harsh, unyielding land, but California was a gentle, bountiful garden. Travelers could reach New Mexico only by dangerous overland trails, while California was accessible by both land and sea. California's ports opened toward the Far East, promising an expansion of trade. And California marked the westernmost possibility of continental expansion. For Anglo Americans California was the goal, and New Mexico was just a necessary way station en route to it.

### Settlement

The threat of English invasion from the east and Russian incursions down the Pacific Coast from Alaska prompted the Spanish Empire to take measures to secure the northern frontier. Accordingly, two overland expeditions and two ships embarked toward California in 1769 to blunt the Russian threat. The four parties rendezvoused at San Diego and established a mission before sending a detachment north toward Monterey Bay. The mission and presidio at Monterey were dedicated on June 3, 1770; the remainder of the eighteenth century saw the Spanish erect a line of missions and hamlets along the coast from San Diego to San Francisco.

Missions made up the predominant aspect of the Spanish presence in California, with a relatively few soldiers and colonizing families representing the secular community. At the turn of the century, the Franciscans claimed twenty thousand Mission Indians under their care, while the remainder of the Hispanic population numbered some twelve hundred scattered along five hundred miles of coastline. As in New Mexico, the converted Indians provided a supply of labor: under the tutelage of the friars, they learned the tasks of farming and ranching and the skills of carpentry and weaving. Members of the secular community not engaged in government or the military devoted the bulk of their energies to ranching. The emphasis on ranching, which increased during the second quarter of the nineteenth century, tended to isolate the *californios*. The ranchos became the focal points of society, self-contained entities of extended families and employees. Without the intricate networks that characterized New Mexican village life, the combination of sparse settlement and ranch life meant that *californio* society did not rest on a solid foundation of *los hombres pobres*.[32]

Like New Mexico, however, California was isolated. Distance, desert, and increasingly hostile Apaches separated the far western corner of the empire from Mexico City.[33] Californians made some attempt to expand settlement eastward into the Central Valley. Enough migrants arrived to raise the Spanish population to eight thousand by 1826. Contact with English and Anglo American trading ships dated from 1790; they and occasional Russian vessels coming south from Sitka provided some contact with the larger world.[34] But, by and large, isolation marked the "romantic period" of early California, and isolation nurtured a provincial mentality of uniqueness that flowered into a desire for autonomy from Mexico after independence—a trend that aided Anglo American infiltration.

### *Land*

The most significant thing about land in California was the secularization of the missions. Authorized by the Mexican Constitution of 1824, secularization in California began in 1831. In the words of historian Leonard Pitt, secularization "was California's most important event before the discovery of gold."[35]

Broadly speaking, secularization was designed to break the power of the church by transferring its lands to the secular society and elevating the neophytes—its Indian charges—to citizenship. In actuality, as the process worked out in California, it created an extremely wealthy elite out of what had been a moderately influential group of rancheros, and it decimated the Mission Indians. Prior to secularization, *californios* shared power with the Franciscans and with government-appointed officials. After secularization and the concurrent political autonomy achieved in 1836, the rancheros became the undisputed leaders of California, competing only with each other. The Mission Indians, on the other hand, went from a "secure, authoritarian existence [to] a free but anarchic one."[36] The neophytes either blended into the lower classes in the villages, worked on ranchos, or disappeared by joining their "wild" counterparts.

But for the rancheros secularization was a windfall. Some eight hundred individuals shared in the division of eight million acres of prime ranch land. From 1836, when native Californian Juan Bautista Alvarado became governor, until 1846, under the administration of Pío Pico, aggressive or well-connected *californios* could, through purchase, lease, or grant, acquire estates of up to 500,000 acres.

The new landed wealth raised to new heights the hide and tallow trade portrayed by Richard Dana in *Two Years before the Mast*. But the huge estates produced by secularization intensified the ranch-centered social structure of the colonial era and inhibited, even undermined, the development of an intricate social fabric like New Mexico's.

The boom was short-lived. Anglo Americans arrived hard on the heels of the last dispersal of mission lands. The Land Law of 1851 established a three-member commission empowered to rule on the validity of title as defined in Spanish and Mexican law, with rejected claims reverting to the public domain.[37] As in New Mexico, bringing California practices in line with Anglo American procedures proved an exercise in confusion, fraud, and intimidation. But it happened faster in California. In the north, where the Gold Rush attracted the newcomers, violent squatters, clever lawyers, and obliging moneylenders virtually destroyed the *californios'* ranches by 1856. Rancheros in the dry, gold-poor south survived somewhat longer. But even there, mismanagement, unpaid mortgages, back taxes, and, ultimately, more Anglos dissolved the old *californio* landholdings by the 1880s.[38]

Secularization rearranged California's political structure dramatically, but change and turmoil marked all politics in the decade and a half before the war with the United States.

The liberal spirit that spurred Mexican independence and shook all of Latin America influenced many young *californios*. Scions of prominent families like Mariano Vallejo and the brothers Andrés and Pío Pico yearned for education, freedom of expression, and self-government. They reacted against religious institutions first. Men refused to participate in devotions until by the end of the Mexican regime only women, children, and neophytes attended mass, and many of the gentry refused to pay their tithe.

The new political spirit had other effects as well. Beginning in 1831, *californios* launched a series of rebellions and internal power struggles that stopped only with the Bear Flag Rebellion in 1846. The most important uprising occurred in 1836, when Juan Bautista Alvarado drove Governor Nicolás Gutiérrez from the province and gained virtual self-rule for California.[39]

Two other trends appeared during this era of turmoil. First, an anti-Mexican sentiment spread among the gentry, rooted in the tradition of provincial isolation and fueled by Mexico's attitude that California was the end of the world. Leonard Pitt describes California as a "Siberian work camp" for Mexico, a place to relocate convicts and other *cholos* (scoundrels).[40] The blatant misconduct of many of the *cholos*—drunken brawls, thievery, and killings—made natives conscious of their California birth. Pitt dates the use of *californio* as the preferred term of self-identification from the postindependence recolonization of undesirables by Mexico.[41] The change in name, however, did not reflect a California "nationalism." Social attachments remained primordial and were based on family, ranch, and immediate locality. The largest sphere of effective unity evolved from a north-south hostility centering around Monterey and Los Angeles respectively.[42]

A receptivity to Anglo America was the second trend evident between 1825 and 1846. Those fired by the spirit of *liberalismo* found the theory of American government attractive. The maritime trade strengthened this attraction. Trade turned the products of the rancheros' land into wealth and provided the luxury goods essential to a grand style of living. The traders blended easily into California society, and many chose to remain. Like the Santa Fe traders, merchants and retired ship officers often married into local families and swore allegiance to Mexico. But, as in the Santa Fe experience, they never abandoned their hope that the United States would one day acquire the province.

### Infiltration, War, and the Deluge

*Californios* welcomed commerce and appreciated the theory of the U.S. Constitution, but they were not blind to the potential danger from the United States.

Alvarado's 1836 rebellion that realized autonomy for California had been aided by Isaac Graham and forty riflemen, who returned to their holdings disgusted that he had not pressed for independence à la Texas.[43] Commodore Thomas Ap Catesby Jones captured Monterey in 1842, erroneously assuming that war had broken out between Mexico and the U.S. He replaced the Mexican flag when he discovered his error, but the incident graphically illustrated that the U.S. government wanted California. In the 1840s, the arrival of settlers to the Sacramento Valley—who, unlike the traders, remained aloof from and even hostile toward California society—provided additional evidence of U.S. designs. And, since 1843, *californios* had been urged by U.S. Consul Thomas O. Larkin to cast off Mexican "tyranny." Torn between anger at Mexico's California policies and the attractiveness of Anglo American economics and governmental theory, on the one hand, and a growing dislike of the racist, anti-Catholic Anglo American settlers coupled with a deep-rooted patriotism, on the other, *californios* remained uncommitted.[44]

On June 6, 1846, a group of Anglo riflemen captured General Mariano Vallejo at his Sonoma ranch and declared the establishment of the Bear Flag Republic. *Californios* viewed the incident not as an act of war but as pure banditry, and they ignored it. Subsequent depredations by the "grimey adventurers" who formed the *osos* (bears), followed by Commodore John D. Sloat's arrival in Monterey and Captain Archibald Gillespie's occupation of Los Angeles, drove the *californios* to arms. Guerrillas under José María Flores forced Gillespie to surrender, and outnumbered lancers under General Andrés Pico defeated Kearny at San Pascual in "one of the few skirmishes north of the Rio Grande worthy to be called a battle."[45]

Anglo America won California at the treaty table, not on the battlefield. The initial plans for transition to Anglo American rule provided for significant participation by *californios*. The Gold Rush changed all that and turned a relatively peaceful and equitable transition into total defeat. The deluge of gold hunters brought strange institutions, new laws and legal procedures, and racial hostility. *Californios* not only lost their land, they were also driven from the gold fields. The racial hostility was compounded by numbers of Mexicans and South Americans also attracted by the lure of gold. *Californios* equated them with the *cholos* of previous decades, but to the Anglos they were all "greasers."[46]

The abrupt, roughshod takeover produced anger and violent resistance from the *californios*. But, lacking the base of time, tradition, and numerical strength enjoyed by the New Mexicans, California resistance flared intensely and was then extinguished by the flood of newcomers.

California and New Mexico mark the poles of the northern outposts' experience. Texas stands midway between these extremes, in terms of age, colonial society, the nature of Anglo encroachment, and the patterns of resistance.

## Texas

Spanish settlement in the region annexed as the state of Texas was older than that in California and younger than that in New Mexico. Midway in time, Texas also underwent both the New Mexican and California experiences. The fact that the state of Texas began as two distinct Spanish colonies accounts for this contradiction. One colony, Tejas, began at the Nueces River and extended north and east in a defensive arc against the French, and later English, incursions. The other, Nuevo Santander, lay along both sides of the Rio Grande from the river's mouth to what are now the two Laredos.

### *Tejas*
The history of Tejas exhibits striking parallels to the history of California. The Crown established Tejas, like California, to combat a foreign threat, in this case, the French pushing westward from Louisiana. Again like the northwestern province, Tejas numbered few inhabitants and sheltered an elite that chafed under imperial restrictions, demonstrated ambiguous pulls between autonomy and Mexican patriotism, were quickly outnumbered by Anglo American migrants, and were soon swallowed by the new regime.

But the parallels are not perfect. Tejas neither enjoyed California's maritime commerce nor achieved the autonomy that gave the rancheros temporary economic and political ascendancy. The separation of Tejas from Mexico, moreover, occurred in a context of extreme violence, and violence sanctioned by the Remember-the-Alamo myth characterized "normal" interaction between Anglo and *mexicano* to a much greater extent than in either California or New Mexico.

Settlement of Tejas began in 1690 with the founding of Mission San Francisco de los Tejas northeast of present-day Crockett, Texas.[47] A thin band of missions and presidios stretched from San Juan Bautista del Rio Grande near present-day Gerro, Coahuila, through San Antonio and eastward toward the Sabine River, expanding and contracting according to foreign threat, Indian attacks, and available funds. The inhospitable geography and the hostile Apaches and Comanches discouraged colonists. Even by the early nineteenth century Tejas had a population of no more than five thousand, concentrated in the towns of San Antonio, Goliad, and Nacogdoches.

Tejas missions did not realize the success of their California counterparts—only four survived at the end of the colonial area. Ranching and farming supported the population. The centralized trade policies of imperial Spain irked *tejanos* just as much as they did *nuevos mexicanos* and *californios*; illicit cattle drives and general smuggling with Louisiana through Natchitoches offered only a partial antidote. By the nineteenth century, disenchantment with their situation under colonial administration led many of the *tejano* elite to foment revolution, either as separate independence movements, or as part of the drive for Mexican independence.

Mexico opened the doors for alien colonization in Texas in 1820, and Stephen F. Austin established the first Anglo colony.[48] The legislature of Coahuila and Tejas passed a colonization law in March, 1825, that enabled an Anglo American settler to obtain 4,500 acres for fifty dollars payable over a six-year period.[49] The law produced a flood of immigrants. By 1830, an estimated twenty thousand Anglos lived in Tejas, outnumbering *tejanos* by a ratio of five to one. The effect of the Colonization Act of 1825 on the population of Texas is often equated with the effect of the Gold Rush on the population of California.

The influx of Anglo Americans created tensions that mounted through the decade. Despite the technicality of swearing allegiance to Mexico that was one of the conditions for settlement, most *americanos* brought traditions about land ownership, language, law, and government that they had no intention of giving up. Internal turmoil in Mexico added to the tensions. *Tejanos*, like *californios*, sided with the Federalists in the hopes of making Tejas an autonomous state of the Mexican nation. Anglos and *tejano* Federalists joined in a series of maneuvers that culminated in the Texas Revolution in 1836, the same year that the Federalist Alvarado led an uprising that gained autonomy for California.[50]

The Texas Revolution, however, achieved independence, although it was an independence that Mexico refused to acknowledge until 1845, when, in an unsuccessful attempt to forestall U.S. annexation, the Herrera government offered diplomatic recognition to the Republic of Texas.[51] Warfare, therefore, continued after 1836, with the disputed territory between the Nueces and the Rio Grande serving as the battleground between *americano* and *mexicano*, between Federalist and centralist.[52]

Immigration from both the United States and Europe continued to swell the non-*mexicano* population after 1836. The legend of

Santa Anna's cruelty and the continuing bloodshed on the border raised tensions between *tejanos* and Anglos. The fact that most *americano* migrants came from the South and brought a social order predicated upon skin color that they could easily apply to *mexicanos* intensified the blatant racial hostility. Juan N. Seguín, for example, had fought with the rebels and had been elected mayor of San Antonio. Yet, by 1844, just eight years after the Battle of San Jacinto, mob action drove him to exile.[53]

Few in number and poor in resources, native Texans stood little chance in the face of the growing, hostile population. The census underscores the situation: according to the 1850 enumeration, *mexicanos* made up only 5 percent of the population.

### Nuevo Santander

The Tejas experience resembles that of California in many of its major aspects. Nuevo Santander, on the other hand, shares many of the characteristics of New Mexico history.

Like Tejas and California, Nuevo Santander was founded to combat potential threats to the Spanish Empire. In the middle of the eighteenth century, the Crown saw the Gulf Coast from Tampico to the mouth of the Guadalupe River as vulnerable to the French and English adventurers roaming the Gulf and to Indians who had been squeezed north and east by the pressure of Spanish expansion. Accordingly, Colonel José de Escandón received the appointment to colonize. After several reconnoitering expeditions, Escandón chose the Rio Grande Valley. Between 1749 and 1755, he founded twenty-four settlements on both sides of the river from its mouth to the two Laredos, all but one of which still exist.[54]

Nuevo Santander developed as a self-contained, relatively cohesive community focused upon the Rio Grande. It was tangential to the main roads between San Antonio and Coahuila and surrounded by almost impassable brush country and hostile Indians. As a result, a fairly closed pastoral community arose, supported by a mixed economy similar to New Mexico's: land next to the river was divided in small irrigable strips, with grazing in the back country. Although Matamoros boasted fifteen thousand inhabitants and a small merchant class by 1835, most of the people lived in small villages, and the social relationships based on family and immediate locale gave Nuevo Santander a primordial orientation similar to that of New Mexico. And, like New Mexico, this closed pastoral community tended to view others—whether *mexicano* or Anglo—as *fuereños* or *extranjeros*.[55]

Anglo American encroachment followed a course like New

Mexico's as well. Merchants and lawyers landed at Brownsville and used economic inducements and the intricacies of Anglo American law to insinuate themselves into the community and acquire land. But the Valley experience contained elements not found in New Mexico. From the mid-thirties, Valley people were drawn into conflicts that New Mexico largely ignored: the Federalist wars, the Texas Revolution, and nine years of border warfare after San Jacinto. From the perspective of Valley *mexicanos*, the war with the United States was just another phase in a struggle that had been going on for more than a decade, and conflict continued into the next century. The war, however, had one lasting impact. It turned the unifying river into a dividing line, thereby bisecting a cohesive community of almost one hundred years' standing. As in New Mexico, Anglos did not gain complete ascendancy in the Valley until the twentieth century. But, unlike the situation in New Mexico, that domination was accompanied by bloody skirmishes that were cast in terms of the border: its artificiality, its symbolic meaning, and its strategic possibilities.

Mexicano residents in all of the areas acquired by the United States faced the same problems. Property rights made up one set of concerns; justice in the courts and from officers of the law made up another. On a daily basis, the differences in language, religion, and appearance caused friction and hostilities that nagged constantly, like a dull toothache. In sum, the issue for *mexicanos* was self-preservation—self-preservation not only in the literal sense of physical survival, although often the problem was that basic, but also in the more general sense of living the way they wanted to. Their struggle was to preserve their time-honored, socially established structures of meaning.

Differences in the Anglo American advance in each area cloaked the problems in various guises. Differences in the historical backgrounds of *mexicanos* shaped the specifics of their responses. But, within a fairly narrow range, the problems were the same, and *mexicanos* drew their responses from a fairly limited repertoire of tactical possibilities.

In Texas, nineteenth-century resistance sprang almost entirely from the Valley. The most important feature about the Valley after 1848 was the newly imposed border. Resistance ran the gamut from individual outbursts of rage to planned and coordinated uprisings, but all of the resistance was cast in terms of the border. The border was at once a concrete and specific factor that had to be dealt with and a symbolic statement about their situation for all *mexicanos* north of Mexico. A look at resistance on the Texas Border provides an introduction to *mexicano* resistance in the nineteenth century.

# CHAPTER 3

# The Border

Mexicanos in nineteenth-century Texas shaped their resistance to Anglo American control in terms of the new border created by the Treaty of Guadalupe Hidalgo.

Folklorist James Reed, in discussing the border between England and Scotland, observed that "The Border is not a line but an area, in many respects historically and traditionally an independent region."[1] The same is true for the lower Rio Grande border. Within six years of its founding, Nuevo Santander numbered almost nine thousand colonists clustered in tight village units along both sides of the Rio Grande.[2] The thick growth of chaparral that covered the back country caused settlement to focus on the Rio Grande, and the river became the lifeline of the community that gave both water and social access. Relatives and close friends lived on both sides of the river, and often north bank villages were extensions of those from the south bank. Off the major north-south arteries between Tejas and the interior, outsiders rarely troubled the colony. A close-knit society developed there, supported by subsistence agriculture and grazing and possessed with a regional consciousness exemplified by the use of the term fuereño—outsider—to identify Mexicans from elsewhere.

The new international boundary literally cut through the heart of Nuevo Santander as the province was entering its second century of existence. Valley residents now faced the demand to change the traditions of a lifetime. The unifying river became a barrier; relatives and neighbors on the other side were now supposed to be treated as foreigners in a foreign land.

Californian and New Mexican communities, in contrast, were transferred whole to the new regime. The surveyed boundary from San Diego to El Paso ran through desert and the lands of hostile Indians; the Rio Grande from El Paso to the Laredos flowed through much the same kind of territory.[3] The war and the treaty did many

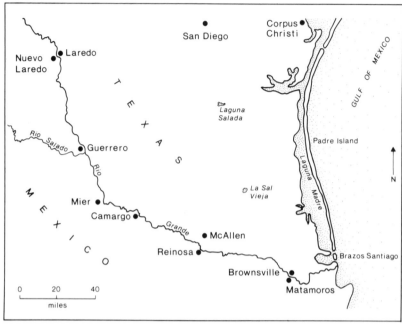

Map 2. The Lower Border

things to *californios* and *nuevos mexicanos*, but they did not abrupt-
ly sunder the regionalism that, after the family, formed the basis for
their strongest social attachments. But Nuevo Santander was torn in
two.

Several things can happen when a new international boundary
bisects a community. The change disrupts. Law, currency, political
systems, economic policies, and procedures both statutory and cus-
tomary no longer mesh. The disruption is inconvenient, and it is
also an affront, a constant reminder of defeat. Inconvenience and insult lead to tension. The awareness of change, of being occupied by a
foreign power, feeds the desire for reunion. Those not under the conquerors' rule encourage and support reunion, and the asylum offered
on the other side makes harassment, sabotage, and guerrilla warfare
strategically possible. The conquerors know this too, and they are
likely to use the violence inherent in the police powers of the state
in an attempt to solidify their hold. But unless violence is carried to
the level of terror, it usually serves only to increase hostility and
conflict.

The tradition of regional unity kept irredentist sentiment high along the Lower Rio Grande Border until well into the twentieth century, and the violence perpetrated by local law enforcement officials, the Texas Rangers, and the U.S. Army added to the incentives for reunion. But other factors joined with these general "border" characteristics to make violence the most distinguishing facet of cultural interaction along the Rio Grande during the remainder of the century. For one, *mexicanos* outnumbered *americanos*. For another, the historic isolation of the Lower Valley was not truly ended until the completion of the railroad to Brownsville in 1904 opened the region for corporate farming, intensive land speculation, and the other aspects of Anglo development. Third, the police arm of the state was accompanied by a vicious racism on the part of Texas officers that contributed to what would now be called police brutality and that allowed Anglos who murdered *mexicanos* to go unpunished. The political wars of Mexico added a fourth element; *mexicanos* in Texas often participated in them, and the example of revolution inspired the people of the Border to seek redress through violence. And finally, frontier life made *mexicanos* just as familiar with and experienced in the armed defense of their communities as were Anglo American pioneers.

Prior to Mexican independence, life in Nuevo Santander followed a rhythm of pastoral tranquillity broken occasionally by Comanche attacks. Although the movement for independence itself did not affect the colony to any great extent, the Federalist wars and the Texas Revolution inaugurated a series of violent confrontations that continued through the remainder of the century and into the next.

## The Tradition of Border Dispute

The Battle of San Jacinto in 1836 marked the independence of the Republic of Texas, but Mexico did not acknowledge Anglo American control of the province until 1845. For nine years, Mexico maintained that Tejas was a Mexican area in a state of rebellion until, in an attempt to forestall U.S. annexation, the Herrera regime tendered the Republic an offer of diplomatic recognition.[4]

Diplomatic protocol aside, the conflict between Mexico and the new Anglo American republic centered around the border. Texas claimed all of the land north and east of the Rio Grande. President Mirabeau Lamar carried this position to its logical conclusion by sending an expedition to conquer New Mexico in 1841.[5] It failed miserably, but left a bitter legacy of hate and distrust between Texan and *nuevo mexicano* expressed in the saying: "Pity poor New Mexico. So far from heaven and so close to Texas."[6] But most of Anglo Texas's efforts to realize the boundary claim came through raids aimed at the Lower Rio Grande communities, while *mexicanos* countered by attempting to keep the Republic confined north of the Nueces, the traditional boundary of Tejas. The brushland between the Nueces and the Rio Grande—Nuevo Santander's rangeland or "backyard"—became the arena for constant skirmishing between *americano* and *mexicano*.

The nine years of conflict ran the gamut from outright banditry to more formal military actions. The foundation of bandit-guerrilla activity was raiding for cattle and horses. Bands of Texas "cowboys" penetrated south of the Nueces, rounding up thousands of head of livestock in what they claimed was retribution for property destroyed during the Revolution. Their vaquero counterparts crossed the Nueces in retaliation and returned driving equally large herds. Not infrequently, *americano* and *mexicano* riders met and fought.[7]

Three related trends built on the raiding and marauding base. First, the Federalist disturbances which broke out in northern Mexico in 1837 added to the level of violence.[8] The northern Federalists wanted an independent nation carved out of northern Mexico. The opportunities for excitement, plunder, and infiltration of Mexico attracted many Anglo Texas allies. The planned Republic of the Rio Grande of 1840–1841 offers a clear expression of this regional ideal, which continued as a motivating sentiment into the twentieth century: delegates to the organizing convention came from the states of Tamaulipas, Nuevo Leon, Coahuila, and "that portion of Texas lying west of the Nueces"; and the boundaries of the proposed republic included "all of Tamaulipas and Coahuila as far north as the Nueces and Medina Rivers, respectively, and extending south to the Sierra Madre, including Nuevo Leon, Zacatecas, Durango, Chihuahua and Nuevo Mexico."[9]

Indians provided another complication. Increased settlement brought pressure to bear on Indian tribes in adjacent areas, particularly the Comanches, and the border turmoil created attractive conditions for raiding and plundering Anglo and *mexicano* communities alike.[10] Repeated Mexican attempts to form alliances with the Comanches in order to reconquer Texas added another layer to the problem of Indian attacks.[11]

Reconquest formed the third violent trend that built on the raiding tradition. Rumors of Mexican invasion swept through Texas regularly. Periodically, Mexico massed troops along the Rio Grande in a show of strength. Occasionally, Mexican troops marched past the Nueces: Mexican forces occupied San Antonio twice in 1842, in March and September.[12] Anglo Texans retaliated with the unauthorized and ill-fated Mier expedition, the defeat of which added to the Remember-the-Alamo myth of Mexican cruelty and cowardice.[13]

For Nuevo Santander, the Mexican War was another event in a decade-long conflict. The boundary dispute that allowed Zachary Taylor to report that he had been attacked on American soil dated from 1836. Fighting with cowboy raiders, irregular militia, and regular troops had gone on for years. Rancheros from both sides of the Rio Grande joined the Mexican army at the battles of Palo Alto and Resaca de las Palmas and harassed Taylor's column throughout the march to Monterey.[14]

But the war made a difference. It brought the Border, and the Border brought gringos. Many of Taylor's men elected to remain in the Lower Valley and enjoy the fruits of victory. They remembered which side their new neighbors had been on, and their memories did not make them charitable. Other Anglo adventurers arrived, lured by the possibilities afforded by war and its aftermath.[15] The newcomers began to exert themselves almost immediately, and land was what they aimed at first.

Historian Walter Prescott Webb asserted that after 1848, "the old landholding families found their titles in jeopardy and if they did not lose in the courts they lost to their American lawyers."[16] Adverse court rulings and lawyers' fees paid in land were two ways that Anglo American law separated the new citizens from their property. Law enforcement, or its absence, was another. A ranchero's cattle would be killed or stolen. If economic ruin did not convince him to sell, then he would be charged with and convicted of rustling, which usually convinced his widow.[17] *Mexicanos* in the Lower Valley believed that Anglo peace officers not only turned a blind eye to this intimidation, but actively participated in it. Thus, along the Border, the Texas Rangers were known as *los rinches de la Kineña*—the Rangers of the King Ranch.[18]

The Border remained a rough frontier area for decades after the treaty. Hostile Indians, bandits, and other hard cases added more violent dimensions to the hostilities between conqueror and conquered. The "oxcart war" of 1857 between Anglo Texan and *mexicano* freighters offers a dramatic, but by no means isolated, example of the potential for violence in the region.[19] But the Rio Grande was easy to cross, and *mexicanos* had numerical superiority. The years immediately following the war witnessed the same kind of friction that had gone before, intensified by the fact that social authority was now in new hands. The actions of the new authorities outraged Border residents almost daily. In 1859, *mexicano* outrage crystallized around a man named Juan N. Cortina.

## The Cortina War

Juan Nepomuceno Cortina was born into a respected Border family at Camargo, on the south bank, in 1824.[20] As one historian put it, Cortina "received his education in the turbulent politics of northern Mexico"; that is, he came to manhood during the years of the Federalist wars.[21] He enlisted in the national guard of Tamaulipas and fought against Taylor's command. Cortina was among the petitioners who in 1850 requested Congress to form a Territory of the Rio Grande from the region south of New Mexico.[22] The request was not granted, but nonetheless, Cortina moved to the north bank in 1855 and began ranching on a portion of his mother's estate.

Thirty-five years old in 1859, Juan Cortina was a man of mature vigorous years, from a prominent family, experienced in military affairs, and with a history of opposition to Anglo Americans. He was, in short, a natural leader of the society split by the new border. His family's property, the Espíritu Santo land grant, had been diminished by the Anglo courts. Cortina's pride rebelled against the gringo law officers whose arrogance rose as Anglo merchants and lawyers increased their inroads in the Valley. Twelve years under Anglo domination had built a volatile fund of anger and resentment in Cortina and his people that needed only a spark to ignite it into open war.

A law officer struck the spark. On July 13, 1859, in Brownsville, Cortina saw city marshal Bob Spears pistol-whipping a drunken vaquero who worked for Cortina's mother. He shot Spears and left town with the vaquero. Two months later, Cortina led an estimated sixty riders into Brownsville, where they released all of the mexicano prisoners in the jail, sacked the stores of particularly obnoxious merchants, and executed four Americans who had killed mexicanos and had gone unpunished.

Influential citizens, including the Mexican consul in Brownsville and Cortina's cousin, persuaded him to leave the city. Two days later, however, Cortina issued a proclamation that enumerated the grievances of his band and vowed that they would continue to fight for justice. Apparently, further pleas from mexicano residents of Brownsville convinced him to disband; in any event, Cortina did not strike again until Brownsville police captured one of his lieutenants, Tomás Cabrera. Regrouping, Cortina threatened to destroy the city if his man was not released. A joint force made up of Anglos and Mexican national guardsmen lent by the Liberal government, which did not want to disrupt U.S.-Mexican harmony, attacked Cortina on October 22. They suffered a resounding defeat. Cortina controlled the countryside and kept Brownsville under siege.

The arrival of the Texas Rangers inflamed the situation. In exasperation, the Rangers hanged Cabrera, despite earlier promises from Brownsville leaders that he would receive a fair trial. Cortina responded with a second proclamation and renewed his attacks. *Mexicano* riders swelled the size of his army. Noncombatants refused to help state officials and volunteered supplies to Cortina instead. Cortina's statements and actions won widespread approval from the people of the Border, and the combination of popular support and successful skirmishes kept Cortina master of the Rio Grande for the remainder of the year.

General Juan N. Cortina, 1866. Photo by De Planque, Brownsville and Matamoros. Laredo Archives, St. Mary's University, San Antonio, Texas. Copy from the University of Texas Institute of Texan Cultures.

It took the U.S. Army to defeat the insurgents. Troops under Major S. P. Heintzelman accompanied by a force of Texas Rangers under Colonel John S. Ford defeated the rebels at Rio Grande City on December 27, 1859. Sporadic fighting continued into the new year, but Cortina was now confined to sniping and harassing actions as he moved along both sides of the border pursued by American and Mexican troops. The aftermath of the rebellion saw Anglos, principally the Rangers, retaliate indiscriminately against all *mexicanos* in a fit of bloody terrorism.

Gringos called Cortina a bandit and attributed the uprising to the inherent characteristics of a vicious race who wanted plunder and the chance to "execute summary vengeance on all towards whom [they] had *private* grudges" (italics added).[23] Americans on the Border were acutely conscious of being in the minority—numbering only three hundred against twelve thousand according to one contemporary estimate[24]—and conscious of their disproportionate economic and political power. People occupying a privileged status often find it necessary to justify themselves in terms of the "natural" order of things and to attribute any signs of discontent to a biological or moral flaw of the complainers. But contemporary Anglo accounts of the uprising sometimes allowed traces of guilt or glimmerings of awareness of oppression to show through. Accounts of the Brownsville raid said that Cortina's raiders had shouted "Death to Americans; *viva la republica Mexicana*; and threatened to hoist the Mexican flag on the staff of our deserted garrison," clearly attributing a political motive to the raiders.[25] Another account explained the raid by saying: ". . . under a polite exterior, the deepest, settled hatred exists in the Mexican mind towards us," an expression suggesting that there might be legitimate grievances against the newcomers.[26]

Anglos made occasional lapses which hinted that Cortina and his followers were something other than bandits; Cortina asserted unequivocally that the movement aimed to bring justice to his people. The first proclamation, issued two days after the Brownsville raid, explained that in the name of "the sacred right of self-preservation" Cortina and his men were trying to "put an end to our misfortunes." Cortina laid the blame on a "secret conclave. . . [that] persecute[s] and rob[s] for no other crime than that of being of Mexican origin."[27] Cortina described the Brownsville raiders as "clothed in the imposing aspect of our exasperation" and went on to warn that though they might have to lead a "wandering life . . . our personal enemies shall not possess our lands until they have fattened it with their own gore."[28]

Cortina's two proclamations emphasize three major complaints: loss of land either through legal manipulation or through intimidation; the impunity with which Anglos killed Mexicans; and the arrogance of Anglo American racism, "so ostentatious of its own qualities."[29] While the grievances against the Anglos are expressed long and eloquently, the remedies are brief and vague. Beyond swearing to correct injustices and exterminate the "tyrants," the only specific proposal suggests that *mexicanos* "repose their lot under the good sentiments of the governor elect of the State, General Houston."[30] A tragic aura, arising from phrases like "a wandering life" and "I am ready to offer myself as a sacrifice to your happiness," joins with the ill-defined proposals to give a hopeless quality to the undertaking. The grievances and the anger are real and powerful, but there is no corresponding conviction of hope for the future.

The Cortina War was planned and coordinated, widespread and momentarily effective: for three of the seven months that it lasted, Cortina controlled the Lower Rio Grande Border. It was a resistance movement that grew out of Border culture and was limited by Border culture as well. The conflict carried two major themes: the tradition of community unity in the face of the international boundary, and the personal nature of the undertaking. The revolt formed around a charismatic individual who responded to assaults on individuals for whom he felt personally responsible; the cause of the problems and the targets of the raids were specific people judged to be guilty of wrongdoing. Although Cortina's proclamations stressed that he spoke for U.S. citizens deprived of their rights, he used the Border as one region; Anglos used this crossing of the river to brand all insurgents as "Mexicans" and thereby deny the legitimacy of their complaints. Cortina's subsequent career continued to be shaped by this regional affiliation: he fought with the Mexican Republicans against the French in the battle of the Cinco de Mayo, and he rode as an *enganchado*—Union agent—against Confederate Texas during the U.S. Civil War.

The tradition of regional unity distinguishes one aspect of Border orientation and *personalismo* another. Both are undergirded by tradition, the sense that things were the way they ought to be before the gringos came. The real goal of Cortina's revolt was to return to the old ways, the proper ways, by getting rid of the evil gringos. Since the solution was to purge the community of evil, the revolt itself was the solution, and elaborate proposals for the future were unnecessary. Since, however, the United States was so strong and Mexico so unsettled, and since evil is a constant in the human condition, a realistic man did not assume that he would be successful. Still he had to try.

Many others also tried. Cortina was joined by other Border fighters who combined the dual roles of *enganchado* and *juarista* (a Benito Juárez supporter), and this double activity continued through the century, underscoring the regional sentiment in Border culture. But before there can be resistance movements, there must be people who are willing to resist. The essential materials for any form of resistance are individuals who refuse to submit, who will "break before they bend."[31] The Border sheltered many proud people, and the most outstanding were remembered in ballads called *corridos*. The saga of Gregorio Cortez provides a good picture of the values and attributes that formed the basis for the resistance that came out of nineteenth-century Border culture.

## The Saga of Gregorio Cortez

The story of Gregorio Cortez, who "defended his right with his pistol in his hand," captures much of the *mexicanos'* situation in Texas at

Gregorio Cortez and his guard. Courtesy Hunter Collection, Humanities Research Center, The University of Texas at Austin. "—¡Ah, cuánto rinche . . . / para un solo mexicano!" ("Ah, how many rangers / Against one lone Mexican!") (From the Ballad of Gregorio Cortez, in Américo Paredes, "*With His Pistol in His Hand*," p. 172.)

the turn of the century.[32] It began in 1901 with a brief flurry of gunfire and ended in 1913 after a legal fight waged by Hispanic Texans. The battle grew out of a confrontation between Anglo lawmen and a *mexicano* farmer. Set in a context of mutual mistrust and hostility, specific cultural problems—three errors in translation by a "bilingual" deputy named Boone Choate—touched off ten days of turmoil that reached epic proportions.

On June 12, 1901, Karnes County Sheriff W. T. (Brack) Morris, an experienced Texas peace officer, set out with two deputies in search of a "Mexican" horsethief. They were armed but unencumbered with a warrant. The lawmen learned that Gregorio Cortez, a rancher and farmer who had lived in the county for some eleven years, had recently traded a horse to a neighbor. Morris and his party went to question him, arriving as Cortez, his brother Romaldo, and their families were resting after the noon meal.

Whether Morris actually suspected Cortez or merely wanted information is not clear. Three mistakes by Choate, the translator, rendered the question academic.[33]

The officers first spoke to Romaldo, asking if Gregorio was there. Romaldo turned, saying, "*Te quieren*," literally, "You are wanted." In

Spanish, this is a common way of saying "Somebody wants to talk to you." To a barely fluent Anglo deputy, it sounded very close to an admission of guilt.

Morris then asked, through Choate, if Cortez had traded a horse (*caballo*) to a name named Villarreal. Cortez said no, meaning that he had not traded a *caballo*, but a mare, a *yegua*. Hearing the negative, Morris then told Choate to tell Cortez that he was going to arrest him and moved closer, drawing his gun. After Choate's translation, Cortez answered, "You can't arrest me for nothing," which Choate took to mean "No one can arrest me." Gunplay followed that left Morris dead on the spot and Romaldo fatally wounded.

Cortez became a hunted man. At first on foot, later mounted, he eluded posse after posse—some numbering over three hundred men—leading Texas authorities on a ten-day, five-hundred-mile chase toward Laredo—the border and safety. The lone Cortez almost made it; a vaquero betrayed him to the Texas Rangers as he rested, preparing to cross the Rio Grande at night.

A series of trials ensued that lasted almost four years. Cortez was charged with horse stealing and three counts of murder (Morris and two other lawmen). He was found not guilty by reason of self-defense for killing Morris, not guilty of horse theft, and not guilty of killing a posse member named Schnaebel. The Court of Criminal Appeals upheld his conviction for the murder of a man named Glover, however, and on January 2, 1905, Cortez entered Huntsville to serve a life sentence. Governor O. B. Colquitt pardoned him in 1913, and Cortez returned to the Border where he was born. He died in 1916, probably of natural causes, although both legend and family tradition maintain that he was poisoned.

The saga of Gregorio Cortez is remarkable not only because it tells how one *mexicano* responded to a serious threat, but also because of the folklore that developed about him.

Daily newspaper bulletins and word of mouth kept Texans abreast of the ten-day chase, and the successive failures of the pursuers embarrassed and infuriated the authorities. *Mexicanos* rallied in support immediately after the capture: the Miguel Hidalgo Workers' Society of San Antonio initiated the fund raising to support the defense. Support lasted through the years of litigation and did not stop until Colquitt's pardon; one man's violent outburst produced a sustained legal campaign that won after a twelve-year fight.

Ballads or *corridos* appeared along with the fund raising. The practice of commemorating conflicts in song was firmly established along the border; *corrido* fragments that describe the Cortina War still survive, and the form probably developed earlier. The *corridos* about Gregorio Cortez depict the Border peoples' ideal man and their perceptions of life under Anglo domination. The principal theme is the morality of Cortez's actions. He had defended his right. Similarly, his flight is unquestioned. It was the only possibility in Anglo Texas.

In the songs, Cortez appears as the model of virtue: modest and dignified, not boasting or frivolous; industrious and talented—the best vaquero, horseman, and farmer around—not acquisitive but content with the traditional occupations and skills; courageous, loyal, compassionate, proud, and unrepentant—in both legend and fact he never wavered from his claim that he was in the right. Cortez is the quintessential embodiment of traditional Border values, and his capture, according to the *corridos*, follows tradition, too: he is betrayed by a Judas, a *vendido*—a sellout.

Anglo Texans divided in their attitudes toward Cortez after his capture. Grudging admiration surfaced amidst the vituperative outpourings during the chase, and his conduct during the trial won many Anglos, including many of his pursuers, to his side. And Cortez was found not guilty of killing Morris, indicating that Anglos, too, thought that he had a right to defend himself.

On the other hand, many Anglos saw Cortez as a vicious specimen of a corrupt and inferior race. They called for his lynching, trumped up charges against him, abused and terrorized his family and other *mexicanos*. This sentiment remained alive throughout the era. One newspaper responded to the pardon with a vehement attack against the "chicken-hearted Governor" who had freed a "Mexican who took the lives of American citizens."[34]

The *corridos* depict a man of spirit who properly defends his rights. His successes against overwhelming odds make for a prideful exhilaration. But tragedy permeates the story. According to the *corridos*, Cortez knows in advance that he will be betrayed, but he accepts his fate. He, personally, can defeat the Rangers, but his people are not as gifted, and their vulnerability is his. His pardon does not justify working within the system but rather reinforces the moral correctness of his position. Even his oppressors must admit that Cortez is on the side of justice. But the pardon is a hollow victory, for the treacherous Anglos poisoned him. The vision is tragic, almost predestined, although not in a Calvinistic sense. Neither is there an other-worldly aspect that promises a final eternal reward. Rather, the world is unjust, and evil enemies will win. A good man's fate is to struggle, knowing that victory is in the fact of struggle, not in its success.

Gregorio Cortez was both a product and perpetuator of Border culture. As folklorist Américo Paredes demonstrates, the facts of his life conformed to pre-existing legend: "It was almost as if the Border people had dreamed Gregorio Cortez before producing him, and had sung his life and his deeds before he was born."[35]

From the Cortina War to the twentieth century, life along the Lower Rio Grande Border followed a pattern of uneasy accommodation punctuated by outbreaks of violence. Anglo cattle barons consolidated their holdings and tried to act like *patrones* toward the *mexicano* workers. In some areas, influential *mexicanos* were able to gain some measure of control; Brownsville, for example, had a *mexicano* sheriff by 1890. But tensions were never far from the surface, and the overwhelming attitude of *mexicanos* living on the border was that they were living in a part of Mexico occupied by a foreign power. *Corridos* honoring those who fought bravely against Anglos, or against the friendly regime of Porfirio Díaz that cooperated with Anglos by sending "outlaws" back across the border, kept the attitude alive. Sometimes the songs honored bandits like José Mosqueda, who struck against Anglos by committing the first train robbery on the Brownsville–Point Isabel railroad. Sometimes they commemorated peaceable common folk fighting Anglo injustice as Gregorio Cortez did, and sometimes they honored revolutionaries like Catarino Garza, whose attack against the Díaz government was stopped by U.S. forces.[36] But the common themes of the songs of border conflict were resistance against the foreign Anglos and unity with the people on the south side of the Rio Grande. These motives created one last major uprising along the border between 1915 and 1917.

## Los Sediciosos

Brownsville was connected to the outside world by rail in 1904, and a new wave of Anglo migrants and developers upset the balance worked out during the preceding fifty years.[37] Heightened discrimination accompanied the economic dislocation brought by the new influx of Anglos. The discrimination was not new, particularly in its violent forms. Gregorio Cortez's almost reflex use of his pistol came from a deep-seated understanding of what was likely to happen to a *mexicano* when an Anglo lawman drew his gun. But the use of the "shoot first and ask questions later" technique of law enforcement increased during the first two decades of the twentieth century, as did the number of *mexicanos* killed by Anglo mobs. The rising tensions led to the formation of the Congreso Mexicanista that met at

Laredo in 1911 in an attempt to deal with the problem of violence.[38]

The Mexican Revolution also contributed. Under the dictatorship of Porfirio Díaz, relationships between the United States and Mexico were cordial. Díaz and the *científicos* (literally, the scientists) sought to modernize the Mexican economy. One of their major efforts to this end involved enclosing the common lands of the *peones* into commercial plantations that produced cash crops. The Díaz regime welcomed American investment and encouraged the United States to import Mexican laborers, thereby reducing the surplus population created by enclosure. Because he wanted to please the United States and to inhibit revolution against himself, Díaz cooperated with U.S. authorities by returning fugitives north of the Rio Grande. Just as the Border had been strongly Federalist and supportive of Juárez, it was also pronouncedly anti-Díaz. When the revolution broke out, many Border residents became actively involved. The increased Anglo presence combined with the inspirational example of the revolution to lead Border *mexicanos* on a planned movement of violent resistance.

A man named Basilio Ramos was arrested and taken to Brownsville in January, 1915. Authorities found a plan for revolt, scheduled to begin on February 20, among his possessions. Dated January 6, 1915, at San Diego, Texas, it has become known as the Plan de San Diego.[39]

The document identifies nine signatories who make up the provisional directorate of the movement. It goes on to describe the organizational structure of the revolutionary force, called the Liberating Army of Races and Peoples, detail the timing of the uprising, and lay out fundamental policy: every North American male sixteen years of age or older will be killed; when cities are captured, municipal authorities will be appointed immediately "that they may preserve order."[40]

The goal of the revolt is the establishment of an independent republic that reunites both sides of the Border, a vision first expressed almost a century before in the documents of the Republic of the Rio Grande. The plan, therefore, springs from the time-honored regional identification of the Border *mexicanos*. Reunion is the goal; annexation with Mexico might occur "if it be thought expedient."[41]

Another aspect of the plan indicates the broadening horizons of the *mexicano* world view. Indians, Orientals, and blacks will be recruited for the Liberating Army of Races and Peoples as well, forming a coalition of third world peoples who share the experience of Anglo oppression. But, although appealing for help against a common enemy, the plan sees each group as occupying separate areas:

Indian lands "which have been taken from them shall be returned to them . . ."; blacks will be aided "in obtaining six States of the American Union . . . [and] they may form from these six States a Republic."[42] The plan describes a cooperative venture by distinct peoples who share a common enemy in order that each group may establish a separate nation.

No uprising took place on February 20. A revised Plan de San Diego, a Manifesto to the Oppressed Peoples of America, did appear on or about that date.[43] Nothing much happened for the next four months. Then, beginning in July, 1915, a series of raids swept the Lower Rio Grande Valley, accompanied by an undated manifesto calling all *mexicanos* in Texas to take up arms.[44] The raiders were led by Luis de la Rosa, a former sheriff of Cameron County, and by Aniceto Pizaña, from a respected ranching family near Brownsville.

Between July and November in 1915, *los sediciosos* burned railroad trestles, stopped passenger trains, raided the Norias Ranch that was part of the King Ranch holdings, and fought a number of skirmishes with U.S. Army detachments and Texas Ranger patrols. The raids ceased during the winter, but then began again during the summer of 1916.[45]

Anglos on the Border struck back. Citizens formed vigilante Law and Order Leagues, and the U.S. Army and Texas Rangers moved through the area. The Rangers attacked with such indiscriminate viciousness that even Walter Prescott Webb's sympathetic pen called it "an orgy of bloodshed" and "revenge by proxy."[46] General Funston, commander of the U.S. forces in the region, feared that the army's reputation would suffer through association with "peace officers who are such scoundrels."[47] The estimates of *mexicanos* summarily shot or hanged without trial range from three hundred to five thousand.

Recent scholarship demonstrates that Venustiano Carranza, then very close to winning his battle for control of the Mexican Revolution against Emiliano Zapata and Pancho Villa, used the raiders as a device to win U.S. recognition of his regime and to get General Pershing's punitive expedition withdrawn from Mexican soil.[48] There is evidence that Carranza not only encouraged *los sediciosos*, but also supplied funds, officers, and troops from his army and in general directed the whole enterprise.[49] Historians Charles Harris and Louis Sadler draw this picture of Carranza: "Viewing Mexican Americans as a useful fifth column, Carranza skillfully played on their hopes and fears as a means of exerting pressure on the United States. When his policies shifted, they were cynically abandoned."[50] Carranza's role in the raids helps to explain the pattern of the attacks and their abrupt cessation after he withdrew his support. But the only explanation for the willingness of de la Rosa and Pizaña to participate in what, in hindsight at any rate, looks like a wild and impossible scheme is the depth of Border community feeling and the extreme hostility toward gringo rule. And the reign of terror instituted by the Rangers in response to the raids shows why these attitudes remained so entrenched in Border culture.

After *los sediciosos*, armed protest against Anglo domination was confined to individuals who refused to submit. Movements of self-preservation in Texas began to explore other ways to carve out enough space for survival and comfort under United States rule. But nineteenth-century violent resistance in Texas left a legacy that influenced subsequent efforts.

Violent resistance in Texas covered the entire spectrum of armed protest used by *mexicanos*. The Border gave a particular emphasis and focus to protest that New Mexico and California did not share, except in the overarching sense that *nuevos mexicanos* and *californios* were also "foreigners in their native land."[51] Resistance in Texas built upon proud individuals who were part of the community, people called "social bandits" in Eric Hobsbawm's terminology. The Border witnessed endemic friction and violence that occasionally flared into planned and coordinated uprisings. Modifications and adjustments in goals and tactics appeared over time: Cortina's personal identification with his movement and the identification of evil individuals as the cause of the problem while "innocent" people had nothing to fear contrasts sharply with the impersonal tone of the Plan de San Diego and threat of total war embodied in the order to kill all males over sixteen. Similarly the vague program of Cortina's uprising is markedly different from the procedures for revolt, the aim of an independent republic, and the cooperation of the oppressed contained in the Plan. But modifications aside, both Cortina's uprising and the Plan de San Diego, and all other resistance in Texas, sprang directly from the perceptions of what was possible and desirable that were inherent in the traditions of *mexicano* culture.

The same was true for resistance in New Mexico and California. Resistance of all kinds builds on a sense of outrage and forms around individuals who are willing and able to fight back.

# CHAPTER 4

# Social Bandits
# and Community Upheavals

Mexicano-americano conflict on the Lower Rio Grande Border ranged from individual outbursts to planned and coordinated attacks. All armed protest on the Border, however, needed the fundamental ingredient of people who believed that resisting violently was possible and legitimate. The same was true of mexicano resistance in New Mexico and California.

Mexicanos reached the conclusion that violent acts were legitimate by measuring their situation against their traditional standards of behavior and structures of meaning; this process moved in complicated and subtle ways, but always with the interaction between world view and present circumstances.[1] Since circumstances differed from region to region and changed over the course of time, violent resistance took many forms. Two of the basic forms through which mexicanos translated anger into action were social banditry and community upheavals.

Banditry and upheavals are quite different, but each expresses the outrage that dominated peoples feel toward those in power. Social banditry involves a small number of active participants and widespread support from the larger community. Community upheavals have large numbers of participants, last for a fairly short but intense period, and appear to be spontaneous, that is, unplanned.

## Bandidos: Individual Rebels and Social Symbols

That mexicano bandits operated in the Southwest comes as no surprise to anyone who has seen a Western movie—they are a staple of Hollywood's clichéd Old West. But what Hollywood omits is that for many bandidos robbery was as much a kind of individual rebellion as it was a way to make money or enliven a dull existence.

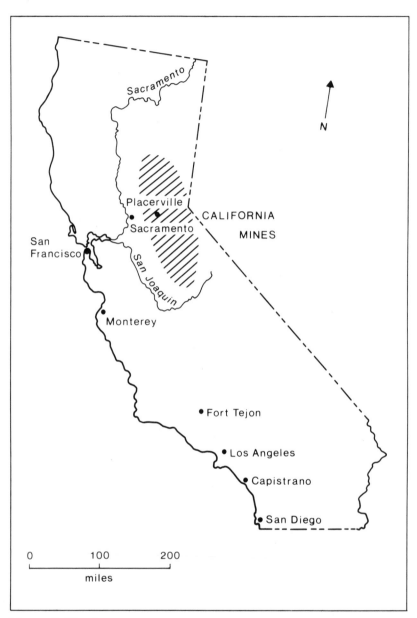

Map 3. California

The thing that separates social bandits from other criminals is the way their own communities regard them. Bandits break laws; therefore the state hunts them as outlaws. But to their own people, they are heroes and defenders, remembered in story and song. For the English-speaking world, the classic social bandit whose legend set the standard for all others was Robin Hood. He robbed from the rich and gave to the poor; he fought against evil government in the persons of Prince John and the Sheriff of Nottingham and for good government in the person of King Richard. And social bandits have appeared and have been remembered throughout the world from the Chinese *Water Margin Novel* to the ballads of eastern Europe and the folklore of Brazil.[2]

*Mexicano* social bandits ran the gamut from men like Gregorio Cortez, who broke no laws until forced to defend himself "with his pistol in his hand," to hard-bitten killers and robbers who gained renown and community approval because they usually attacked Anglos. *Bandidos* covered a wide range of activities and were spurred by a mixture of motives, but *mexicanos* in general saw them as men who refused to submit and who thus symbolized resistance. The story of Tiburcio Vásquez illustrates the circumstances that could lead a man to a career that attained a symbolic impact.

### Tiburcio Vásquez

Tiburcio Vásquez was born in Monterey County, California, on August 11, 1835; he was thirteen at the signing of the Treaty of Guadalupe and fifteen when California joined the Union as a state.[3]

When he was sixteen, in 1851, Vásquez and several others were accused of killing a constable named Hardimount at a fandango in Monterey. Anglos immediately formed a vigilante committee to avenge the lawman and summarily hanged a man named José Guerra. Vásquez fled to the mountains. Although he always maintained he was innocent of the Hardimount killing, the incident launched Vásquez on a life as a bandit that did not end until his execution in 1875.

During the decade of the 1850s, California underwent an epidemic of bandit gangs.[4] The gold fields in the north and the cattle ranches in the south attracted outlaws from all backgrounds. Anglo popular opinion branded most gangs operating at this time as "greasers." This was patently false, but it is true that a large number of *californios*, together with other Latin Americans drawn north by the Gold Rush, did engage in rustling, holdups, and the like. After his flight from the dance-hall knifing, Vásquez probably joined one of the bands in the area.

Nothing distinguished Vásquez from other *bandidos* during the turbulent fifties. He appears to have occupied his time with stage-coach robberies, horse stealing, and cattle rustling, interspersed with periods as a gambler. He was sentenced to San Quentin for horse stealing on August 26, 1857, and escaped, along with forty-one others, on June 25, 1859. Recaptured the following August 17, Vásquez remained in San Quentin until his formal release on August 13, 1863. Arrested again for rustling, Vásquez entered the penitentiary in January, 1867, where he remained until June 4, 1870. Nine and a half of the first nineteen years of his career were spent in San Quentin and the remainder as a bandit and a gambler moving around California.

After his release from prison in 1870, Tiburcio Vásquez began a four-year spree of cattle rustling and robbery that made his name a household word in California and known across the nation. The Monterey grand jury indicted him for murder in January, 1871. Still at large, Vásquez committed a series of robberies in which the victims were left tied and face down on the ground—a technique that became his trademark.

Posses chased him without success; Vásquez roamed almost at will for three years. Then, the robbery and killing of three men at Snyder's Store in Tres Pinos on August 26, 1873, raised a statewide alarm. The day after the Tres Pinos robbery, Governor Booth offered a reward of one thousand dollars for Vásquez, dead or alive. Despite the best efforts of the sheriffs of several counties and the enthusiastic pursuit of vigilante committees, Vásquez remained free and continued to ply his trade. The state legislature authorized the governor to spend fifteen thousand dollars for his capture. In January of 1874, the governor offered three thousand dollars for Vásquez alive and two thousand for his corpse. Vásquez responded by robbing two stagecoaches.

Los Angeles County Sheriff Rowland and a posse of city policemen and deputized citizens finally captured him in May, 1874, after a gunfight in which Vásquez was wounded several times. He was transferred to San José, where, after a continuance on the grounds that important witnesses were missing, his trial began on January 5, 1875. On the ninth he was found guilty, on the twenty-third he was sentenced to death, and on March 19, 1875, after an unsuccessful appeal, Tiburcio Vásquez was hanged.

From mid-summer of 1873 until his death, Vásquez received an enormous amount of publicity. Not only did he electrify the state for the bulk of a year, but the length of time between his arrest and trial allowed a multitude of admirers to visit him in the San José jail, where he sold cards printed with his picture and a short biography.

Major Ben C. Truman, editor of the *Los Angeles Star*, interviewed him, and two newspapermen from the *San Francisco Chronicle* wrote extensively about the bandit.[5]

A number of related factors account for the interest in Tiburcio Vásquez. Bandits have intrigued people for a long time. But he was also a dramatic figure whose exploits corresponded with a national and international rise in interest about the Wild West—Ned Buntline, for example, had already written dime novels about Buffalo Bill and Wild Bill Hickok. Furthermore, Anglos had a secure hold on California by the 1870s, thereby allowing a kind of romanticized interest in *californios* that can be compared to the romanticization of the Indians once they no longer appeared to be a threat.

The English-language press treated Vásquez as something of a social bandit during his trial, and subsequent writers have continued the Robin Hood comparison.[6] As quoted by Major Truman, Vásquez explained that "A spirit of hatred and revenge took possession of me. I had numerous fights in defense of what I believed to be my rights and those of my countrymen. I believed that we were being unjustly deprived of the social rights that belonged to us." He went on to describe his decision to become a bandit: "I got my mother's blessing and told her I was going out into the world . . . to take my chances . . . I should live off the world and perhaps suffer at its hands."[7]

That Anglos should be willing to make a social bandit of Vásquez can be explained in part by their tendency to romanticize the daring and exotic and in part by latent feelings of guilt about the conquest. But certain elements of his long career indicate that he was regarded as a hero by *californios* in general. For one thing, the vast majority of his victims were Anglos. A cynic would argue that he was doing no more than following bank robber Willie Sutton's dictum of going "where the money is." But that argument misses the point about social bandits—they strike out against oppressors. Oppressors are oppressors because they control wealth and politics; to hurt oppressors one must attack them in one or both of these areas.

Second, Vásquez received support and assistance from *californios* throughout his career. The aid and approval from his people is especially apparent during the intense nine-month period during 1873 and 1874: despite the best efforts of California lawmen and the inducements of substantial awards, Vásquez and his men eluded pursuit and struck repeatedly from August to May. A story attributed to Eugenio Plummer, a respected *californio*, illustrates this close relationship. According to Plummer, Vásquez had decided to quit the bandit life and relocate in Mexico.[8] To commemorate this decision, he gave a fandango near Tujunga Canyon the night before his capture. That a hunted bandit should give a party demonstrates that the general population regarded him with approval. Even if the event did not take place, the fact that such an incident can become a part of the oral tradition about a man indicates how he was viewed by his community, in retrospect at least. For *californios*, Vásquez was a man who fought back against the insults and depredations of the Anglos, and he therefore became a symbol of pride and courage for the people as a whole.

The myth of Joaquín Murieta provides another illustration of the importance of symbolic resistance to a conquered people.

### Joaquín Murieta

The debate about whether Joaquín Murieta really existed and terrorized California during the early fifties will probably never be definitively settled. But in a sense the question of his authenticity is irrelevant. As Leonard Pitt observes, "Joaquín Murieta became California's foremost folk legend; the truth may be doubtful but the myth is real." [9]

According to legend, Murieta migrated from Sonora to the California gold fields at the age of eighteen. [10] He arrived in the Stanislaus district in 1850, a peaceable man who endured the insults and outrages of Anglo miners for a year before his pride led him on the path of revenge. Conditions in the gold fields make the motive plausible, and conditions in California in general make the response equally believable.

From 1849 on, Anglo Americans were extremely jealous of "foreign" miners getting "American" gold, and they passed a series of acts aimed at inhibiting or prohibiting non–U.S. citizens from the mines. [11] In theory, these bans did not include *californios*, as they were citizens. But lynch and mob justice, directed particularly against Latin Americans—"greasers"—and Orientals, characterized the California camps until the mid-fifties.

During the same period, bandit gangs began intense activity throughout the state. They decimated the cattle herds en route to market from ranches in Napa, Sonoma, Monterey, and Contra Costa counties, and hijacked payloads from the mines. A number of *californios* responded to insult by revenge through banditry in the initial years after the Mexican War.

During the winter of 1852–1853, Anglo fear and distress about bandit activity crystallized around the figure of Joaquín Murieta. By March, the "Joaquín scare" had the man as mastermind of a conspiracy active across the state. The legislature believed enough in the existence of a Joaquín to create a special ranger company for his capture, and the governor put up a thousand-dollar reward on his authority. A statewide manhunt for someone as ill-defined as a "Joaquín Muriati, or Murieta, or Ocomorenia, or Valensuela, or . . ."[12] was hardly a prudent undertaking; voices of sanity and judiciousness, however, were able only to put a three-month limit on the bounty.

The ranger company returned from the field with a head pickled in a whiskey jar just as the bounty was to expire. The captain, Harry S. Love, claimed that the head had once been attached to the body of Joaquín Murieta, and a grateful legislature awarded him five thousand dollars. The generosity of the reward for such a vague identification of the culprit and timely success of the manhunt prompted some observers to comment that more than one head must have been pickled in whiskey. In any event, the jar and its contents remained on display in San Francisco until lost during the 1906 earthquake.[13]

The point about Joaquín Murieta is not whether he existed but the fact that Anglos and *californios* alike thought that he did. Overt hostility between conqueror and conquered was at a high during the early fifties. *Californios* struck out in many ways against the tangible manifestations of Anglo control, and Joaquín focused their anger and resentment. Anglos knew of this hostility, and their eagerness to believe in a criminal mastermind indicates the depth of their fear.

The epidemic banditry in California is indicative of the extreme social dislocation produced by the conquest and the Gold Rush. The fact that Joaquín was supposed to have come from Sonora illustrates one important aspect of the dissolution of *californio* society: the Gold Rush broke California's isolation from Mexico and Latin America. Miners from Chile, Peru, and the Mexican state of Sonora flocked to the diggings. *Californios* had traditionally remained aloof from *cholos*, and they continued to try to do so. But the Anglos' blindness to distinctions of citizenship allowed them to lump all Latins together as "greasers," thereby adding intense discrimination to the other factors contributing to the collapse of the tenuous society of Old California.

### Social Bandits in Texas and New Mexico

Social banditry in Texas and New Mexico was less intense, but lasted for a much longer time than in California. The legend of Gregorio Cortez shows that the ideal Border hero was a peaceful man who resorted to the violent defense of his "right" only under extreme provocation. Other Border heroes fell short of the Cortez standard. José Mosqueda robbed a train, Mariano Reséndez was a smuggler, and Alejos Sierra died the "way men should, fighting on horseback"; they and many others are remembered in *corridos*.[14] Brave individuals willing to fight to the death against the gringo are the people honored in the Border tradition: they are the ones who exemplify and keep alive the spirit of resistance against Anglo domination.

Anglo domination of New Mexico came about through a comparatively slow process of insinuation and attrition that gradually added a new element to the traditional complex of social relationships. Lines of combat, consequently, were much less clearly drawn than in Texas and California, and when violence erupted it tended to involve whole communities. But brave people willing to defend their "right" to the death formed the fundamental ingredient of New Mexican resistance too. On the land grants of central New Mexico people still tell stories of Juan de Dios Ortega's fights with Texas cowboys.[15] The words *muy hombre* and *mucho hombre*—much of a man—punctuate reminiscences of José Chávez y Chaves, a bandit and sometime deputy sheriff of San Miguel County. Even bandit chief Vicente Silva, who murdered his wife as the crowning act of a particularly vicious career, is remembered with traces of admiration and pride.[16] And Elfego Baca, whose talent for self-promotion makes it difficult to separate fact from fancy, has now joined the roster of *mexicanos* who would not submit.[17]

Men like Tiburcio Vásquez, Gregorio Cortez, and Juan de Dios Ortega fought back alone. Theirs were individual rebellions. They had no plans for social change, and their goals did not go beyond revenge or self-protection, the righting of specific wrongs, or a vague wish to return to the old ways. The methods with which they struck back—attacks, and then using unsettled areas and the support of their communities to elude pursuit—depended upon the peasant situation of a society based on agriculture and exploited by others, whether aristocrats, governments, lawyers, banks, or conquerors. According to Eric Hobsbawm, "Social banditry of this kind is one of the most universal social phenomena known to history,"[18] and he goes on to say that it is "not a programme for peasant society but a form of self-help to escape it in particular circumstances."[19] The advent of economic development, efficient communications, and public administration destroys the environment which nourishes social banditry as a form of protest and rebellion.

*Mexicano* communities in California, Texas, and New Mexico remembered in ballad and story the brave ones who refused to submit, who would break before they would bend. The tales stressed the virtue of physical courage and described settings in which violent response was the most admirable course of action. The folklore about *bandidos* kept pride alive and provided examples for other forms of violent resistance when provocation was great enough. Social bandits rebelled and in turn inspired resistance during the transitional period of the nineteenth century. Community upheavals were another basic way that *mexicanos* resisted violently.

## Community Upheavals

Social banditry springs from individual anger and becomes a shared symbol. Community upheavals are collective actions. Bandits do act, of course, and upheavals join the common memory and become symbols. But upheavals differ from banditry in that they require large numbers of people who respond to a provocation in an almost identical fashion.

Urban riots are the most familiar community upheavals in contemporary life, and the writings of historian George Rudé or the *Report of the National Advisory Commission on Civil Disorders* are two sources among many that explore the phenomena. While there are a number of differences between the London riots of the eighteenth century and those of Watts, all community upheavals require a period of tension and frustration that is viewed in the same way by a group and the common tendency to react violently to a "last straw" incident. Two of the most graphic incidents of *mexicano* community upheaval took place in southern California during the decade of the 1850s.

### *Race War in Los Angeles*
The period of greatest tension between Anglos and *californios* in Los Angeles after José María Flores drove Captain Gillespie from the city was the week of July 19–26, 1856.[20] Trouble started when Deputy Constable William Jenkins shot a man named Ruiz while attempting to repossess a guitar. Ruiz was a man of universally good reputation. He had returned home to find his wife struggling with the constable over the instrument. Jumping to the rescue, Ruiz grabbed the deputy from behind, and the deputy, in a panic, drew his gun and fired. Ruiz lingered a day, receiving a steady stream of visitors, before dying. His funeral was highlighted by the "largest procession of its kind ever seen in Los Angeles."[21]

That night, after the funeral, *mexicanos* concluded that Jenkins would be acquitted by Anglo law, so they attacked the jail in order to hold their own trial. The sheriff and five deputies repelled the mob, although the sheriff received a head wound. The Anglo community feared the attack was the start of a "Mexican revolution." They jailed twelve innocent *californios* and turned the city into a garrison on alert, complete with four military companies, including a group of former Texas Rangers living at nearby El Monte and a troop of *californios* led by Andrés Pico. After several uneasy days in the garrison punctuated by random shots fired from outside the perimeter, the troops swept the countryside. Several alleged rebels were captured, but as a compromise to allow the release of Jenkins, all charges against them were dropped.

The "race war" erupted out of six years of rising tensions between gringo and *mexicano* that built on the lawlessness that afflicted southern California from 1850. Robberies, murders, and general drunken disorder escalated during this period, perpetrated by people from all races and national backgrounds. Forty-four homicides were recorded in Los Angeles County, with a population of only 2,300, in 1850–1851. The sheriff's office went vacant for long periods, even at a salary of ten thousand dollars a year.[22]

Anglo Americans reverted to their old standby, the vigilante committee, in the summer of 1852. The situation had reached crisis proportions, and many of the *californio* elite supported and participated in the vigilante movement. It soon became evident, however, that the committees used a double standard of justice: the vast majority of the lynchings conducted by the committees involved the Spanish-speaking.[23] Los Angeles witnessed its first "legal" execution after the conquest in 1854, and the victim, a man named Herrera, was undisputedly guilty of murdering his wife; the *mexicano* community did not dispute his guilt, but wondered if the gringo judge would have passed the death sentence on a fellow *americano*. When the well-known and well-regarded Ruiz was killed by the Anglo deputy, it provided the "last straw" example of double justice.

The Los Angeles race war illuminates the fundamental weakness of the native Californian society in dealing with the severe threat posed by the newcomers. As *californios* like Andrés Pico had traditionally viewed other Latin Americans as scoundrels, they tended to blame the crime wave on the newcomers—the Sonorans, Peruvians, and Chileans—or the liberated mission neophytes. Pico and other prominent Californians cooperated with the Anglos, or at least the more moderate among them, thus splitting the *californio* community along class lines. The fact that the rebels were relatively easily dispersed after the assault on the jail points out the lack of a developed social structure among *los mexicanos pobres*. Since *los pobres* as a group were made up of poor *californios*, neophytes recently severed from the missions by secularization, and recent arrivals from Sonora and points south, the lack of cohesiveness is not surprising. The alliance of the elite with the Anglos intensified the fragmentation.

Anglo behavior during the incident displayed several characteristics about the conquest that apply both to California and to other parts of the Southwest. The double standard of laws and punishment indicates the ingrained racism of the Anglo American orientation, an attitude, of course, that Anglos did not confine to Hispanic peoples. The viciousness of the Texans—nurtured on the myth of the Alamo and reinforced by their participation in the Mexican War—demonstrates their particularly aggressive brand of racism, a trait they carried with them wherever they went.[24] And the readiness of the Anglo Americans to see a mass insurrection in a relatively well-focused and contained upheaval shows the extent of their insecurity and hints at latent guilt: they knew they were conquerors, not liberators.

Early the following year, a somewhat different incident produced a markedly similar response.

### The Flores War

Juan Flores was twenty-one when he escaped from San Quentin in 1856, in the midst of a sentence for horse stealing.[25] Flores returned to his native region as the head of more than fifty *mexicanos* whom he had recruited from the territory between San Luis Obispo and San Juan Capistrano. It has been called the "largest bandit aggregation ever seen in California."[26]

Men joined the Flores gang for various reasons. He was apparently a young man of personal magnetism and style; accounts of his trial and execution uniformly describe Flores as good-humored, witty, and well-mannered. The opportunity to avenge personal slights and insults attracted some, while the War of the Reform that had just broken out in Mexico may well have inspired others to turn to guerrilla tactics as a means of expressing and redressing grievances.[27] It is clear, however, that the thought unifying all of Flores's riders was the desire to strike out against the Anglo American regime in one way or another.

Flores decided to operate out of San Juan Capistrano. He requested aid from two local ranchers. Both turned him down; angered, Flores shot the second, a German settler named Charles Fluggart. His men then broke into three shops in the town. The merchants escaped to Los Angeles, where one, Miguel Krasewski, reported that the gang had shouted antigringo curses during the attack. Krasewski also claimed that he had overheard references to a troop of five hundred

Mexicans waiting in the hills nearby, the vanguard of a massive invasion.

The Anglo community of Los Angeles interpreted the news from San Juan Capistrano as the beginning of a full-scale rebellion. Sheriff Barton and six deputies set forth to reconnoiter. They ran into some of Flores's riders, and a twelve-mile running gun battle ensued in which Barton and two of his deputies were killed.

When the three survivors returned to Los Angeles, the city once more girded to face an army of "Mexican revolutionaries" en route to "kill the white people." Once again Andrés Pico and the Texans from El Monte formed detachments to meet the challenge. In the first encounter with the Flores band the informal militia captured a number of "rebels"; they hanged them in order to prevent their escape. After eleven days of combing the countryside and meting out death sentences when they were deemed appropriate, the Los Angeles troops had crushed the upheaval and returned to the city with most of the gang in custody.

When the fighting was over, fifty-two suspects crammed the Los Angeles jail awaiting the judgment of the vigilante court. On February 14, 1857, the committee voted to execute Flores. The vigilantes hanged three others on succeeding days and then handed the remaining suspects over to the official courts.

The Flores War lasted a relatively brief time and involved unusually large numbers for a raiding operation. While Flores and his lieutenant, Pancho Daniel, were seasoned bandits, a significant number of their followers had no previous outlaw experience. The public, open-warfare nature of their actions—capturing San Juan Capistrano, for example—qualifies the Flores War as an upheaval, qualitatively different from the raids of a Tiburcio Vásquez but without the program or organization of a Cortina War. The readiness with which the Anglos of Los Angeles saw a political rebellion in the making and the viciousness of their response, particularly the behavior of the bloodthirsty Texans from El Monte who acted like "voracious lions rushing in upon unfortunate victims with a frenzied appetite,"[28] show that they, too, viewed the disorder as something apart from the run of "normal" violent crimes.

Other incidents in California approached the level of community upheaval. *Californios* elsewhere in the state, angered by the double standard of arrest and punishment, responded against vigilante committees. In Santa Barbara, for example, *mexicanos* blocked vigilante justice and turned the prisoners over to the authorized courts, where Spanish-surnamed jurors found them not guilty.[29] Incidents such as the Salt War near El Paso or the Horrell War in Lincoln County, New Mexico, represent other examples of times when *mexicano* frustration and rage coalesced into the collective violence of community upheavals.[30]

Social banditry and community upheavals were the two most basic ways that *mexicanos* struck out against an oppressive social and political order. Compared to banditry, and other forms of collective violence as well, upheavals occurred rarely, and the reason lies in the nature of the *mexicano* communities on the one hand and the nature of the Anglo presence on the other.

Upheavals occur when generally held anger focuses around a specific issue or particular manifestation of injustice. The triggering incident can range from the price of bread to the forcible arrest of someone on a crowded city street; an upheaval can spring spontaneously from an event, or it may come after an interval of community discussion, rumor, or even speeches. An upheaval may be entirely leaderless, a true mob, or it may have leaders who incite and even attempt to control and focus action. But no matter the type, in order to take place, upheavals require a setting, a shared experience, and a willingness to consider violence as an acceptable course of action. The setting must be in a relatively concentrated population with a developed network for spreading information quickly. The shared experience must include a widespread, fairly long-term body of examples and beliefs about the way the dominant group treats the subordinate group. And violence must be a sufficiently frequent alternative in the popular experience—symbolically if not in everyday life—to make violent response appear to be generally warranted in some circumstances.

*Mexicanos* viewed violence as a possible course of action, an orientation valued in their cultural tradition and reinforced by their frontier experiences. Anglo Americans' violent treatment of the conquered people strengthened this predisposition: violent action invites violent reaction, and all *mexicano* community upheavals in the nineteenth-century Southwest occurred in a context of violence initiated by *americanos* through either informal or authorized agencies. But the numerical weight of the Anglo presence differed in Texas, New Mexico, and California; it differed in northern and southern California; and it even differed in Los Angeles and Santa Barbara. Numerical differences corresponded to differences in treatment so that rarely did a whole *mexicano* community share feelings of resentment, triggering incidents, and perceptions about how to respond. In addition, since *mexicanos* practiced a subsistence or peasant economy that spread them in small clusters across the countryside, concentrations of people with efficient channels of communication were equally rare. Of the two basic ways of expressing outrage, *mexicanos* employed individual rebellion most frequently; given the nature of their social structure, when *mexicano* resistance expanded to units larger than individuals it usually took forms that involved the considered judgment of the communities as a whole.

Violent resistance in California never expanded beyond basic outrage. The secularization of mission land and the internal political turmoil that accompanied autonomy from Mexico had left California's young and small society in a state of flux during the decade preceding the war. The conquest and the Gold Rush brought a flood of newcomers that swamped the unsettled world of the *californios*. They resisted through banditry and occasional upheavals for a quarter of a century, a resistance that began almost immediately. Hostility was so great during the first decade of American rule that William Ingraham Kip described travel conditions thus: "When I see a Mexican approaching, I cock my rifle and cover him with it. At the same time calling him to raise his hands away from his lasso which hangs at his saddle-bow. In this way I keep my rifle on him until he has passed and gone beyond lasso distance."[31] The turbulent fifties, with the guerrilla warfare against squatters in the north and the general statewide epidemic of banditry, were followed by the sixties, in which a roster of Spanish-surnamed badmen headed every wanted list: Tiburcio Vásquez was the last and most famous of a long line. By 1880, the combination of Anglo American population increase, efficient communication and administration, and the loss of land that drove *californios* to the "Mexican" barrios of the towns and cities had quashed the banditry as a form of social protest.

Natural catastrophes like famine or earthquakes and human catastrophes like war tend to increase banditry. This was certainly true for California. Even allowing for nostalgic exaggeration, accounts of California before the Anglos came indicate that banditry was almost nonexistent. During times of extreme social dislocation, banditry can be the forerunner or spearhead of major uprisings or rebellions.[32] This did not happen in California. The disparate elements of the poor *mexicanos* never developed a group cohesiveness during the nineteenth century: native *californios* held themselves separate from the but recently "liberated" mission neophytes, and neither group built any affinity with the migrants from Sonora and Durango, Chile and Peru. With no sense of community, *los mexicanos pobres* did not follow the example of the bandits and attempt a social revolution.

The *californio* elite might conceivably have focused resistance, but they welcomed the Anglos, or at least the economic opportunities and political institutions that accompanied the change in sovereignty. The native elite lost ground quickly in the north, but they held out and even enjoyed fleeting prosperity in the south until the 1880s. Spanish-surnamed residents accounted for some 25 percent of the population in the southern counties, and this "Spanish" vote allowed some individuals from the old families to run for and even win elective office. Caught between a dissolving social order and the inexorable and increasing pressure brought to bear by the Anglos, some few assimilated, while others sought to adjust to life with other Latin Americans in the growing barrios. And those who would not submit followed the path of Tiburcio Vásquez until the social base that made social banditry possible also disappeared.

Resistance in California was intense but brief, a product of the hopeless anger of tough but alienated individuals. In Texas and New Mexico, however, resistance persisted into the twentieth century. It involved considered community undertakings as well as the outbursts of individuals who had had enough; it was frequently the result of reasoned councils that, given the information and perceptual orientations available to them, viewed their plans as anything but hopeless.

One kind of community resistance developed in the context of long-term, endemic sniping or engagements between factions of relatively equal strength. The history of the Maxwell Land Grant of New Mexico, crosshatched over time with competing factions, captures the essence of resistance through long-term skirmishing.

CHAPTER 5

# The Maxwell Land Grant:
# A Setting for
# Long-Term Skirmishing

New Mexico's governor, Manuel Armijo, awarded the Maxwell or Beaubien-Miranda Land Grant in 1841; over the years, the various owners of the grant pressed claims for as much as two million acres, land that tumbled eastward from the crest of the Sangre de Cristo Mountains toward the high plains.[1] Controversy accompanied the grant award, and *mexicano* settlers, Anglo miners and ranchers, and Eastern and international financiers kept the vast tract tangled in controversy for the balance of the century. The gradual exertion of Anglo control over the Maxwell mirrors the pattern of attrition and insinuation by which Anglos gained dominance in New Mexico. Long-term skirmishing was a way of life on the grant until 1900, and its history illustrates the conditions that produce this kind of resistance.

Armed resistance in the form of long-term skirmishing shares many of the traits associated with classic feuds. Like feuds, it often spans a generation or more. Like feuds, skirmishing involves groups of relatively equal strength, takes place in areas where the police arm of the state is weak, and occurs among people for whom violence is an acceptable course of action. The level of conflict describes peaks and valleys in intensity, with some guarded intermingling and intermarriage during the lulls, but with the consciousness of fundamental alliances always present so that the sides regroup quickly when the action picks up.

The analogy between skirmishing and feuding is not perfect. Feuds are usually conceived to be between families or clans like the Capulets and the Montagues or the Hatfields and the McCoys, while skirmishing takes place between larger social associations. Feuds are often of such long-standing that warring factions cannot remember what started them, thus giving feuds an irrational quality to the modern eye. Skirmishing, on the other hand, responds to a real threat—in the case of *mexicanos* in the Southwest, threats to life and land; while it may include the irrationality of race prejudice and eth-

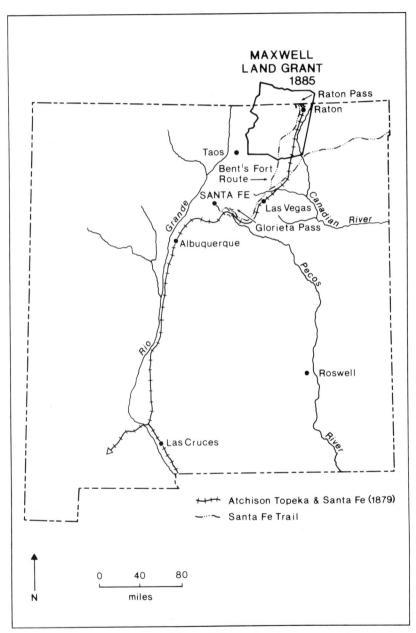

Map 4. New Mexico Territory: Maxwell Land Grant

nic hostility, resistance through skirmishing is a considered choice, however doomed the benefit of hindsight may make it appear.

People fighting to protect homes and families engage in skirmishing; they are not like social bandits who strike out against oppression in individual rebellions. Although they share the characteristic of community participation, skirmishes differ from upheavals in the length of time they last and the degree of decision making involved. Despite the elements of community participation and some planning, skirmishing differs from movements like the Cortina War in the size of the group of resisters and the scope of their actions: they have no program beyond preserving things the way they are, maintaining the status quo in the immediate area. The autonomous and self-sufficient *mexicano* communities in many parts of New Mexico Territory fought the gradual *americano* advance during the nineteenth century with long-term skirmishing; the land claimed by the owners of the Maxwell Land Grant was one major arena.

The Santa Fe trade created the Maxwell Land Grant indirectly: Armijo made the award to a New Mexican *político* and his business partner, an *extranjero* merchant. *Mexicanos* in Taos saw the grant as a dangerous example of *americano* infiltration into New Mexico and they quickly lodged a protest.

## Settlement and Conflict: The Early Years

On January 8, 1841, Guadalupe Miranda and Charles Beaubien petitioned Governor Armijo for a tract of land east of Taos, beyond the mountains, which they would "reduce to possession" for the good of the department.[2] Beaubien, a French Canadian who had followed the fur trade to the Southwest, was a naturalized citizen of Mexico, a leading merchant, and a prominent figure in the American Party of Taos; Miranda, a native of Chihuahua, was a resident of New Mexico, a government official, and a close associate of Armijo. The last factor probably accounts for the speed with which Armijo honored their request, for three days later the governor issued a decree granting them the land.[3]

Formal possession did not take place until February 22, 1843, when Cornelio Vigil, alcalde of Taos, testified that the boundaries had been ridden and the proper cornerstones set in place. Vigil described the boundaries of the grant as beginning

> below the junction of the Rayado River with the Colorado, and in a direct line toward the east to the first hills, and from there running parallel

with said River Colorado in a northerly direction to opposite the point of the Una de Gato, following the same river along the same hills to continue east of said Una de Gato River to the summit of the table land, from whence, turning northwest to follow said summit until it reaches the top of the mountain which divides the waters of the rivers running towards the east from those running towards the west, in a southwest-wardly direction until it intersects the first hills south of the Rayado River, and following the summit of said hills toward the east to the place of beginning.[4]

This imprecise description and the "elasticity" of surveyors' chains later in the nineteenth century led subsequent owners of Beaubien and Miranda's estate to claim more than two million acres. Questions about the validity of the grant under Mexican law, opposing interpretations on the part of different Secretaries of the Interior, and changing policies by successive grant claimants confused the situation and led to resistance against the grant owners.

The Taoseños, led by Padre Antonio José Martínez, argued that the grant overlapped with lands given to Charles Bent by the Taos Pueblo, that it infringed upon the grazing rights of *mexicano* farmers, and that it threatened the buffalo herds that were an important food source for both Indians and *mexicanos*. Martínez also contended that the grant did not conform to Mexican law on two counts: it was far larger than the maximum that two individuals could receive, and it violated Mexican prohibitions against foreigners or naturalized citizens owning land in frontier areas.[5]

Martínez's opposition proved a temporary obstacle. The departmental assembly approved the tract as granted on April 15, 1844. Beaubien began settlement, but Kearny's occupation of Santa Fe and the subsequent revolt in Taos ended his efforts.[6]

The beginnings of permanent settlement in the region remain obscure. Testimony taken during the 1870s by both challengers and defenders of the grant claimants mention inhabitants at the time of formal possession. The boundaries described in Vigil's statement were known and recognized, swore one witness, "especially by all the old settlers who were here at the time the grant was made."[7] Other witnesses supported Martínez's contention about grazing rights: "Nobody claimed it [the Moreno Valley]," asserted crusty, eighty-four-year-old William Brownell. "It was used as public land and the people of Taos used it to graze their cattle . . . it was too cold for cultivation."[8] Kit Carson testified before U.S. Surveyor General Henry Pelham in 1857 that he had seen settlements on the Rayado River in 1844 and had himself built a home in the area in 1845, and that at the time of U.S. invasion, two hundred acres were being farmed and fifteen thousand head of livestock grazed on the grass-lands of the grant.[9]

Whatever the actual state of settlement north and east of Taos when Beaubien and Miranda made application, it is clear that the area was well known to both native New Mexican and Anglo adventurers. Vigil's use of place names attests as much. Fur trappers and Indian traders of many nationalities had roamed the region for decades. The Santa Fe Trail cut across a portion of the grant; buffalo hunters and rancheros had visited the region annually.[10] But, the technicalities of land title and number of permanent residents aside, by both New Mexican and Anglo American standards, northeastern New Mexico was a frontier before Beaubien and Miranda claimed ownership, and it remained a sparsely peopled area throughout the nineteenth century. *Los mexicanos pobres* played a large part in settling the region, expanding east from Taos and north from San Miguel County, at least until the 1890s.[11]

## Maxwell Gets the Grant

Lucien Bonaparte Maxwell, Charles Beaubien's son-in-law, had settled on the land by 1848. Another French Canadian who had followed the fur trade to New Mexico, Maxwell married Luz Beaubien in 1844 and soon went to work for his father-in-law.[12] He became the only member of either grantee's family to take an active interest in the grant and the first person to realize significant profit from the estate.

The archetypal New Mexican entrepreneur, Maxwell fused New Mexican methods with opportunities brought by Anglo Americans, trying anything to turn a profit. Rancher, landlord, merchant, army contractor, and Indian agent, he was a vigorous man who ruled his domain in the grand manner of a benign don or *patrón*, while taking advantage of every change in economic conditions and government organization.[13]

Maxwell got well on his way to becoming the richest man in northern New Mexico without a clear title to the land that brought him his wealth. His right to the grant derived from his wife's future share of her father's interest in the estate, and Beaubien's title was not clear. Miranda had returned to Mexico after the U.S. invasion, but he still maintained an interest in his northern holdings. Other claimants complicated title, and the United States had not sanctioned the grant.[14]

A major hurdle was cleared in 1857. U.S. officials had to winnow fraudulent land titles from the valid. U.S. Surveyor General Henry Pelham held hearings regarding the Beaubien-Miranda claim and decided that the grant was legitimate according to the "laws and customs of the Republic of Mexico, the decisions of the Supreme Court of the United States, and the Treaty of Guadalupe Hidalgo."[15] Congress followed Pelham's recommendation and confirmed the grant in 1860.[16]

Pelham judged, and Congress agreed, that Beaubien and Miranda had received a legitimate grant, but the surveyor general and Congress acted without benefit of survey. The only legally acceptable description of the land in question was Alcalde Vigil's statement of 1843. In effect, Pelham and the Congress affirmed that the Beaubien-Miranda interests possessed clear title to some land, but precisely where and how much was still debatable.

Pelham's judgment gave Miranda an opportunity to sell his share. He offered it first to his partner. Beaubien refused, but he arranged negotiations between Miranda and his son-in-law. On April 7, 1858, Maxwell received the deed to Miranda's half-interest in the grant for the considerations of $1,000 cash, an additional $1,000 to be paid by July 1, 1858, and $500 due when "the Congress of the United States of American [*sic*] shall have passed favorably on the . . . Claim or Grant."[17] Beaubien died in 1864, and Maxwell purchased the interests of the other heirs; by 1867 he was the grant's sole owner.[18]

Maxwell oversaw a sprawling, personal domain. He pursued a variety of enterprises with great energy, and tried to get *los hombres pobres* to recognize his rights as proprietor. While Maxwell pressured residents to pay rent or purchase title from him, these attempts were more a matter of pride and precedent than profit. Ranching, commerce, and government contracts gave Maxwell his wealth.[19] Only one man, he could not reach into every mountain valley to exact tribute, even had he wanted to; in addition, he was not sure of the boundaries to his land.[20]

In 1866, the discovery of gold high in the mountains started a rush of prospectors and miners to the western parts of his land that made Maxwell modify his role of benign *patrón* over a slowly developing empire. Ranchers and homesteaders moving west after the Civil War also increased the *americano* population on his estate, and towns began to spring up across the countryside.[21] Clear title, dramatic increases in settlement, and profitable activities run by other people on his lands changed Maxwell's casual attitudes toward his rights as landlord. He strove to receive consideration for each mining claim filed and each town lot sold and began to actively claim all

of the land circumscribed by the boundaries as described by Alcalde
Vigil. Maxwell did not claim the Moreno Valley, Ute Creek, or any
"such damn thing until after gold was discovered there," according
to blunt William Brownell.[22] He met with only partial success—the
number of settlers and the swiftness of the changes forced him to
concentrate on the miners, and he remained lax in getting ranchers
and farmers to recognize his title—but between 1866 and 1870 he
intensified his efforts while simultaneously battling the surveyor
general of New Mexico, the commissioner of the General Land Office, and Interior Secretary Jacob D. Cox in an unsuccessful attempt
to get the grant patented according to Vigil's boundary description.[23]

The boom in northeastern New Mexico attracted the attention of
big money. On September 5, 1870, Lucien and Luz Maxwell sold
their entire estate of "2,000,000 acres more or less" to a group of English capitalists for approximately $1.5 million.[24] The Maxwell Land
Grant and Railway Company was born.

## Investors Take Over

Changing the form of grant ownership from an individual's personally supervised estate to a corporation of international investors
planning large-scale development threatened all residents on Maxwell's lands. But confusion on many levels accompanied the change
in ownership and organization.

Title was one problem. Congressional approval in 1860 stated
only that Beaubien and Miranda possessed a valid grant but did not
say how much, and Maxwell had been inconsistent in his claims. Officials trying to bring Spanish and Mexican practices into line with
U.S. law arrived at eleven square leagues as the maximum allowed
an individual under Mexican land policy. By this standard, the Beaubien-Miranda grant could cover no more than twenty-two square
leagues, or 97,600 acres. In 1869, Secretary of the Interior Cox ordered the grant surveyed not to exceed this amount.[25]

A group of speculators headed by Jerome Chaffee, a future senator from Colorado, paid for their own survey based on Vigil's description. The surveyor's notes, received by the Interior Department
in November, 1870, indicated that the grant encompassed the two
million acres cited in Maxwell's deed. But the new Secretary of the
Interior, Columbus Delano, refused to issue a patent based on this
survey, arguing that the congressional confirmation of 1860 was the
equivalent of a patent, and furthermore refused to change the twen-
ty-two-league limitation set by his predecessor.[26] In 1874, the Interior Department complicated the situation by declaring the land part

of the public domain, and homesteaders began to file claims in the disputed area.[27]

Despite these setbacks, the company pressed for recognition of the largest possible amount of land. The new owners fought the Interior Department in the courts and in Congress; at the same time they moved to exert their rights over grant residents. A widely distributed notice ordered all miners to report to John Collinson at Cimarron before September 10, 1870, or suffer ejectment as trespassers.[28] This deadline came only three days after the company received Maxwell's deed and when no agency of the U.S. government recognized the company's claim to more than 97,600 acres.

The miners refused to comply. Company agents and law officers met armed resistance. Elizabethtown rioted on October 27, 1870, requiring the use of troops, and again on April 18, 1871, bringing Governor William A. Pile to the scene. Willow Creek miners met on June 10, 1872, and resolved that the company had no authority to exact rents, a position heartily endorsed by the miners of Elizabethtown.[29]

Finding the miners difficult, the owners turned to stock raisers and farmers in an effort to gain recognition of company title and, incidentally, to realize some income. On March 28, 1873, district court convened at Cimarron with a docketfull of ejectment suits against small farmers and ranchers. The settlers responded with a mass meeting at Cimarron on March 30.[30] Squatters' clubs formed at Cimarron and Elizabethtown, joined forces, and prepared to protect their members with guns if necessay. Shooting incidents began on May 1, 1873, and escalated over the next year and a half. In January, 1875, Sheriff O. K. Chittenden informed Governor Samuel B. Axtell that he could no longer enforce the law.[31]

Violence increased during the fall of 1875, reaching its height in the aftermath of the murder of Thomas J. Tolby. Tolby, a Methodist minister, had vigorously attacked both the Maxwell Land Grant Company and the Santa Fe Ring. The discovery of his body in Cimarron Canyon on September 14 sent emotions to a new pitch on the grant, spawned a vigilante movement that resulted in the deaths of three *mexicanos* and the extralegal "conviction" of an Anglo politician, and sent the various factions on the grant into strange alliances.[32]

## The Competing Groups

The turmoil following Tolby's death illuminates the complex relationships among the people who struggled over the grant.

By the mid-1870s, the grant's population divided into four basic groups: *americano* miners, ranchers, and farmers who denied that the land was anything but public domain, many of whom had initiated claims with the General Land Office and who suspected all territorial politicians; officers, agents, and lawyers of the company; adherents of the Santa Fe Ring; and poor *mexicanos* who continued to migrate to the sheltered valleys along the Cimarron, Poñil, and Vermejo rivers.[33] Logically, the company men and the Santa Fe Ring should have been close allies; members of the Ring had been influential in forming the company, and they used their influence to try to extend the company's claim to the full two million acres.[34] By the same token, both *mexicano* and *americano* settlers should have allied against the grant forces.

When the dust settled after the Tolby affair, the alliances were reversed. Company lawyer Frank Springer defended O. P. McMains, another Methodist minister and anti-grant leader who was charged with the murder of Cruz Vega, a victim of vigilante justice.[35] Both grant and anti-grant factions joined in damning the Santa Fe Ring and the *mexicano* people who, it was believed, kept the Ring in power.

This polarization was temporary, and there are explanations for it. Financial problems, poor planning, and internal dissension had plagued the Maxwell Land Grant Company from the start, compounding the legal complications over title.[36] Although members of the Santa Fe Ring had played prominent roles in company affairs, they were loyal only to themselves. Taking advantage of the company's weakness and their control of county and territorial government, the Ring levied exorbitant taxes on grant and settler property alike, then purchased the holdings at delinquent tax sales.[37] Further, the Ring passed a bill in the territorial legislature attaching Colfax County courts to Taos County, where the Ring was sure of controlling the juries.[38] Finally, all circumstantial evidence pointed to agents of the Ring as murderers of the Reverend Tolby.[39] Neither the grant faction nor the anti-grant faction of Anglos had reason to favor the Santa Fe Ring during the 1870s.

Neither faction saw any reason to embrace the *mexicano* settlers either. To the company, the native New Mexicans were an irritating, unprofitable group whose presence challenged authority and impaired the attractiveness of their holdings. Other problems occupied the company at this time, but officers knew that *mexicanos* stood in the way of complete company control and would have to be dealt with eventually.

Anglo settlers had no love for native New Mexicans. Many were Texas cattlemen who brought their Remember-the-Alamo attitudes to the mountains,[40] and most were Protestants harboring bitter anti-Catholic sentiments.[41] The settlers and the company agents shared a contempt for the "backward" agricultural methods of the natives and a belief that the Santa Fe Ring depended upon *mexicanos*. For example, one of the major objections to having the courts attached to Taos County was that the juries would be entirely native. Complained Frank Springer, "Out of a voting population of over seventeen hundred, not over seventy-five at the utmost can understand the English language." And even worse, county *jefe* Pedro Sánchez controlled both grand and petit juries through the "satanic" Penitente brotherhood that practiced "barbarous, bloody exhibitions of self-torture."[42]

*Mexicanos* stayed aloof from the conflicts of the seventies. The company did not challenge them directly, so *los hombres pobres* did not ride against the company.[43] The death of a Methodist minister caused no *mexicano* outrage; the location of the courts did not concern native subsistence farmers. Of the *americano* factions fighting for control of the region, the Santa Fe Ring behaved in the most familiar manner. The Ring made a conscious effort to woo *jefes políticos*, and many of the Ring's local agents were *mexicanos* who knew how to win native support. Through a judicious use of rewards and threats of legal action that could be relieved only through proper performance at the polls or in the jury box, the Ring manipulated native New Mexicans.[44] But to *los hombres pobres* seeking to live as they had always lived—in self-contained groups nestled along mountain streams—these were things of little importance; if casting a vote in a certain way meant that one would be left alone, it was not an unreasonable price.[45]

## Dutch Ownership

In 1877, the Interior Department interpreted a U.S. Supreme Court decision as negating Cox's eleven-square-league rule, and the commissioner of the General Land Office ordered the Maxwell Land Grant surveyed according to the landmarks in Alcalde Vigil's description.[46] The new survey revealed that the grant encompassed 1,714,764 acres. Congress issued a patent for this amount in 1879, although one of the surveyors was a brother of Santa Fe Ring kingpin Stephen Elkins and this blood relationship, "referrable to the interests of the owners," provided grounds for litigation during the eighties.[47]

At the same time that Congress and the Interior Department

strengthened the company's claim to the land, the problem of dissension within the company directorate was solved. On March 18, 1880, Dutch bondholders received masters' deeds to the entire estate.[48] The Dutch determined to make their investment pay.

Under Dutch leadership, company officials moved to control all the land within the boundaries authorized by the congressional patent of 1879. They followed three tacks in dealing with their holdings: outright sale, the formation of subsidiaries to develop resources, and leasing to settlers.[49] Their favorite tactic was the short-term lease. In theory, short-term leases generated income without depriving the company of assets, and by signing a lease a settler acknowledged company ownership. Managers of the Maxwell reasoned that leases would spike settler opposition, would buttress the company's title claims, and would be an income-producing stop-gap until the company could develop the grant itself.

The Dutch plan aimed at making tenants of people who had experienced few controls. *Mexicanos* had moved into northeast New Mexico in a steady flow that outran the reach of government, too far from Santa Fe and too scattered to be worth the enumerator's notice for either the 1850 or 1860 U.S. census. Most migrated after 1848 without even the formal organization of a community land grant. In the early territorial years, only Lucien Maxwell tried to control the haphazard clusters of farms and ranches east of Taos.

The discovery of gold in 1866 brought Anglos who clamored for familiar American political institutions. The Maxwell Grant was part of Taos County, but Taos was two days away in good weather. In response to Anglo demands, the territorial legislature created Colfax County in 1869. All but 265,000 of the more than 1,700,000 acres patented as the Maxwell Land Grant by Congress in 1879 lay within Colfax County boundaries.[50] But while Anglos wanted government, they didn't want the company.

## The People on the Land

The 1870 census credits Colfax County with a population of only 1,992; the 1880 census enumerated 3,398; by 1890, the number of people had jumped to 7,691. Probably 600 persons lived on the grant in 1870, and this figure had quadrupled by 1890.[51]

The Maxwell Land Grant Settlers Book, a census completed by the company in March, 1887, reveals more about the residents that the owners were trying to subdue. Farmers and stockmen, and their property, concern the company; this census lists neither miners nor

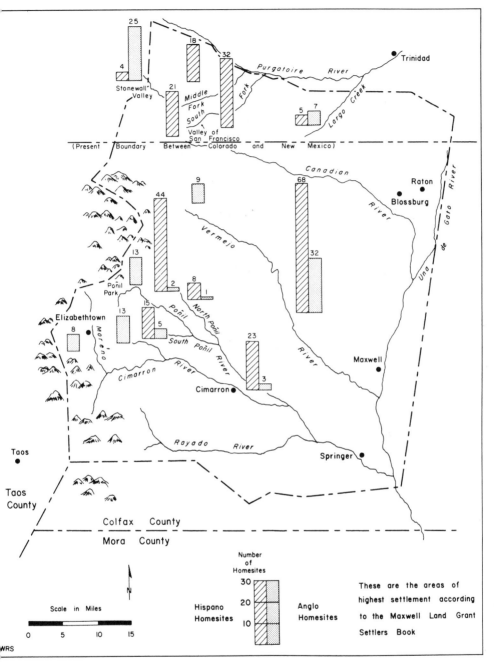

Map 5.  Maxwell Land Grant, 1885

residents of such towns as Maxwell or Springer.[52] Excluding miners and townspeople, the company counted 505 separate holdings, ranging from the barest of subsistence farms to large cattle ranches. Some settlers had lived on the land for less than half a year at the time of the company inventory; many traced back their tenure for more than twenty years.[53]

The pattern of settlement sketched by the company census is of ethnically homogeneous clusters of homesites concentrated in fifteen areas, with isolated holdings scattered across the remainder of the grant. The Vermejo River, bisecting the grant on a northwest-to-southeast line, attracted the largest number of farms and ranches. Of the one hundred holdings along this river, sixty-eight were occupied by *mexicanos*, with the nine ranches in Vermejo Park all belonging to Anglos. Information is not complete, but many sites had been taken up at least ten years before, and probably much earlier.[54] On the average, the *mexicanos* farmed at a subsistence level. Most cultivated between twenty and fifty acres of irrigated land, usually planted in wheat or oats, put up very little, if any, fencing, and ran perhaps twenty to thirty sheep or goats. Few possessed many cattle or horses. The Anglos, living on the Vermejo, were generally more prosperous, farming sixty to eighty acres in crops similar to those of the native New Mexicans, having more invested in improvements such as fencing, and in some instances running large herds of cattle. They, too, had enjoyed possession for a time, over ten years in some cases, often obtaining their land from earlier *mexicano* settlers.

The Poñil and Cimarron river valleys, running parallel to the Vermejo to the south, held the next largest concentration of settlers. The land along the three forks of the Poñil supported seventy-five settled places, eight of which belonged to Anglos, while the Cimarron Valley had twenty-six, three of which were *americano*-occupied. The people along the Poñil tended to farm much larger fields than did their neighbors on the Vermejo, but they did not have much livestock. Their investment in buildings and fences was somewhat greater than that of their neighbors to the north. A like pattern emerges along the Cimarron, where some settlers cultivated up to 160 acres, and several grazed large flocks of sheep. Anglos along these watercourses prospered on the same scale as the *mexicanos*.

Further north, in Colorado, settlement concentrated along the forks and tributaries of the Purgatoire River. The South Fork boasted thirty-two sites, all *mexicano*, with a mixture of very small and fairly large farms and several large ranches. Occupants here traced their title back twenty years or more. The Valley of San Francisco and the Middle Fork valley shared similar settlement patterns. The people living along both valleys, on twenty-one and eighteen sites respectively, were all *mexicanos*. The Middle Fork was much poorer than either the Valley of San Francisco or the South Fork; whereas the latter two show several prosperous holdings, the farms on the Middle Fork were marginal, with little invested in improvements and almost no livestock. Again, many settlers could trace title and occupancy back more than twenty years.

*Americanos* predominated in the broad Stonewall Valley at the head of the Middle Fork of the Purgatoire where they occupied twenty-five of the twenty-seven homesites. Here, farms tended to be large, and most settlers were recent arrivals, although one man claimed sixteen years of residency.

Anglos owned less than half of the 505 homesites recorded by the company in 1887. Few were near populous *mexicano* areas. *Americanos* grouped together in parks or in valleys that had not been occupied by the native New Mexicans. When Anglos intermingled with Hispanos, they usually purchased land from the previous occupants. By honoring *mexicano* claims, by taking up unoccupied parkland, or by setting up ranches in isolated areas avoided by *mexicanos* because of the absence of water for irrigation, the Anglos minimized conflict with native New Mexicans.

Partitioning grant land along ethnic lines did not prevent all conflicts. Those that surfaced impeded cooperation against the common enemy. Geographic segregation also worked against cooperation: it reduced friction between settlers, but it inhibited the growth of a sense of community against "the merciless company of land thieves." [55]

The Maxwell Land Grant Company sought to impose its authority on a varied group. Resisting the company were large ranchers, such as the Manby brothers, who claimed twenty-five thousand acres at Castle Rock Park, [56] smaller ranchers and farmers sprinkled over the grant, and a host of *los hombres pobres*. Not all residents challenged the grant's authority; some had signed leases, some had purchased their holdings outright. [57] But large bands of reluctant tenants confronted the directors.

Neither the new owners nor congressional patent quieted dispute. The Santa Fe Ring continued to play settler against company for its own advantage; litigation continued that sent two cases to the U.S. Supreme Court. The Department of the Interior still harbored doubts about the correct amount of land. Thomas Donaldson, writing about the state of the public domain in a report of the Secretary of the Interior for 1884, said of the "notorious" Maxwell Land Grant that with "a forced assumption of the applicability of a judicial decision in another case and a tortuous construction of a general letter of advice from a succeeding Secretary, this office resurrected the extinguished claim for excessive quantity and passed it to patent without written decision." [58]

Four decades after Armijo had awarded the tract, the status of the Maxwell was no more settled than at the beginning. For Anglo settlers, the company represented a criminal obstacle to their right to take up land in the public domain; for *mexicanos*, the company stood as the most tangible Anglo threat to their way of life. A tangle of factions began skirmishing in earnest in 1870, and the skirmishing continued well into the 1890s, with sides forming, dissolving, and reforming in a kaleidoscope of alliances. During most of the seventies, *mexicanos* remained relatively aloof from the conflicts for the simple reason that they and their holdings were not directly threatened. They were aloof but not immune; occasionally *mexicanos*, too, responded violently to the threat posed by the company or by competing Anglo settlers. For the next decade and a half, however, direct pressure on *mexicano* grant residents increased. As it did, *mexicano* skirmishers moved to the forefront among the company's opponents.

# CHAPTER 6

# Violence on the Maxwell and War in Lincoln County: Two Examples of Skirmishing Resistance

The physical and human geography on the Maxwell Land Grant provided a fertile environment for skirmishing resistance. The rough and sparsely peopled land dotted with small homogeneous communities made skirmishing tactically possible; the several competing factions of relatively equal strength made skirmishing strategically attractive. The intensification of company pressure after the Dutch bondholders gained control added the element of provocation and stimulated *mexicano* grant residents into armed defense of their property for more than a decade.

## Violence on the Maxwell: 1880–1900

Notices ran in the Cimarron *News and Press* during the winter of 1880–1881 warning all grant residents to make arrangements with the company or face prosecution. Suits against farmers and ranchers who refused to deal with Maxwell agents followed in the spring.[1]

Settlers responded with squatters' clubs. As in the seventies, the company moved first against Anglos, and initial resistance followed Anglo patterns: petitions to federal officials, litigation, and politics. But the threat of violence lay behind all opposition tactics, a fact driven home in 1882 when armed men prevented the sheriff's sale of Reverend O. P. McMains's property.[2]

### Sparring

McMains was the most vocal critic of company procedures and company claims, and gave resistance a degree of coordination and focus. He published *The Comet* in Raton, won a territorial council seat in 1884 on an anti-grant platform, and wrote innumerable letters to influential people across the country asking that the Maxwell patent be disallowed.

On July 15, 1881, McMains filed a petition with the Secretary of the Interior requesting that the Maxwell title be set aside because it violated Secretary Cox's twenty-two-square-league ruling of 1874, and because of alleged fraud in the survey of 1877. On advice from the U.S. Attorney General, the Interior Department took no action and so informed company lawyer Frank Springer. But agitation in Colorado over fraud in the survey and a new U.S. Attorney General induced the Justice Department to sue the company in Colorado district court in 1882. Ultimately, the U.S. Supreme Court ruled for the company in 1887.[3]

Struggle continued while the suit was pending. The company could not rid itself of McMains, who encouraged his fellow settlers to resist even to the extent of breaking previous agreements.[4] Company lawyers brought ejectment suits against grant residents and, in 1884, initiated an omnibus suit against one hundred *mexicanos* on the Cimarron.[5] Company managers added to the number of their active opponents at the same time that the validity of title was under serious question. *Americanos* tried litigation first and then turned to arms; *mexicanos* rallied around local leaders in conspiracies of silence leavened with harassment of company agents.

The company managers found legal action slow going and favorable decisions no guarantee that they could actually remove squatters. They turned to Governor Lionel A. Sheldon in the winter of 1885 and convinced him to enforce court judgments with military force. Sheldon authorized the formation of a militia troop commanded by James H. Masterson. Anti-grant adherents gained the governor's ear in turn and convinced him that the militia was nothing more than a band of hired killers. Sheldon disbanded the unit. The militia dissolved reluctantly, and disgruntled "soldiers" provoked incidents with settlers, whereupon vigilantes met in Raton and escorted Masterson and his men to the Colorado line. Other clashes between grant and anti-grant forces followed, and Sheldon called on regular army troops from Fort Union to quiet the disturbances.[6]

While Anglos faced each other in "wars" in the towns, *mexicanos* organized juntas along the Vermejo, Poñil, and Cimarron rivers to strengthen resistance against company agents.[7] *Mexicano* and *americano* opposition to the company followed separate but parallel courses through the first half of the eighties; from 1880 to the early spring of 1887, Maxwell managers made very little headway in extending company control.

### *Fighting*

The U.S. Supreme Court decision of 1887 drove the settlers to frantic action. Concurrent with the favorable ruling, the company had solved most of its financial problems, allowing it to concentrate on affairs on the grant.[8] The Dutch owners placed M. P. Pels on the scene to supervise investor interests. Determined to get rid of squatters, Pels, however, used more tact than had his predecessors. He offered to purchase livestock and to reimburse them for their improvements, adopting the stance that the settlers had acted in good faith in an un-settled situation and deserved fair compensation.[9] By intensifying legal proceedings against all, the new manager triggered stronger, more violent resistance; but by offering reasonable payment, he cre-ated chinks among the settlers.

O. P. McMains responded to the setbacks by attacking on all fronts. He called for a mass meeting at Raton for August 1, 1887, trumpeting that "Only contemptible cowards would tamely submit to be kicked off from public lands as trespassers by an unofficial gang of public land thieves."[10] While McMains whipped up enthusiasm on the grant and tried to instigate government investigations, Pels began his program of amiable persuasion backed by promises of cash. Beginning in July, 1887, Pels journeyed to the Stonewall Valley in Colorado, where he convinced some settlers to yield and tempted others with the company terms.[11]

Prospects did not look as good along the Vermejo. There, in the most populated *mexicano* area on the grant, armed men patrolled the trails. Pels found most settlers unwilling to talk at all; those he met refused to consider leases for less than five years. Even among the Anglo ranchers in Vermejo Park, Pels found none of the willing-ness to deal that was shown by their counterparts in Stonewall. Met with rifles, the company agent was ordered to leave and informed that the ranchers would not vacate their holdings unless ordered to do so by President Cleveland himself.[12]

Pels wrote Cleveland and likened the anti-grant forces to the Ku Klux Klan: company surveyor E. C. Van Deist had been followed from Trinidad to Stonewall by sixteen masked *mexicanos* who pre-vented him from laying out an irrigation ditch in the valley.[13] Presi-dent Cleveland supported the company in a letter to Pels of Septem-ber 27, 1887; that and court action against the Vermejo Park men who had threatened Pels in July weakened the resolve of many set-tlers. Ranchers agreed to talk terms, either for sale or lease.[14]

Despite the victories of 1887 and early 1888, Pels had not won the war. The bondholders were unwilling to provide all of the mon-ey necessary to purchase improvements and livestock from those willing to sell. In addition to a tight-fisted board of directors, Pels faced a stubborn nucleus of resistors. Many *mexicanos* refused to recognize any Anglo decree and continued to migrate into the area, taking up land, building houses, and breaking fields.[15] On July 11,

1888, armed men turned back the sheriff of Colfax County when he tried to serve ejectment orders along the Vermejo. On July 23, an estimated seventy-five armed men, both *americano* and *mexicano*, reinstated George Blosser on his Willow Springs ranch near Raton. In August, three miles of fence encircling a ranch purchased from the company was destroyed. E. J. Randolph, foreman for the company's Colorado herds, notified Pels that twenty-five men had ordered him and his wife off the ranch under pain of hanging. Armed and masked men threatened the contractor constructing an irrigation ditch in the Stonewall Valley; Pels reported that *mexicanos* were stealing and killing company cattle.[16]

Tension on company land on both sides of the New Mexico–Colorado border remained high. Pels dispatched six deputies to the Stonewall Valley to quiet the situation. Instead, a gun battle ensued; the deputies retreated, and the company property was burned. On the Poñil, fourteen masked riders of the Poñil Association ordered the company surveyor from the Poñil Valley, and he received similar treatment on the lower Vermejo.[17]

A handful of *mexicanos* near the headwaters of the Vermejo came to terms, but on the middle Vermejo, Jacinto Santistevan and his son Julien led a disciplined resistance against all company overtures. On the Poñil, twelve *mexicanos* sold out, but most remained staunchly opposed. The few victories chalked up by company agents resulted as much from tension between Anglo and Hispano as they did from the persuasive skill of the agents. When *mexicanos* tried to run company agent Charles Hunt off the Vermejo, the *americanos* in Vermejo Park refused to help. This angered the *mexicanos* to such an extent that many vowed never to aid Americans again.[18]

But through steady effort the company gained ground. By summer 1889, several prominent and troublesome ranchers had come to terms, some *mexicanos* on the upper Vermejo and in the Cienguilla Valley had sold out, and the company surveyor was working with only a minimum of difficulty. By December, even George Blosser indicated a willingness to deal. By the beginning of 1890, the company had spent over seventy thousand dollars purchasing settlers' improvements and had effected more than one hundred leases for terms of from one to five years.[19] Order, by company definition, although order established with some compromise, seemed to have been achieved.

Optimism was ill-founded. The company surveyor and the company timber agent were ordered off the Vermejo in December. Maxwell Cattle Company cowhands working Vermejo Park left in the face of threats. *Mexicanos* from the Poñil destroyed 1,500 company fence posts, and houses bought by the company from settlers burned along the Vermejo, Poñil, and Cimarron rivers until only two company-owned ranches were left standing by the middle of April, 1890.[20]

*Mexicanos* and *americanos* participated in coincidental and supportive, not cooperative, attacks. For the Anglos, it was a last fling before yielding to a fate that they now saw as inevitable. From late spring through summer of 1890, Anglo after Anglo capitulated to the company. With some exceptions, notably in the Moreno Valley, the Americans living in the New Mexican portion of the grant signed their peace with the company.[21]

### *Mexicanos Hold the Field*

Such was not the case for the *mexicanos*. George W. Cook, a deputy sheriff delivering injunctions on the Poñil, was wounded—from ambush he said—while returning to his task. It took Cook three weeks to recover. Then, equipped with a writ, he and another deputy named Russell rode to arrest Julio Martínez, their prime suspect. According to Cook and Russell, Martínez was working in his corral when they approached. Seeing the two men, Martínez ran to his house "for a rifle," thereby "forcing" the lawmen to kill him.[22]

The killing aroused the *mexicano* community. On February 21, 1891, Russell and Cook were attacked while engaged in company business along the Vermejo. Russell was killed, but Cook survived and killed one of his attackers. Escaping, Cook rode for aid. By the next morning, a posse of twenty-three men using bloodhounds trailed the attackers to the house of Francisco Chaves. There the posse found an estimated 100 to 150 *mexicanos* and decided that retreat was in order.[23]

*Mexicano* violence remained high following this incident. Crops, fences, and buildings were destroyed; cattle stealing and cattle killing occurred more frequently as the spring wore on. Cowhands were reluctant to risk their lives for the company, and the courts would not act.[24]

Pels realized that the situation was precarious. Preparing for a sustained campaign, he wrote to a Denver supplier requesting hand grenades, but he was reluctant to pursue such an all-out course.[25] Instead, Pels chose to follow a policy of "divide-and-conquer." The last thing he wanted, he wrote in his report to the company board of trustees, was to do anything that might cause this "uneducated class" to form an effective combination. Tact and courteous persuasion, wrote the manager, were the best ways to keep the *mexicanos* divided. A frontal assault, he said, was an imprudent move. At best it would be bloody and costly; at worst it could unify all the *mexicanos* on the grant, maybe all the *mexicanos* from San Miguel County north, and cost the company everything.[26]

The *mexicanos* who presented the major obstacle to a trouble-free company came from the older settlements, where subsistence agriculture predominated. Jacinto Santistevan, who led opposition on the middle Vermejo for years, was one of the wealthiest men in the region. Yet even he had only 160 acres fenced, farmed eighty in corn, wheat, and oats, ran twenty head of cattle, and possessed improvements valued at $300. His two sons, Julien and Santiago, each had fenced eighty acres. Julien farmed twenty, and Santiago, sixty acres in corn, wheat, and oats. Neither possessed any livestock; Julien's improvements were valued at $150 while Santiago's totaled $175. Others whom the company identified as leaders of *mexicano* resistance enjoyed even less affluence.[27]

At the beginning of the 1890s, the company faced bands of angry *mexicanos* fed up with company demands and determined to retain their holdings. They were angry but not organized: neighbors gathered around local leaders and struck against immediate threats with little, if any, communication or planning between the different groups. Occasionally, rage at the behavior of company officials or Anglo lawmen could unite one hundred or more riders, but such aggregations dissolved after attacking a specific target. More often, however, groups of friends burned buildings, killed livestock, and shot at agents as conditions in their immediate community warranted. Their attacks expressed anger and attempted to hamstring the company—at best, they might raise the price of ownership higher than the board of trustees was willing to pay.

### The Company Wins

As Anglo resistance died to a smolder, Pels's divide-and-conquer policy, helped by company willingness to lease land to *mexicanos* for 25 percent of their crops, "thereby sharing the fortunes of the leasee" in a manner most in accordance "with the customs of the Mexicans," began to bring results.[28] The constant pressure wore down the toughest: Jacinto Santistevan, who, in the company's estimate would "fight to the death," left the grant in 1893, although not without a long court battle.[29] By 1896, the Stonewall country was the only openly rebellious area. Violence flourished one last time in December, 1898, with the burning of 130 tons of hay. Without haste, the company organized a posse to serve ejectment writs. Leaving Trinidad on September 25, 1899, the fifteen officers worked slowly up the Purgatoire River, signing six-month leases with those willing to come to terms. The action was so peaceful and the people so willing to deal that the deputies found no one to evict.[30] By 1900, all was calm, and company title was acknowledged.

In many respects, the struggle over the Maxwell and the way the company won control parallels the history of the New Mexico Territory and the way Anglo Americans achieved domination. As was often the case in the territory, the whole Maxwell affair rested upon the paradoxical coupling of elements from Anglo and New Mexican traditions: the company epitomized corporate capitalism, yet its very existence depended upon U.S. recognition of a Mexican land grant. Battle lines gathered a number of distinct factions on each side so that struggles rarely formed along explicit ethnic lines, but common enemies never erased ethnic affiliations to any appreciable degree. Victory came through attrition, not blood: Pels and the board of trustees applied constant pressure, patiently adjusted their tactics, and used arenas outside of the territory—international financial circles, the U.S. Supreme Court, and the legislative and executive branches of the federal government—they did not defeat their opponents on the battlefield. The settlers, on the other hand, had endurance and passion but lacked the resources to compete where the company was most effective, and they suffered from disunity.

Alliances between Anglo and *mexicano* grant residents never went beyond hesitant cooperation accompanied by a wariness that precluded strong union. Jesús Arellano was elected an officer of the Squatters Club of Cimarron in 1873, and Manuel Salazar received similar recognition in 1881. McMains received a great deal of his support in the eighties from both *mexicano* and *americano* small farmers. He could persuade these men to work together and, sometimes, to ride many miles to oppose company actions. But by and large, cooperative ventures were founded on sand. Bands from the two groups might come to each other's aid against a common enemy or, just as often, refuse a call for help. As the *americanos* began to surrender to the company at the end of the eighties, *mexicano* disgust with Anglos rose along with the intensity of *mexicano* attacks.

Cooperation between *mexicanos* was almost as difficult to achieve. New Mexicans living on the Maxwell had not been there long enough to create social structures that defined leadership, maintained channels of communication, or developed a sense of community that went beyond the horizons of the immediate locale. This meant that *mexicanos* reacted against threats to their particular communities and formed around local leaders for specific purposes. They attacked the tangible aspects of the company presence such as cattle, haystacks, fences, or agents, but did not threaten the heart of the New Mexican operation, let alone the international base of the corporation. They caused the company a great deal of difficulty over a number of years, but without widespread organization that could at least control the whole grant, they could be endured until they wore themselves out.

Pels recognized this. The fear that he expressed, and others echoed repeatedly, was that the *mexicanos* in neighboring regions would join those on the Maxwell and forge a movement that could sweep all of northern New Mexico.[31]

Pels's fears never materialized, and he followed his careful program of dividing and conquering. The device of mimicking a *patrón* by taking a percentage of crops for rent proved the deciding blow: in effect, it manipulated *mexicano* traditions in order to obtain precedents recognized in Anglo courts; once done, the company could eliminate *mexicanos*, who did not understand the rules of the game, one by one. Anglo settlers knew the rules of the game and, except for diehards like McMains, knew the game was over by 1890; *mexicanos* did not, and their fiercest resistance took place after the *americanos* had capitulated.

Long-term skirmishing also occurred in a number of other regions in New Mexico. The conflicts in Lincoln County illustrate a variation on this basic theme.

## Lincoln County: 1870–1890

Fighting broke out in Lincoln County, two hundred miles south of the Maxwell Land Grant, during the 1870s. *Mexicano* settlers, *americano* freebooters, and Texas cattlemen made up the groups involved, and they allied and fragmented in a series of feuds and wars for control of the grasslands that lasted well into the 1880s. Like Colfax County, Lincoln County was a fringe area where recent *mexicano* migrants faced the vanguards of Anglo expansion; unlike Colfax, neither Spain nor Mexico had granted any land in the region. But, as in the north, the struggles proceeded on two levels: competition for land and water and disagreement about what constituted proper land use and valid title.

Novelists, moviemakers, and Western history buffs have raised the Lincoln County War (1878–1880) to legend. Scholars assessing this storied conflict see it as a struggle for economic and political control between an established band of Anglo opportunists affiliated with the Santa Fe Ring and a competing faction of Anglo newcomers.[32] This interpretation is well documented for the struggle between 1878 and 1880, but focusing on these years overshadows ethnic conflicts that preceded and followed the legendary gunfights and

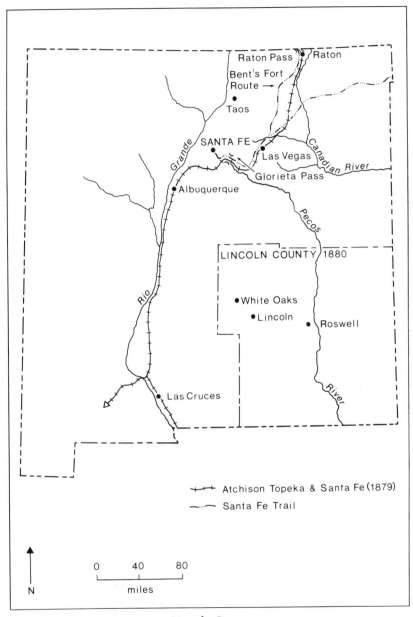

Map 6. New Mexico Territory: Lincoln County

obscures the pattern of ethnic affiliation that underlay the famous battles.

The lower Pecos Valley received the last impulses of New Mexican expansion before the counterwave of Anglos lapped westward from Texas toward the grazing lands of New Mexico. Mescalero Apaches lived in southeastern New Mexico, and roaming bands of Comanches passed by frequently. *Comancheros* [33] and buffalo hunters led the *mexicano* advance; by the end of the Mexican regime and the beginning of the American, native New Mexican farmers and herders had filtered southeast through the mountains and settled along the Rio Hondo and Rio Bonito, eastward-flowing tributaries of the Pecos. [34]

General James H. Carleton arrived in the territory in 1862 at the head of the California Volunteers. Too late to assist in driving Sibly's Confederate forces from the area, he turned to extinguishing the hostile Indian threat. Defeating both the Mescaleros and the Navajos by the winter of 1863, Carleton placed the conquered peoples on a reservation in what was to be Lincoln County. The reservation and nearby Fort Stanton became the dominant economic factors in the area. [35]

The territorial legislature created Lincoln County in 1869. Sparsely peopled and sprawling, neither *mexicano* nor *americano* resident had much regard for governmental institutions. Economic life centered on sheep and cattle raising supplemented by some corn, barley, bran, and wild hay; surpluses were sold to either Fort Stanton or the Mescalero reservation. The few resident merchants gained control over the region through the extension of credit and reaped large profits in supplying the two federal agencies. [36]

Lawrence G. Murphy, a wandering Irishman who entered New Mexico with the U.S. Army, began a store in 1869 at Placitas, later Lincoln, the county seat. He used his friends in the army to monopolize supply to Fort Stanton, credit at his store to corner the county's produce, and both to run the Mescalero reservation for his own benefit. By the early 1870s, L. G. Murphy and Company was the major force in county economics and politics and had a working alliance with the Santa Fe Ring. [37]

But competition with Murphy in the form of Texas cattlemen had already appeared. As early as 1867, John H. "Jinglebob" Chisum recognized the economic potential of the reservation and fort, and settled near the present site of Roswell, where he ran some seventy-five thousand head of cattle. [38] More Texans followed, and competition between Murphy and the newcomers intensified, with *mexicanos* caught in the middle, resenting and resisting both.

The Texans moved into an unsettled area and brought with them a disposition for violence fed by the Civil War, intensified by a tradition of blood feuds, and supplemented with a contempt for native New Mexicans. *Mexicanos* had hated Texans since the days of the Texas Republic; the Texas-based Confederate invasion during the Civil War was not, to New Mexican minds, a part of the grand strategy between the Union and the Confederacy, but just another in a succession of Texan attempts to conquer New Mexico.[39] Migration of Texas cattlemen represented a new invasion by traditional enemies; their arrival complicated the tensions between native settlers and Anglo speculators already milking Lincoln County.

On January 27, 1874, the *Santa Fe New Mexican* announced that Lincoln County had exploded into an "unfortunate war between the Texans and the Mexicans." Five brothers named Horrell transformed the county from a state of guarded watchfulness to one of open war. Leaving Lampasas County, Texas, after a bloody feud, the Horrells had begun ranching along the Rio Hondo in 1873.[40] On December 1, 1873, Ben Horrell and four friends got drunk in Lincoln and, in the course of their recreation, shot Constable Juan Martínez when he tried to quiet them. The gunfight that followed left Ben Horrell and two companions dead. The surviving brothers demanded an investigation. When their request was denied, on the grounds that their friends had been killed while resisting arrest, the Horrells planned their own vengeance.

Although unthinking racial hatred and the crudest kind of frontier violence sparked the "unfortunate war" and characterized many of its encounters, the rapid spread of severe conflict indicates the extent of divisions among county residents. The Lincoln incident was followed by a series of bloody skirmishes that left thirteen dead by the end of December. News of disorder reached the territorial capital; on January 7, 1874, Governor Marsh Giddings offered a $500 reward for the capture of Zacariah Crompton, E. Scott, and "three other persons by the name of Harrold [sic]."[41]

The reward resulted neither in the capture of the Horrells nor in the end of violence. Deputy Sheriff Joseph Haskens was pulled from his bed in Lincoln and murdered "for no other reason than that he had a Mexican wife."[42] Captain James F. Randelett summarized the situation for the adjutant general:

> The civil law is powerless and has no active execution except a lawless posse led by one Juan Gonzales, a noted murderer and horse thief. This man Gonzales pretends to act as (and I believe is actually) a deputy sheriff.
>
> No white citizens would surrender to this Villain and his posse with a show for anything but a barbarous death.

The Mexican population have nothing to fear from Gonzales and commit crime with impunity unless some action is taken by authority sufficient to control the elements at work.[43]

Bloodshed continued well into February. The *Santa Fe New Mexican* reported that "every man met is armed to the teeth," and that ranches up and down the Rio Hondo were deserted and "could be purchased for a song."[44]

The pressure from *mexicanos* proved too much for the Horrells and their followers, and they retreated back to Texas.

Like most conflicts in New Mexico, the war between the Texans and the Mexicans was not simply a race war. Lawrence Murphy and his chief ally, Sheriff William Brady, joined with the *mexicanos* in a public meeting to form a vigilante committee to cope with the Texans.[45] Murphy was less concerned with Texans' racial attitudes or encroachment on *mexicano* grazing land than he was with their threat to his economic and political dominance. The alliance between the Irishman and the *mexicanos* did not last long.

Soon after the Horrells' defeat, County Clerk Juan B. Patrón, whose father had been killed in a particularly brutal Texan attack, became convinced that Murphy had instigated the whole affair. According to Patrón, Murphy had loaned the Horrells money, encouraged the fighting, and then took over their land when they were driven from the territory.[46] The Lincoln County War of 1878–1880 developed in this climate of violence and mistrust.

The arrival of Alexander A. McSween, a lawyer from Kansas, and an English gentleman-rancher named John H. Tunstall posed a new threat to Murphy's virtual monopoly. The newcomers secured the tentative support of Chisum and started a rival bank and store. Fighting broke out in December, 1877, lasted more than two years, and involved a confusion of factions. Basically, Murphy and his successors, James J. Dolan and John H. Riley, formed one side and received support from Thomas Catron and the Santa Fe Ring; opponents to the Murphy-Dolan forces gathered around McSween and Tunstall and included Chisum and his cowboys, many Anglo small ranchers and farmers, and most of the Mexican people, led by Juan Patrón.[47]

Violence was so intense that it precipitated the removal of Governor Samuel B. Axtell. His successor, Lew Wallace, declared martial law and commissioned Patrón to raise a company of mounted rifles to restore order.[48] But Wallace could not quiet Lincoln County until he issued a proclamation of general amnesty. No victor emerged. In the end, McSween and Tunstall were dead, the firm of Dolan and Riley was bankrupt, Chisum had moved to the Texas Panhandle, and *mexicanos* continued to joust with *americanos* for land and water.

Violence during the 1870s polarized the several groups in the county into uneasy alliances, but ethnic tensions remained close to the surface. A citizens' meeting at Lincoln during the height of the war called the troubles "a continuation of feuds dating back five or six years" and admitted past hostility between ethnic groups by resolving that it had ended: ". . . we recognize with inexpressible pleasure the good and united feeling that binds all our people Mexicans and Americans together."[49]

With the return to a semblance of order, Texans resumed migration to southeastern New Mexico, and *mexicanos* continued to fan out eastward.[50] Native New Mexicans, by and large, grazed sheep; Anglos usually herded cattle. Competition for land and water in the public domain prompted battles between occupations that were ethnically identified. During the eighties, territorial governors received letter after letter describing conflict between cattlemen and sheepmen in Lincoln County.

By mid-decade, according to one Anglo sheepman, the situation was hopeless. He wrote Governor Ross that the Lincoln County Stock Growers Association had ordered him out of the county several times and that the sheriff was among the association's representatives delivering the ultimatums. The sheepman ignored the threats, whereupon his flock was killed. He swore out complaints with the Fort Stanton justice of the peace, writs were served, and a trial was held. All defendants were acquitted. He then received another order to leave, and he sadly concluded that "cow men are largely in the majority in this neighborhood and it is utterly useless to think of receiving any protection whatever from the civil authorities. . . ."[51]

Yet Ross's correspondent recognized that he received considerate treatment: the deputation that ordered him out of the country after the futile trial told him that they were on their way to meet a flock of four thousand sheep and that they would "show them no quarter, as they were Mexicans."[52]

Cattlemen answered that perfect harmony existed "excepting in isolated cases where wandering bands from other countys . . . owning no water and paying no taxes . . . have been invited to move on."[53] *Mexicanos* grazed wandering flocks and paid no taxes; nothing in their experience in southeastern New Mexico prepared them for "owning" water, remaining on a specific range, or paying taxes. Furthermore, cattlemen claimed that the two industries were incompatible:

> There can be but one opinion in regard to the enforcement of the law, that all men are entitled to its protection.
>
> But sir, so long as men attempt to pasture sheep on Government land without owning water . . . there will likely be trouble.

> You are yourself aware Sir, that cattle cannot thrive on the same range
> with sheep, and that therefore sheep will have the power of ruining the
> cattle interests of the Territory.[54]

Four points of friction produced the conflicts: competition over
basic resources, differences between concepts of land use and ownership, the believed incompatibility of the industries, and ethnic
hostility. Grazing land can only support limited herds, and stock
raisers on semiarid prairies were especially conscious of this; control of fixed assets underlay much of the tension between *mexicano*
and *americano*. But disagreement over valid use and ownership
played an equally important part.

Both groups agreed that most of the land in Lincoln County belonged to the public domain. To *mexicanos* this meant that they
could roam it at will. To Anglos this was not enough; somehow exclusive, individual rights had to be transferred to public property.
The General Land Office did not allow ranchers title to enough grazing land for large operations, so an informal method of attaching
grazing rights to water rights evolved. Ranchers got title to sections
along a stream, river, or other body of water; by consensus, Anglos
agreed that a rancher's range covered all grazing land served by this
water.[55] Under this system, *mexicanos* suffered a double disadvantage: they were not used to thinking of water as owned by individuals; moreover, to participate in the Anglo method meant dealing
with the alien land offices under the terms of the unfamiliar homestead laws.

As their numbers increased, and as modern techniques of both
capitalization and management became more necessary, Lincoln
County cattlemen relentlessly strove for supremacy. Concluded one
Anglo lawyer: "That the cattle men are determined to drive sheep
from the range here in defiance of law, right or any other consideration except the promotion of their own personal ends is evident."[56]

As on the Maxwell, *mexicanos* lost control in Lincoln County
through attrition, not abrupt defeat in combat. In the north, a single
company focused the struggle; in the south, a loose coalition of
Texas ranchers and Eastern-owned cattle companies led Anglo encroachment. The former relied upon congressional patent and U.S.
Supreme Court decisions and used only enough force to maintain
occupancy and bring constant, eroding pressure to bear on the settlers; the latter combined the preemption procedures of the General
Land Office, local courts, peace officers, and unpunished—if not
condoned—intimidation to solidify their position. Conflict between
Anglos broke out in both areas, slowing the *americano* advance and
contributing to the effectiveness of skirmishing as a delaying tactic.

Nevertheless, the fundamental struggle took place between *mexicano* and *americano*.

After a generation of skirmishing, the company won control of the north. By the turn of the century, migration, intimidation, and manipulation had earned for southeastern New Mexico the title of "Little Texas" for reasons amply demonstrated by this editorial entitled "The Guileful and Aromatic Greaser":

> Judging by the standard of decency usually endorsed by the *New Mexican* we presume the Mexican is "entitled to all the rights and privileges of American citizenship" in Valencia and Rio Arriba counties, in fact, is the cream of society, but among the intelligent people of this valley he falls into the niche that God Almighty intended when he put on the impress of color. It was Texas men and Texas money that brought forth the gushing fountains and made this the fairest vale in New Mexico. If a single native has ever spent a dollar in developing this great work, we have never heard of it. The only element of commerce or business that appeals to the Mexican is the retailing of the seductive tamale and his elective franchise, and the expense of the thing was too much for the Eddy County candidates so he was quietly left out of the primaries.[57]

Skirmishing between cattlemen and sheepmen over land occurred across the New Mexico Territory during the nineteenth century. Governor Edmund G. Ross complained to the commissioner of the General Land Office that "native inhabitants who have long been in possession are now ousted from their homes by persons who are permitted by the local land offices to make filings for the land occupied by them," a situation, continued Ross, that caused "much trouble . . . crime and bloodshed."[58]

Two letters written by Governor Ross give a capsule summary of the cattleman-sheepherder conflict in the territory. The first, addressed to a cattle company, sprang from violence in Rio Arriba County:

> I understand very well, and so do you, what a cow-boy or cattle herder with a brace of pistols at his belt and a Winchester in his hands, means when he "asks" a sheepherder to leave a given range. It means instant compliance or very unpleasant consequences to the herder and his flock. That has been the unvarying history of the controversy between cattle and sheep man in this territory. . . . You sent these men, with your cattle upon a quarter of the public domain that has been occupied exclusively by these Mexican sheep herders for a generation or more . . .[59]

The second letter, written to Don Jesús Luna, sheriff of Valencia County, shows what happened when *mexicanos* dominated an area:

As you well know, I have in practically every instance where outrages have been perpetrated upon sheep men by cattle men, offered a reward for the capture and punishment of the perpetrators; I have done this because the sheep men appeared to be at a disadvantage, and there seemed to be need of such a course. In this case, however, the conditions are different. The sheep men in your county are very largely in the majority, and the peace officers are all sheep men. It is in your power, and it is your duty, to thoroughly investigate this case and bring to justice the men who killed Meshimen, or at least ascertain who was wrong in the matter.[60]

Social banditry, community upheavals, and long-term skirmishing are variations of the same basic theme: they are attempts on the part of conquered or subordinate peoples to fight back against the most severe aspects of the dominant regime. Resistance grows in a climate of widespread and clear-cut tension and hostility between the two; the particular form it takes depends upon the circumstances enjoyed by the contending parties and their perceptions about what is possible and desirable. As resistance comes from the same general conditions, types of resistance frequently overlap or interact so that they are not distinct categories but points on a scale. Bandits played a prominent role in the upheaval called the Flores War, for example, while the El Paso Salt War contained elements of long-term skirmishing and of planning and coordination as well. But, qualifications aside, *californios* concentrated the bulk of their violent resistance into a quarter-century of social banditry spiced with a community upheaval or two. *Mexicanos* of the lower Rio Grande border can be seen as skirmishing over some seven decades in a resistance that subsumed social banditry and occasionally jelled into more ambitious uprisings that hinged upon the tradition of community on both sides of the Rio Grande.

Resistance in New Mexico can also be characterized as skirmishing over decades, with leavenings of social banditry and community upheavals. But late in the nineteenth century, San Miguel County—geographically midway between the Maxwell Land Grant and Lincoln County—was the setting for a movement that reached the level of planning and coordination. The San Miguel uprising differed from the Cortina War and the raids of *los sediciosos* on two points: it evidenced no affiliation with Mexico, either formal or informal; and it sparked a political movement. The short-term success and ultimate failure of the San Miguel uprising illuminates the strengths and limitations of *mexicano* resistance during the nineteenth century.

# CHAPTER 7

# Trouble in San Miguel County

On the night of April 26, 1889, masked and armed horsemen rode toward a ranch near the village of San Geronimo in San Miguel County, New Mexico Territory. Two Englishmen named William Rawlins and Frank Quarrell claimed the ranch, which boasted four miles of new wire fence erected at a cost of over $750. The masked band leveled the entire fence, leaving only kindling and glittering fragments. Neither posts nor wire would ever fence anything again.[1]

## Las Gorras Blancas

The destruction of the fence that spring night began a wave of organized violence that swept San Miguel County for two years. Night-riding *mexicanos*, called Las Gorras Blancas or White Caps because of their masks, directed most of their enmity against large landholders.[2] The raiders attacked the fences that were the immediate cause and most prominent symbol of their grievances, and fence cutting remained their basic tactic, but they expanded their targets to include crops, buildings, people, and such examples of Anglo American technology as railroads and lumber mills. The movement centered around conflicts over land tenure and land use, but it involved the Knights of Labor and the People's Party, received the attention of the Secretary of the Interior, and provoked concern on Wall Street and in foreign investment circles. Striving for ethnic solidarity and touched by egalitarian and anticapitalistic ideology, the White Cap movement gave dramatic proof of Mexican American discontent with the Anglo territorial regime.

San Miguel County was an apt setting for bitter conflict between New Mexico's cultural groups. Easily reached from Santa Fe by Glorieta Pass, the San Miguel area received the first settlements of

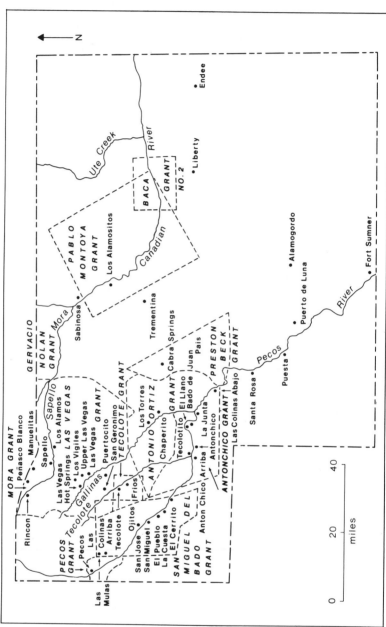

Map 7. San Miguel County, New Mexico, 1890

expanding Hispanic New Mexico. In 1794, Spain granted a tract of some 315,300 acres to Lorenzo Márquez and fifty-one others, a tract which became known as the San Miguel del Bado Grant.[3] Other settlers followed, either settling within the bounds of the initial grant or obtaining other lands in the region. Between 1794 and 1845, the Spanish and Mexican governments made fourteen grants, ranging in size from 574 to 827,621 acres, in what is now east-central New Mexico.[4]

The San Miguel country was also a center of the new Anglo American forces at work in New Mexico. Las Vegas, founded in 1835 as the nucleus of settlement for the Las Vegas Grant, had been a way station on the Santa Fe Trail. Kearny made his first declaration of U.S. sovereignty over New Mexico from the roof of a house facing the plaza of Las Vegas.[5] Indian reservations and the army joined with growing livestock interests, both Anglo and Hispanic, to provide incentives for the burgeoning commercial and banking enterprises of the town. When the Atchison, Topeka, and Santa Fe Railroad arrived in Las Vegas on January 1, 1879, Las Vegas rose to the first rank of New Mexico cities and changed its cultural balance—"New Town," East Las Vegas, sprang up around the depot on the east side of the Gallinas River. The railroad heightened tension between Hispano and Anglo and intensified competition for resources.[6]

### Millhiser v. Padilla

Land was the primary resource in San Miguel County. On August 20, 1887, a civil suit, *Phillip Millhiser et al. v. José León Padilla et al.*, commenced in Las Vegas. This case delineated the differences between the two traditions and underscored the complexity of relationships among the competing elements from these traditions. Litigation consumed more than two years and helped precipitate the violence of 1889 and 1890.

The plaintiffs, Phillip Millhiser et al., doing business as the Las Vegas Land and Cattle Company, had obtained ownership of land within the Las Vegas Grant by purchasing interests from some of the original grantees, their descendants, and legal representatives. Millhiser and his partners argued that the purchases included not only house lots and cultivated fields but also a fractional interest in the grazing or common lands of the grant. The total, they contended, passed in absolute ownership to undivided units of land to which no other party possessed any rights or privileges.[7]

The defendants held that the Las Vegas Grant was a community grant, and while residents owned house lots and irrigated fields, all inhabitants enjoyed equal rights to the common land's pasture, water holes, timber, and firewood. Change in patterns of ownership, access, or use, asserted the defendants, required the consent of the community as a whole.[8]

The suit attracted widespread attention throughout the county. The local Knights of Labor assembly helped form the Las Vegas Land Grant Defense Association to raise money for the defense. As three members of Local Assembly Number 4636 explained to Terence V. Powderly, National Grand Master Workman: ". . . the land grabbers fenced up our public domain where they chose, without the shadow of a title. Or if they purchased a tract of land with a title, they would fence in ten times as much as they bought."[9]

The Noble and Holy Order of the Knights of Labor viewed land speculators and large landholders as part of the complex of bankers, lawyers, monopolists, and intermediaries that prospered at the expense of the people. The Knights, a loose confederation of local assemblies, allowed each assembly to recruit members and focus on issues according to local conditions. Local autonomy and a strong belief that the land belonged to the people made it natural for the Las Vegas Knights to support the *mexicano* defendants against the claims of a speculative company.[10]

The three groups involved in the suit operated from different assumptions. The speculators were trying to establish the principle of private ownership of large tracts of land. To do so, they first had to argue for the validity of the Las Vegas Grant under the terms of the Treaty of Guadalupe Hidalgo, for such a ruling would remove the grant from the public domain. Once this was established, Millhiser and his coplaintiffs would contend that the grant had been awarded to the individuals listed in the petition, grant, and settlement documents. This, in effect, made the Las Vegas Grant a private grant awarded to a group, and thus, by purchasing interests from the original grantees, the buyer would obtain title to discrete units.

The defendants agreed that the Las Vegas Grant was not part of the public domain, but they argued that it had been awarded to a community, not to individuals, for the purpose of encouraging settlement, and that no portion could be alienated without communal consent. The Knights opposed bigness, exploitation, and speculation, not the concept of private ownership of land. As their phrase "public domain" indicates, they did not believe that the land in question had been stolen from anyone but the United States government. *Mexicanos* and the Knights could join against large-scale Anglo manipulation, but their lack of agreement about the "unoccupied" land foreshadowed future discord.

On October 28, the court appointed Colonel R. W. Johnson as

master to take testimony and report. On July 3, 1888, he concluded: "The complainants in this action have no legal or equitable right, title or interest in or to the lands in controversy in this suit, and there is, therefore, no merit in their bill, and the same should be dismissed at their cost." [11]

Chief Justice Elisha V. Long considered the master's report for a year, then issued a fifty-eight–page opinion. Long agreed that the Las Vegas Grant was a community grant and that the plaintiffs had no case, but he offered no solution for future settlement. [12] The plaintiffs withdrew on November 25, 1889, and paid all costs, hoping to prevent Long's opinion from setting a precedent in favor of the community land grant concept. While they were successful in preventing Long's opinion from becoming a decision, Long included his opinion as part of the record of the trial. [13]

Public interest had been high during the two years. Public meetings were held and expenses of the defense met through public subscription. The opinions of Johnson and Long appeared to support the concept of community grants. Clearly, these opinions supported the community grant claim for the Las Vegas Grant, and that principle seemed to apply to most of the grants in the area.

### The Raiding Begins

During the two years that *Millhiser* v. *Padilla* was under consideration, new fences continued to enclose large portions of grant land in amounts ranging from one thousand to more than ten thousand acres. [14] With a feeling of outrage fed by desperation and encouraged by the belief that the United States government would support them, *mexicanos* in San Miguel County moved to direct, violent anti-Anglo action. The Anglo Knights who had allied with the *mexicanos* in the civil suit now sought to disassociate themselves from the movement. Although their class sensibilities and political beliefs made them hostile to the speculators, the Knights could condone neither the violence nor the ethnic overtones of the protest. Furthermore, *americano* Knights had little understanding of the *mexicanos'* method of communal land use and little sympathy for the "ignorant Mexicans" who were swelling the ranks of their order. [15]

Rawlins and Quarrell rebuilt their fence twice, only to have it leveled both times. On the last occasion, one cowhand was shot through the leg and his mount killed as he rode out to defend the ranch property.

Other landholders received their share of attention. Two Anglos in Fulton, on the San Miguel del Bado Grant, found threatening notes on their property in July, ordering them off the land. They refused to leave, and Las Gorras Blancas attacked in December, destroyed their fences, shot one man through the leg and the back of the neck, and burned the store of the other. One complained to the governor that "there was a plot of land fenced in not over one hundred yards from my house belonging to a Mexican which was not touched."[16] Northwest of Las Vegas, in the mountain village of San Ignacio, Las Gorras Blancas visited José Ygnacio Luhan three times during June and July of 1889, destroying his fences and burning his crops, farm machinery, and sawmill. Earlier in the spring, the house of territorial Surveyor General Edward Hobart burned to the ground. Even County Sheriff Lorenzo López received threats. He, being an astute man, opted for the better part of valor and took down his fences on demand.[17]

The authorities tried to retaliate. As early as May 3, 1889, twenty-six indictments were returned against twenty-one individuals for fence cutting.[18] Although the indictments were brought in the spring, the accused were not tried until November, in the fall term of the district court. Interest in land grants was still high: the master's favorable report was public knowledge, Judge Long's opinion was believed to coincide with that of Colonel Johnson, and fence cutting and related activities had been steadily increasing before the first alleged fence cutters were brought to trial.

Those in power were divided. The district attorney, the probate judge, and the assessor were adamantly opposed to the fence cutters and argued for the strongest measures possible to stop the depredations. Sheriff López took a less militant stand, always asserting his willingness to serve any lawful warrant placed in his hands, but complying with White Cap demands when personally threatened.

Judge Long was in a quandary. A Democrat appointed to the bench by Cleveland, he was serving his last term as Chief Justice of New Mexico before resigning to enter private practice in Las Vegas. He agreed with Johnson, who was a close business associate, that the Las Vegas Grant was a community grant and that private occupation of grant lands as attempted by Millhiser was illegal. Long was determined to make such an opinion part of the official record of the trial. On the other hand, he was against Las Gorras Blancas. As a jurist, he could not tolerate extralegal, violent expressions of discontent. As an Anglo American, he was repelled by the ethnic overtones of the movement. As an incipient businessman who looked for growth in the Las Vegas area, he could not support a situation that discouraged the migration of people and capital. Therefore, at the very time that he was preparing his opinion on *Millhiser* v. *Padilla*, and while the cases against the twenty-one fence cutters waited on his docket,

Long urged the grand jury to bring more indictments against fence cutters.[19]

The *Las Vegas Daily Optic*, the leading newspaper of the county and one of partisan Republican tendencies, maintained a policy of quiet antipathy toward the problem. As a paper which sought to attract new wealth and people to the county, it tried to ignore the disturbances. When silence was not possible, the *Optic* denounced the "lawless mobs," although recognizing, implicitly, a certain element of justice in their position. The paper agreed with Judge Long that "the cutting of fences is an unlawful act and the offenders should be sought out and punished; that if the people in the neighborhood where these fences were built were aggrieved by their construction, there were other and legal ways of reaching the men who constructed them . . . people of San Miguel County are not ready to turn their government over to a self-constituted mob, who propose to take the administration of the law in their own hands."[20]

The last two months of 1889 were a busy period for the Fourth District Court of New Mexico. At midnight on November 1, sixty-three masked, armed horsemen galloped into the plaza of West Las Vegas. Although they left without doing any damage, they surrounded first the courthouse, then the home of District Attorney Salazar, and finally the jail, in warning to Salazar and the grand jury and in expression of support for the indicted. Judge Long called the demonstration an attempt at intimidation by the "secret organization of fence cutters" and urged the grand jury to redouble its efforts to find more indictments against them.[21]

The grand jury complied. On November 9, Long ordered Romaldo Fernández jailed for contempt because he refused to answer the questions of the jury. The *Optic* observed that "it is thought that he knows much more about fence cutting than he desires to tell." Three days in the county jail loosened Fernández's tongue only slightly. He admitted that he had passed by two White Cap meetings, one at Salitre attended by about forty-five men and the other at El Burro, but said that he did not know any of the participants. He was ordered back to jail, for Judge Long found it hard to believe that a long-term resident would not have recognized anybody at either meeting.[22]

The first of the fence cutters, Bernabel Gallegos, was brought to trial on November 19. The *Optic* greeted this development with confidence, assuring its readers that the evidence was strong against Gallegos and that this case should break the back of the organization throughout the county. Two days later, when the jury returned a verdict of not guilty, and the prosecution dismissed the charges against the other twenty, the *Optic* reassessed its analysis: "This case had no special relation to the association known as White Caps, but grew out of a dispute over the rights to fence in a certain tract of land in this county." [23] The *Optic* then warned, however, that

> While these particular acts of fence-cutting are supposed to have no direct connection with the regularly-organized body of fence cutters, yet the result in these cases may fairly be considered as foreshadowing the outcome of all those which hereafter may be brought for that crime. They show with what jealousy the people watch the fencing of large tracts of lands, which they, with some color of reason, regard as public, insofar, at least, as wood, pasture and water are concerned. It will be a very difficult matter to obtain a jury who can be persuaded into punishing their fellow citizens and neighbors for the commission of acts, though illegal, that they, in their own hearts, feel to be right and about the only adequate and speedy remedy at their command. [24]

Neither the release of the first twenty-one accused fence cutters, nor the delivering of his opinion upholding the community aspect of the Las Vegas Grant caused Judge Long to ease his demands that indictments be found against other members of Las Gorras Blancas. On December 2, the grand jury indicted the recalcitrant Fernández and another man named Felipe Gonzales. On December 10, the *Optic* announced: "It is noised abroad that a number of White Cap arrests are soon to be made. The indictments have been found and placed in the sheriff's hands. Fence cutting has been going forward at a lively rate lately and much more is anticipated."

The twenty-six indictments had been handed down on the last day of district court. They named forty-seven individuals ranging in age from twenty to sixty-five years, among them five members of the Knights of Labor, including the district organizer, Juan José Herrera, and his brother Nicanor. [25] By the second week in December, many had been arrested. Sheriff López telegraphed the governor for fifty rifles to arm special deputies, as he feared that the jail would be attacked "by a mob of one hundred strong." [26] All forty-seven were in custody by the fifteenth and were released on bond the following morning to a hero's welcome in front of the courthouse.

The *Optic* viewed these events with characteristic ambivalence. Despite the grudging acknowledgement of legitimate grievances contained in its discussion of the Gallegos acquittal, the newspaper editorialized on December 13 that the county should "Hunt Them Down." There "is little, or no doubt," the newspaper stated, "that there is a secret organization in this county, whose ranks have been recruited from the ignorant classes, and that this organization is lawless in its inception, spirit and purpose." Yet three days later, the *Op-*

tic asserted on one page that "our fence-cutting problems have been exaggerated," while on the next page it complained of the "loud and wild demonstration in the street" following the release of the accused and could not understand why Judge Long had set bail low enough so that all could pay.[27]

The Christmas season brought a fragile truce to Las Vegas and San Miguel County. White Cap activity had increased steadily since the spring. The town of Las Vegas had witnessed two large and dramatic demonstrations of support for the movement. One group of accused fence cutters had gone free, and others were free on bail and lionized by their supporters. The turmoil in the county was discouraging investment. As early as August, the *Optic* had published a letter from one "Old Resident," evidently a real estate broker, who complained of losing two thousand dollars in commissions because of the "secret gathering of men" destroying fences in the area. The "Old Resident" said that this state of affairs was known not only in the territory but also to "strangers and men who come here from the east and other points, to make investments in purchasing land and improved ranches."[28]

Ownership of the Las Vegas Grant remained unsettled, and a movement began in the town to effect a compromise. The proposal, supported by a cross section of the business community, both Anglo and Hispanic, argued for a division of the grant. One portion would be reserved for the original grantees, their heirs and assignees, and the remainder would be held in trust for the town of Las Vegas by the county commissioners. "Thrifty, industrious farmers," envisioned the *Optic*, would purchase these lands and the proceeds would go to the town for public use.[29]

A divided county waited for the spring term of district court. One group still maintained the Millhiser position that by buying up fractional interests in grants, a purchaser obtained absolute ownership to large, undivided quantities of land. Las Gorras Blancas upheld the counter position that grant land was communal property and could not be alienated without consent of all residents. Two other points of view were also current. One held that all land not specifically occupied by individuals or families was public domain and should be thrown open to homesteaders. The other argued that community lands belonged to towns and should be open for sale and settlement for the benefit of municipal coffers.

Las Gorras Blancas remained active enough during the winter to keep the county aware of their existence. On two occasions, bands of masked men rode at night through the streets of Las Vegas. Their first visit was an unsuccessful attempt to steal the indictments from the district attorney's office. The second, in early March as signs of spring brought renewed vigor to raiding activity in the countryside, involved a very large body of men who posted copies of the White Cap platform in both East and West Las Vegas.[30]

The platform lacked a specific program but presented a good picture of their attitudes and of the people and institutions that the White Caps considered their enemies. The major emphasis was on the rights and interests of the people, particularly those of the "helpless class." They reiterated their concern about the Las Vegas Grant, stating that it was a community grant which should be settled "to the benefit of all concerned." Attacks on lawyers and the judicial system, monopolists and corrupt practices, political leaders and election fraud, race agitation and legal intimidation made up the rest of the document. White Caps were "law abiding citizens" suffering from hunger and desolation because of the "deceitful and corrupt methods of bossism." They warned in closing, "Be fair and just and we are with you, do otherwise and take the consequences." *Nuestra Platforma* was signed "The White Caps, 1,500 Strong and Growing Daily."[31] District Attorney Salazar, who owed his position to the patronage system, called it "revolutionary, anarchistic and communistic."[32]

Night riding resumed at the same time. Eugenio Romero, the county assessor, a wealthy merchant and businessman, member of a prominent family and a formidable Republican *jefe político*, claimed that three hundred masked horsemen, "armed to the teeth," had destroyed six thousand railroad ties that he had contracted to provide to the Santa Fe Railroad.[33] Fence cutting continued, but Las Gorras Blancas expanded their range of operations and concerns. Railroad bridges were burned, tracks were torn up, poles intended for the Las Vegas Electric Light Company were cut, section hands on the railroad were threatened, and teamsters hauling for the railroad were stopped by masked bands and ordered at gunpoint to strike for higher wages. At the beginning, Las Gorras Blancas had made little ethnic distinction in their targets, attacking alike Anglo and Hispano who erected fences around large amounts of land in violation of custom. By the spring of 1890, they had added other kinds of exploitation to the grievances of the "helpless class." These complaints included the stripping of the grants' timber resources by private contractors, Anglo competition in the labor market, and the inequalities in pay scale for Anglo and Hispanic labor.[34]

District court convened in Las Vegas in the spring of 1890, surrounded by a volatile, passionate county. A new judge sat on the bench, a Minnesotan named James O'Brien appointed by President Harrison. When the case of the fence cutters, Juan José Herrera et al., came up, all forty-seven honored their bonds. To District Attorney Salazar's dismay, the three witnesses, whose testimony had justified the indictments, failed to appear. Charging that the White Caps had murdered the prosecution's witnesses during the winter, Salazar petitioned for a postponement. O'Brien ruled that, without witnesses, the prosecution had no case, and dismissed all charges against the forty-seven. Loud cheers from the crowded courtroom greeted the dismissal on May 20, 1890, followed by an enthusiastic meeting in the plaza marked by speeches, whiskey, and celebratory gunshots.[35]

With the dismissal of the forty-seven, fence cutting and related activities climbed to a new level. The sphere of incidents expanded, south to Antonchico and beyond, east to Trementina, and north into Mora County. Complaints of depredations came in from the western part of the county and from neighboring portions of Santa Fe County.[36] Governor L. B. Prince received word that companies of White Caps were organizing in Bernalillo County, throughout Santa Fe County, and seemed to be moving north into Colfax and Taos counties. The Secretary of the Interior began to receive regular complaints.[37] The Atcheson, Topeka, and Santa Fe Railroad ceased buying ties in the county, causing an estimated loss of $100,000 per year to San Miguel contractors.[38] According to the English-language press, business in Las Vegas had ground to a standstill by mid-summer. Not only were the White Caps braking the wheels of commerce, but, as the *Albuquerque Democrat* complained, they were destroying New Mexico's chances for immediate statehood.[39] Secretary of the Interior John Noble began to exert extreme pressure on Governor Prince to quiet the situation.

### Anglos Try to Respond

Prince had been trying to ignore the outbreaks. Engaged in a strong campaign to achieve statehood for New Mexico and burdened with a conception that it was beneath the dignity of the gubernatorial office to acknowledge such messy activities as fence cutting, Prince tried to push the whole situation from his mind. Finally, the combined pressures from Interior Secretary Noble and from agitated speculators who made up a major portion of the Republican Party in the territory, along with the adverse effects that the disturbances were having on his cherished goal of statehood, goaded Prince into action.[40]

The governor began with a fact-finding effort. He wrote to everyone who had been reported a victim of the attackers, and he journeyed to Las Vegas to meet with "leading citizens" in the town and with the alleged leaders of the movement.[41] The task proved difficult and frustrating. As the organization was secret, it was virtually impossible to know for whom to issue a warrant; as the organization was violent, it was difficult to obtain witnesses who would make a sworn statement, "even for a large consideration"; as the juries were drawn from the same kinds of people who made up the White Caps, conviction, even with strong evidence, seemed unlikely. Prince found a further complication in the "apathy and indifference" of the citizens of Las Vegas. A public meeting held in the city on August 16, supposedly to help stop the White Caps, resulted instead in a denunciation of the land-grabbers.[42] Prince concluded that half the population of the town, including the "best" citizens, sympathized with the fence cutting on the Las Vegas Grant. This, reasoned the governor, "prevents that strong public sentiment which we ought to have as an aid in suppressing these outrages."[43]

Prince proposed two steps to a solution. The first was to station one or two companies of U.S. troops in the county, not for martial law but for "moral effect" and to protect the railroad. The second was to employ one or two detectives to infiltrate the organization and thereby gain the necessary evidence so that the normal law-enforcement agencies could bring action. Both were denied. The first was forbidden by Interior Secretary Noble, and the second failed because funds were not available from any source—federal, territorial, or by private subscription.[44]

Neither of Prince's suggestions was unusual for nineteenth-century America. Private detective agencies, such as the Pinkerton organization, were reaching the height of their fame and were frequently employed as investigators by either corporations or governments. Similarly, the nation had seen frequent use of troops, both regular and national guard, in civil situations. The use of troops to restore and maintain order had been widespread during Reconstruction years, and the growing incidence of labor disputes had continued to make their employment a familiar event. New Mexico's governors had frequently called upon the military to help them retain some semblance of control over their territory. Public reaction to using troops in civil disputes was rarely favorable, and their use was regarded as a last resort. Perceptions of what constituted a last resort differed, however, and many people, especially workers involved in labor disputes, rarely felt it had been reached when bayonets filled the streets. In 1890, Secretary Noble obviously did not think that San Miguel County had reached the point of desperation, but the use of troops was a familiar tactic and would be employed again, both nationally and in New Mexico, during the Pullman Strike of 1894.[45]

Violence remained at a high level in San Miguel County. One observer said that politicians had attached themselves to the movement, and he prophesied that the evils would not cease nor "the guilty leaders be detected, until after the coming election."[46] This prediction proved to be partially correct; from the turmoil emerged a new political alignment that was to win the next two elections.

# CHAPTER 8

# Las Gorras Blancas:
# A Secret Gathering
# of Fence Cutters

Fence cutting was not unique to the *mexicanos* of San Miguel County. The introduction of barbed wire, "the devil's hat-band," to the open ranges of the trans-Mississippi West during the 1880s touched off vicious fence wars from Texas to Oregon; *mexicanos* responded with tactics similar to those used by others in the West threatened by enclosures.[1]

Open-range cattle ranching was the first Anglo enterprise to use the vast, semiarid New Mexico grasslands; its aura of romance and promise of huge profits attracted many Eastern and foreign investors. Profits could be immense because land and water were free. Open-range ranching required a sparse population, a demand for beef in the East, and consensus as to what constituted a "range." Over-grazing, over-production, and bad weather helped burst the open-range cattle bubble by the mid-eighties. Increased population, especially small farmers who took out title under the homestead laws, threatened the cattleman's free use of land and water. Small farmers supported their title with a new invention, cheap but effective wire fencing. Barbed wire ended casual use of the public domain and initiated the transition from cattle ranching to controlled stock raising.[2]

The transition was not smooth. Ranchers attacked homesteaders whose fenced crops cut off their herds from water. Small ranchers attacked large operations possessing the foresight and the capital to enclose land, whether they owned it or not. But by the end of the decade, most ranchers conceded that they needed some kind of title to their grazing land.

The outbreak of fence cutting in San Miguel County fit into the times. New Mexico's grant lands attracted cattlemen who saw an opportunity to acquire title to more land than the General Land Office would allow them from the public domain. The inhabitants on the grants complicated matters. Their residence created precedent for the title that the ranchers sought. But their presence challenged the new holdings. Vague and conflicting Hispanic practices and a tangled body of law and imprecise boundaries opened loopholes for the interlopers. Anglo ranchers, Anglo farmers, and Hispanic opportunists—who read the signs and hoped to take advantage of the new order—put up fences where none had stood before. Las Gorras Blancas struck at the fences and other manifestations of encroachment that threatened their existence.

## The World of the White Caps

No one publicly admitted to being a White Cap, and contemporary observers differed in many of their interpretations of the organization. To make sense of the evidence and accusations that survive, it is necessary to begin with the first settlement of the region early in the nineteenth century.

### *Social Background*

In 1794, Lorenzo Márquez and fifty-one others, all heads of families from Santa Fe, petitioned the governor of New Mexico for a tract of land on the Rio Pecos, at the place commonly called El Vado ("the ford"), "where there is room enough, not ony for us, . . . but also for everyone in the province not supplied [with enough land to live on]." They described their specific tract at El Vado as bounded "on the north [by] the Rio de la Vaca from the place called the Rancheria to the Agua Caliente, on the South the Cañon Blanco, on the east La Cuesta with the little hills of Bernal, and on the west the place commonly called the Gusano," an area of approximately 315,000 acres. If granted their request, they promised to enclose themselves "in a plaza well fortified with bulwarks and towers, and to exert ourselves to supply all the firearms and ammunition that it may be possible for us to procure."[3]

Their request was granted on November 26, 1794, with the provisions that "the tract aforesaid has to be in common, not only in regard to themselves but also to all settlers who may join them in the future," and that the building of their plaza, the opening of ditches, and all work proper for the common welfare "shall be performed by the community with that union which in their government they must preserve." The last paragraph attests that the boundaries had been walked, that all understood that the pasture and watering places were in common, and that possession had been taken with proper ceremony.

Official occupation took place on March 12, 1803, when the Justice of the Second Note of Santa Fe supervised the equitable division of farming land and the apportionment of both fields and house plots by drawing lots. He also marked out the boundaries of the village of San Miguel del Bado, including a large portion of land downriver "which is necessary for the inhabitants of this town who may require more land to cultivate, which shall be done by the consent of the Justice of said town . . ."[4]

The documents picture a homogeneous body of settlers. House and farm plots were drawn by lot, all work for the common good had to be distributed fairly throughout the community, and all pasture lands and watering holes were free to all. Communal ownership of the bulk of the grant land was the only condition mentioned twice in the grant decree. Despite the humble station of the settlers, they were expected to manage their local affairs "with that union which in their government they must preserve." Concerns of their government included the construction and maintenance of the village, defense, distribution of additional farming land, and, of continual importance, the distribution of irrigation water and the maintenance of the *acequias*.[5] To an Anglo American eye, the grant documents picture a cooperative Hispanic variation on the Jeffersonian image of the sturdy yeoman farmer.

The grant was intended to be open to additional settlement. The petitioners requested land for themselves and for any others who needed enough land to live on. In 1794, fifty-two heads of households received the grant, but in 1803, fifty-eight households participated in the drawing of lots, indicating that this provision was more than just a formality. Others followed, either settling at San Miguel or establishing new villages within the grant's boundaries. As people moved to the region, or as population increase overtaxed the resources of the original tract, the Spanish and Mexican governments made other awards. The Antonchico Grant, a 383,850-acre tract down the Pecos from San Miguel, was given in 1822 to Salvador Tapia et al., settlers migrating from San Miguel del Bado. In 1835, Juan de Dios Maese and others received 496,450 acres called the Las Vegas Grant, centered around a large meadowland on the Gallinas River. It was the ninth tract awarded in the region. By 1845, fourteen awards had been made that supported approximately ten thousand people.[6]

These grants range from the crest of the Sangre de Cristo Mountains to the slope of the Canadian escarpment.[7] Altitude varies from nine thousand feet in the west to three thousand near the Texas panhandle. Streams of varying volume and dependability seam the

western portion on a southeastwardly bias, becoming proportionate-
ly less frequent the greater the distance from the mountains. Only
two rivers cut the entire region—the Pecos, rising from the snows of
the Sangre de Cristos and carving a deep path as it travels on its
southern journey to meet the Rio Grande above Del Rio, and the Canadian, describing an eastward loop en route to the Red River. As
one resident observed, "They are not great rivers." [8]

It is varied, broken land with rainfall rarely exceeding sixteen
inches annually. Temperature, vegetation, and terrain differ markedly throughout the area, from the rugged mountains on the west, with
good stands of timber and sheltered valleys, to the dusty brown-green
high plains of scrub piñon, short grass, and rock broken by mesas,
isolated hills, cañons, and occasional rolling meadows on the east.
Streams and waterholes determined the location of settlement every-
where. Except for a few isolated areas, irrigable land was not sufficient to provide a livelihood, and everyone ran some livestock. [9]

Life in San Miguel County, before the railroad aroused the ambitions of Las Vegas, followed a pattern of capricious predictability: [10]
capricious because of the uncertainties of health, weather, and hostile Indians, but predictable in the ways that people confronted the
chancy business of living. Settlers grouped together in small communities along waterways, tilling what land they could for staples
and roaming with their herds or flocks over the hills and eastward
toward the Llano Estacado. Village size depended upon the avail-
ability of arable land and water; when population threatened these
resources, settlers moved on to establish a new village on unoccupied land.

There were differences. The families in one community might
be independent farmers, tilling their fields and grazing their small
herds on the common land, occasionally selling wool or animals for
small cash income. In other villages, one or two clans rose above the
rest, owning almost all of the livestock and employing most of the
village as herders. An entire hamlet might work for one *rico* as wage
labor; some occupied a middle ground, herding for a *rico* or a merchant on the *partido* system, which offered the prospect of independence. A few farmers, fortunate in the quality of land and the
amount of water available, produced a surplus and regarded themselves as somehow apart from the *pastores* and vaqueros. [11]

The general pattern was of house lots and fields held in specific
ownership and pastureland open to all. Grant boundaries were
vague and unimportant, with spheres of use sanctioned by custom.
Whether or not a tract was granted to an individual or to a community made little real difference, for wealth and power depended

upon the size of herds and the number of people a *patrón* employed, not on exclusive use and title to a quantity of land. Before Anglo Americans arrived and demanded that the land be measured and tagged with the name of an owner—an individual, a corporation, or a government—both grant and crown land was used in common by those who could.[12]

A few merchants and traders also participated in this pastoral life. Many hamlets supported small shopkeepers who supplied basic commercial needs. The *comanchero* trade provided an additional source of income. Until the arrival of Anglo investment and the railroad, Las Vegas was one of three prominent villages in the area, the other two being Antonchico and Puerto de Luna, seats for traders to the Comanches.[13]

Public schools were nonexistent. The Church offered the only available education. If a village had a priest, he was often the most educated man in the community and served as an intermediary who dealt with the written demands from the outside world. Others in a village might read and write—the storekeeper, if there was one—and they too served as *escribanos* for their neighbors.

*Ricos* topped the social scale. With large holdings of livestock and often extensive mercantile interests, they claimed descent from the conquistadores and sent their children to private school in Santa Fe and perhaps on to St. Louis University or Notre Dame. Their influence derived from wealth, family, and interest in affairs throughout the territory; they provided territorial legislators and county officials. *Ricos* and local *patrones*—those who employed a number of people in a given area and who, through wealth, family connections, and personality, could exert a great deal of local influence—provided the leadership for the region as a whole.

It would be a mistake to assume that a hegemony of *ricos* and *patrones*, with the aid of the priests, controlled a docile population of *los hombres pobres*. Just as there were gradations within the broad category of *ricos*, so were there differences among *los pobres*. As the case of the San Miguel del Bado Grant demonstrates, the whole adult male population participated in certain group decisions. Of continual importance were the *acequias*. After their construction, they required yearly cleaning and repair. Equitable distribution of water had to be insured, a touchy problem in a land where lack of water meant starvation. A *mayordomo de acequia* and a committee responsible for the use of water were elected each year to supervise the irrigation system. The communities chose alcaldes to distribute lands and to adjudicate minor civil and criminal disputes. Cooperative work had to be done, and this too was a part of local govern-

ment. In some villages, this kind of cooperation even extended to
planting and harvesting. As one resident of the San Miguel del Bado
Grant described his town:

> The people of El Cerrito used to elect a *conservador* each year. He acted
> as a sort of governor of the village. The people had to do what he told
> them to. In those times the people would work together in planting and
> harvest time. The *conservador* would call men to work and could deter-
> mine which work should be done first. When someone wanted to hire a
> man he had to come to the *conservador*. He could determine who could
> have the job. Always he would select the family that needed work the
> most. In that way the needy were usually provided for. In case they were
> not, he could ask the people for money or grain to give the *pobres*.[14]

Political experience in dealing with crucial local problems was
an important element of life for the people clustered in the adobe
and stone houses along the streams of San Miguel County. Naturally,
a political elite developed among *los pobres*. Leaders could rise because they came from respected families, because they enjoyed more
material success than their fellows, because they were adjudged
good and wise, or because of personality, influence, or power deriv-
ing from the support of a *patrón* or *rico*. Just as naturally, factions
developed. Rare was the village that was not divided into two groups,
usually along family lines.[15]

The political world of the region encompassed a complex network of relationships between factions at each point on the social
scale. Support or opposition was determined not by ideology but by
the tangible elements of immediate material benefit, by considerations of prestige, or by the more ephemeral factors of admiration or
hate. Competition was for power, not for change, a logical situation
when there was agreement about the basic structure of life. One student of New Mexican politics observed that if indeed the *jefe político* dominated New Mexican politics among the Spanish-speaking
communities, there were many *jefes* in constant competition for the
same constituency.[16] A present resident of Las Vegas expressed the
same sentiment more forcefully: "If the *patrones* really controlled so
well, why were there so damn many political parties?"[17]

The Anglo Americans shared a region with a people that they
did not understand. They saw dirty, ignorant, lazy natives dotting a
vast land which, to Anglo American eyes, was unclaimed and un-
used. Occasionally they could discern a *rico* from among the masses
of backward and superstitious *mexicanos*, but they had little conception of the complex patterns of relationships and customs.

It was not an easy situation to comprehend. Isolation characterized the life in each village, but it was an isolation tempered by the mobile aspects of a grazing economy and was further broken down by the pattern of settlement which contained many villages in all parts of the region settled by delegations from older villages.[18] Each village on a grant maintained a unique identity, as did each grant, yet there was both conflict and cooperation between villages on the same grant and between grants.[19] This duality between isolation and interaction was enhanced by the coming of the *americanos*. As the Anglos increased in number, the villages tended to withdraw into themselves. Yet the Anglos brought increased opportunities for wage labor and markets, thereby intensifying the mobility and interaction.

Just as there were opposing themes of isolation and interaction, so too were there paradoxical threads of aggression and passivity. When the Anglos arrived, they came to a region of expanding settlement. The Hispanos were still settling and conquering New Mexico, ever-extending their control, when the westward advancing fringes of Anglo America arrived; hardly the behavior of a static culture. But the New Mexican concept of expansion did not include the Anglo's concept of upward mobility or getting ahead. It was expansion along traditional lines, an expansion primarily "to live." Among *los pobres*, the goal was a comfortable existence in their terms. This meant enough land to farm, enough pasture for stock, enough game to hunt, enough wood to burn, and enough material to build. It meant, should the opportunity present itself, wage labor on the railroad, contract freighting or the like, but only to help one live as one ought to live.[20] To the Anglo, such attitudes were backward and slovenly; to *los pobres*, nothing else made any sense.

Politically, the contradictory patterns of autonomy and dependence ran through a social fabric which most Anglos could not unravel. The *mexicanos'* tendency to support members of their upper classes for county and territorial offices, their lack of concern for "political" issues, and the fact that patronage seemed to be the only determinant of their political behavior led Anglos to the conclusion that these were a placid, *patrón*-dominated people, politically naïve and shot through with corruption. The Anglo did not see the politics of the village and did not understand the areas of autonomy and the mutual obligations and benefits in the seemingly servile system. Neither did the Anglo understand the experience of the people which taught that local affairs were the only ones of importance, that the problems of larger units of government were of no concern, and that unless something offered discernible practical benefit it was of little value. When basic ways of life were as they should be, concern was only for improvement within those ways. When their way of life was threatened, *los pobres* fit neither their servile nor their passive image.

### Threat and Response

By the 1880s Las Vegas began to push for territorial leadership, and an atmosphere of boosterism and boom prevailed; land grant speculation increased apace. Legislators collaborated to pass laws that would virtually strip *los pobres* of their interest in their grants.[21] Men conspired with the surveyor general of the territory and with land registrars, even on the floors of Congress, to gain title to as many acres as they could.[22]

In a very brief time, things happened that promised fundamentally to change the patterns of life in San Miguel County. Furthermore, the people who had traditionally coped with larger political problems were not defending *los pobres*; they were participating in the changes.[23]

San Miguel County's population increased by approximately 3,500, almost all Anglo, in the 1880s, bringing the total to over 24,000.[24] Thirty-five hundred people are not many, but if they represent a hundred ranches and a railroad competing for land, water, and timber previously used by others for decades, change is, in fact, great. In addition to usurping land and water, thereby hampering traditional use, these newcomers were hostile and contemptuous in their treatment of the natives, and they were enlisting the *ricos* and *patrones* on their side. In a county in which the *mexicanos* still enjoyed overwhelming numerical superiority, there appeared to be no peaceful recourse. Civil war broke out in April, 1889.

Governor Prince thought that the White Caps consisted almost exclusively of natives of New Mexico of the "ignorant class." A few "active and educated men" arranged the organization, said the governor, and influenced the people with talk that they were being deprived of their rights, using the Las Vegas Grant as a "special illustration." In Prince's view, members joined to protect their "supposed" rights, but the White Caps, once established, were used for "worse purposes." "Worse purposes," in Prince's estimation, included labor agitation, attacks on corporations, politics, and outright banditry.[25] Another observer called them a "lawless mob of several hundred Mexicans" who committed their depredations "upon the plea that the land belongs to the people, and that they are underpaid for their work."[26] Many observers draw a strong correlation between the White Caps and the Knights of Labor: "The White Caps believe that they are backed by the Knights of Labor of the whole United

States. To understand this, you must recollect that these are Mexicans; that the Mexicans in New Mexico, with the exception of perhaps five percent, are the most ignorant people on the face of the earth."[27]

Not all Anglos viewed Las Gorras Blancas with distaste. Judge O'Brien, writing two months after he dismissed the forty-seven accused fence cutters, told Prince: "To a casual and impartial observer, ignorant of antecedent causes, the so-called outrages are the protests of a simple, pastoral people against the establishment of large landed estates, or baronial feudalism, in their native territory. The term 'White Cap,' when used in any other sense, is, in my opinion, a misnomer."[28]

*La Voz del Pueblo*, a Spanish-language newspaper published in Las Vegas, constantly defended *las masas de los hombres pobres*, and by implication Los Gorras Blancas, against the "capitalists, monopolists and land grabbers," although the paper never overtly condoned fence cutting. Founded the previous year in Santa Fe by Nestor Montoya, a rising young educated Hispano who sought to end the Santa Fe Ring's domination of the territory, *La Voz* moved to Las Vegas in 1890, when Montoya joined Félix Martínez, another Democrat of similar background and ambitions and of greater financial resources.[29]

All observers agreed that poor *mexicanos* made up the rank and file of Las Gorras Blancas and that land was the major issue. Prince, District Attorney Salazar, and others saw the turbulence as the product of outside agitators duping the native population. Salazar accused Juan José Herrera and seven lieutenants of being the instigators and argued that if the leaders were disposed of, the organization would fall apart. He recommended the "strongest measures possible against these people, as the only possible way of putting them to fear, and it is only through fear that they can be persuaded to desist [from] the wholesale destruction of property."[30]

There is a familiar ring to the beleaguered cry that "outsiders" or "evil manipulators" with magical powers caused the unrest, if only because the people were too ignorant to understand their self-interest. There was an organization, but to call it an "outside" one is to misunderstand the nature of the issue and the world of the people who fought for it.

Fence cutting and related activities during this period were organized. The number of incidents, their occurrences in a wide geographical area, and the similarity of targets all indicate cooperation. The numbers involved in most attacks or demonstrations exceeded the capabilities of most single villages.[31] Substantial evidence of nocturnal meetings in isolated places attests to communication and planning. The similarity of costume, of technique, and of methods of signaling—using homemade whistles instead of voice commands— also point to organization.[32] Finally, almost all observers, whether hostile or sympathetic, said that a "secret society" was responsible for the fence cutting.

Many identified the Knights of Labor, or at least district organizer Juan José Herrera and his brothers, as the organizers. The Herreras, the Knights, and *La Voz del Pueblo* denied this charge, but

The Herrera brothers, Juan José, Pablo, and Nicanor. From Charles A. Siringo, *A Cowboy Detective*, facing p. 118.

several factors gave it validity. Herrera had lived for a time in San Miguel County, had left under the cloud of scandalous conduct with a woman, and had joined the Knights of Labor in either Utah or Colorado. The date of his return to San Miguel County is not known, but it is undeniable that he received a commission as district organizer from the Knights of Labor in 1888. He proceeded to establish twenty local assemblies in the county and to begin recruitment in the neighboring counties of Mora and Santa Fe. As Herrera organized his assemblies, Las Gorras Blancas began to ride in the same areas, a coincidence that disturbed several Anglo members of Las Vegas Assembly Number 4636:

> Just how many Assemblies he has organized, we are not prepared to say, but fence cutting and other depredations are by far too frequent occurrences. We understand that there has [sic] been three Assemblies organized in Santa Fe County and fence cutting has commenced there. Now who these fence cutters or self-called 'White Caps' are, we are not prepared to say. But the Mexican people who are being organized as K of L are of the poorer class and consequently they are more ignorant, as they have had no advantages of education, there being but very few schools in the Territory.
>
> Now we, as members of the K of L would request that no more assemblies be organized or Charters granted to those already organized until the present condition of affairs changes for the better.[33]

Las Gorras Blancas and the Knights of Labor correspond on three other points. The White Caps' concern about wage scales and job competition, coupled with strike threats, suggests the involvement of people familiar with labor agitation. The parallel membership between the Knights of Labor and El Partido del Pueblo Unido after August, 1890, their support of major White Cap issues, and the coincidence that the strength of all three lay in the same precincts, lend additional support to the theory connecting the Knights and the White Caps.[34] The last bit of evidence is the oral tradition about Las Gorras Blancas current in both Las Vegas and the villages on the grants. In this tradition, Las Gorras Blancas and the Knights of Labor are identical: the old people say that Las Gorras Blancas was a nickname, but that they preferred to be called Los Caballeros de Labor.[35]

The Knights of Labor, as led by Juan José Herrera, organized or coordinated the fence cutting. That the organization was not indigenous to New Mexico is undeniable. A national union that had grown out of a league of Philadelphia garment workers, by 1885 under the leadership of Terence V. Powderly, it encompassed hundreds of thousands of members. The Knights organized people around an ethical substitute for capitalism, and opposition to land speculation and large landowners played a prominent role in their constitution. Although membership was denied only to manipulators of money and corruptors of morals, recruitment was most successful in industries and trades. The many new members in the early 1880s were primarily wage laborers. The strident demands and militant actions of these workers culminated in the Great Southwest Strike of 1885. Powderly could not cope with these tactics and refused to support his own striking members. Defeat by railroad magnate Jay Gould in 1886, coupled with the clamor raised by the Haymarket Riots that same year, sent the national organization on a long slide to decay and irrelevance. As the Knights lost their national impact, the combination of grievances, their stance on land, and Herrera brought them to life in San Miguel County.[36]

District organizer Herrera was no *extranjero*. Herrera had lived outside of New Mexico for a time, but he was a native of New Mexico. He was originally from San Miguel County, and his family still lived there. He did differ from most of *los hombres pobres*: he had traveled, he could read and write, he published a newspaper for a time, and he was involved in a national organization that meant very little to most native New Mexicans. But he understood San Miguel's people and their problems, and he provided a dimension of coordination to their protest that they lacked prior to and after his active years.[37]

Herrera and his lieutenants coordinated; they did not create. They did not make the issues. Fences went up on common land before assemblies of Los Caballeros de Labor spread across the county. These fences dislocated the way of life of the native people, a way of life that had been sanctioned in grant documents and established custom. The dislocation was severe in a marginal land where the loss of grazing privileges brought starvation near.

Herrera did not create the issue; neither did he provide the techniques of protest. *Los pobres* of New Mexico did not seek redress through legislative assemblies or the vote; nothing in their experience taught them that this would be a fruitful course of action. In their world, peaceful redress of grievances was realized either through judicial arbitration or petitions to the governor.[38] If these avenues failed, only two other choices remained—sullen acceptance or direct action.

Direct action, forceful action, was natural to a culture that remembered a constant hostile Indian threat and placed high emphasis on honor and the stalwart defense of one's rights. Most adults remembered the Comanches who had used the Llano Estacado as a highway between Texas and Mexico. *Comancheros* traded regularly with them, but the commerce did not block out the memory of Indian attacks. Other military memories included the capture of the Texas–Santa Fe expedition near Antonchico in 1841 and the defeat of Sibley's column at Glorieta Pass in 1862.[39] On a personal level, the people of the villages still tell stories and sing *corridos* about individual triumphs over insulting Texas cowboys, and the phrase *mucho hombre*—much of a man—punctuates their tales of men who defended their rights with guns.

Feuds between families occurred frequently and are still not uncommon. The village of El Cerrito on the San Miguel Grant was one of the few villages that did not have two political factions in the 1930s. El Cerrito had once had two powerful families, but disagreements over grazing ranges on the common land touched off a feud in the 1880s that drove one family group from the community.[40] Disagreements over communal resources caused many conflicts. For example, the residents of Bado de Juan Pais accused the *mayordomo de acequia* at El Llano of diverting too much water from their common *acequia madre*. Moving quickly, representatives of the aggrieved community set the ditch gate at what they considered to be the proper position, marked it, and left a note for the El Llano *mayordomo* informing him that he would be hanged if anything was changed. The El Llano official complied.[41]

One problem in determining the extent of White Cap activity, a problem recognized by observers at the time, is to separate reported attacks done for personal reasons from those done by Las Gorras Blancas. The large-scale incidents by masked horsemen are easy to identify, but such incidents as isolated murders, stock mutilation, or burning of buildings are less easy to categorize. A Mr. F. LeDuc, whose wellhouse was burned in March, 1890, thought that he was a victim not of the White Caps but of two "troublemakers" from the neighboring village of Los Vigiles.[42] Violence was a part of life for the people of San Miguel County. Juan José Herrera brought only a higher degree of efficiency to a people facing a common problem and possessed of common tactics for confrontation.

This is not to say that there was a 100 percent correlation between Los Caballeros de Labor and Las Gorras Blancas. Most probably, Herrera organized his assemblies emphasizing as much as possible the tenet that the land belonged to the people, and then used the assemblies as an institution for careful recruitment of White Cap chapters.[43] Membership could vary. In one village the local leader might be a pillar of the community, the *mayordomo de acequia* for example, while in the next he could be a young, dashing bachelor, a quasi-bandit used to a high-risk life and able to command some respect by his personality or reputation for bravery.[44] Sometimes the entire village supported the movement, sometimes a village might be split, and some villages and areas were never won over by the White Caps. The majority of the members were the poor, but sometimes *patrones*, inspired by outrage at injustices or political opportunism, joined.

Building on a sense of ethnic and class identification that grew stronger in the face of racial slurs and economic threats, Herrera forged a movement out of the traditional materials of Hispanic culture. To *las masas de los hombres pobres*, the issues were clear. Traditional use of land led their list, followed by fair and dignified treatment of wage labor. The two spectres of hunger and change motivated most. Perhaps they hoped that they could drive *los extranjeros* from their land and reunite with Mexico. But they would settle for traditional land tenure and fair treatment of labor.

The White Caps enjoyed some success by the summer of 1890. While they were unable to enlist all of San Miguel's *pobres*, they had gained the tacit support of most. Juries would not convict for fence cutting. Governor Prince could mobilize no popular movement against them. Their actions had temporarily stopped immigration, and the courts seemed to uphold their position. If they had not beaten the *americanos*, they had at least effected a stalemate. In August, 1890, the movement took a new tack. On the twenty-fifth of the month, the Optic published a call for precincts to organize and send delegates to the county convention of El Partido del Pueblo Unido.

# CHAPTER 9

# El Partido
# del Pueblo Unido

The thirty-four names affixed to the call for delegates to the county convention of El Partido del Pueblo Unido signaled a realignment in the San Miguel political arena and a transition from terroristic to electoral politics.

The White Cap raids halted Anglo American "progress" in east-central New Mexico; the authorities could not combat the phantom movement, and public opinion supported the White Caps against land thieves. Investors and settlers paused en route to San Miguel County, waiting to see which tack *mexicano* resistance would take.

Conceivably, Las Gorras Blancas could have continued their violent attacks. During the summer, cut fences and burned barns were reported with increasing frequency, and Governor Prince received warnings of unrest spreading to neighboring counties. Fearful *americanos* predicted a war for independence: ". . . quite a large number of them are dreaming . . . that New Mexico can achieve her independence of the United States by driving out the Americans . . . They say, '. . . this country . . . is ours, and we don't propose to have any Americans interfering with our rights.' Ever since the annexation . . . a few hotheaded ignorant Mexicans have talked like the above, but since the labor organizations have come into existence . . . these extreme men have become more numerous and bolder in their declarations."[1]

There is no evidence that the idea of secession, however appealing, was seriously entertained. Las Gorras Blancas held sway only in San Miguel County. Bands appeared in adjacent regions, *los hombres pobres* shared common resentments and grievances, and in the summer of 1890, White Caps enjoyed marginal dominance in a disrupted county. But White Cap supremacy was more apparent than real. It rested on the uneven cornerstones of intimidation and popular sympathy. The first was concrete, but touched only a small segment of the county's population; the second was widespread but intangible and could disappear quickly.

The bitter, angry residents of the countryside saw their way of life being destroyed by incomprehensible methods that violated their standards of order and morality. One purpose overrode all others in drawing the bands of horsemen together: restoration of the traditional use of the common land. Their success threatened to dissolve their organization held together by immediate problems and bounded by local landmarks: with the fences down, the problem no longer existed, and their unity weakened.

Juan José Herrera coordinated common complaints, methods, and leadership into a body capable of obstructing change and expressing discontent, not one that could sustain creative action. By the end of August others recognized that Las Gorras Blancas could go no further. The night riders had exposed serious problems to the full light of the New Mexican sun, and they had created a power vacuum. But Las Gorras Blancas could not fill the void, and El Partido del Pueblo Unido stepped forward to take advantage of White Cap successes. It assumed the mantle of Las Gorras Blancas' moral position by embracing, in form at least, two issues emphasized in the platform of the preceding March: the land question and political bossism. To this nucleus the party added the national anger against monopolies and corporations soon to solidify around the Populists and presented itself as a reform party committed to the welfare of all the people.

## Membership

A mixed bag of Las Vegas *políticos* signed the call for the convention. White Caps Herrera and his brother Nicanor joined young, ambitious native Democrats Félix Martínez and Nestor Montoya. Anglo Knights of Labor and Anglo lawyers and businessmen of the Democratic Party mingled with renegade Republicans unhappy with county leadership. *Jefes* like Lorenzo López saw a chance to increase their power.[2] Idealism, dissatisfaction, patronage, and power spurred the alliance of old antagonists. Opposition to the Republican Party as run by Eugenio Romero in San Miguel and Thomas Catron in Santa Fe was the only point of agreement among the leaders of the party that capitalized on the White Cap outbreaks.

Juan José Herrera, Félix Martínez, and Lorenzo López represent three distinct types within El Partido del Pueblo's upper councils. Herrera, an active man of middle age, was willing to substitute votes and elected officials for raids and posted warnings if doing so would protect and enhance the interests of *los pobres*, but he was wary of Anglo practices. The traditional rights must be maintained; Herrera

Lorenzo López. From campaign biography, *La Voz del Pueblo*, October 29, 1892.

would support no change in established patterns until it was clearly demonstrated that the people, his people, would benefit.[3]

Félix Martínez had a different vision of the coming order. Born in Taos and educated at a "commercial school" in Trinidad, Colorado, Martínez had come to Las Vegas in 1880 at the age of twenty-two and quickly made a mark as an entrepreneur and active Democrat. By 1890, he had served one term in the New Mexico House, another as county assessor, and was on the Democratic Territorial Central Committee. Martínez used his position in the county to plead for the masses in general and *mexicanos* in particular. But where Herrera viewed all aspects of Anglo America with suspicion, Martínez welcomed Anglo political institutions, commercial and technological innovations, and social services like public education. Martínez was not opposed to progress; he only wanted his people to control it in New Mexico.[4]

Lorenzo López was neither a leader of the people nor a proponent of integrating *mexicanos* into the American Dream. Born in 1837 to a wealthy local grazier, López combined the advantages of birth with a strong interest in politics and a judicious marriage into the powerful Romero family. By 1890, he was one of the top two Republican *jefes* in the county, controlling, in Catron's estimation, four hundred votes directly,[5] able to command a large following among the lesser *jefes* and *patrones*, and alternating with his in-laws in the most lucrative and influential county offices. Friction with the Romeros prompted his move to the new party. At "daggers-points" with his wife's family since 1888, Lorenzo López saw in the new party a chance to control San Miguel County without having to share with Eugenio Romero.[6]

El Partido del Pueblo formed out of a coalition of middle-class Hispanos, Anglo laborers and lawyers, and some old style *jefes políticos*, founded upon an angry and rebellious mass of *los hombres pobres*. The *Optic* called it the "mongrel" party and characterized the campaign as one of equal parts "free whiskey, free sheep and intimidation."[7] The newspaper branded El Partido del Pueblo as the party of the White Caps: "'Down with the fence cutters, the despoilers of our citizens,' says Nestor Montoya. All right Don Nestor. That is certainly sage counsel; but then, the people would have more confidence in the sincerity of your purpose, if you would first remove the said persons from your county ticket."[8]

## The Election of 1890

A good partisan newspaper, the *Optic* each day predicted crushing defeat for the upstarts. Even after preliminary returns promised a sweeping victory for the new party, the *Optic* remained optimistic. Eugenio Romero was not worried, the paper assured its readers, for the returns from the outlying precincts were sure to bring victory to the Republicans.[9]

Romero was wrong. Running on an anticapitalist, antimonopolist platform, which in New Mexico meant anti–land-grabber, anti–railroad and anti–Santa Fe Ring, the United People's Party captured every office by an average of 60 percent of the vote. The party supported Democratic incumbent Antonio Joseph for delegate-in-Congress, and this tie with Democrats was maintained through cooperation in the territorial legislature and continued participation in the Central Committee.

Hon. Felix Martinez.

Félix Martínez. From campaign biography, *La Voz del Pueblo*, October 29, 1892.

The precinct returns underscore the importance of the land issue; *mexicano* communities on threatened grants provided the largest margins for El Partido del Pueblo. The returns also point to an independence on the part of the *nativo* voters: almost every precinct made distinctions between candidates, with Anglos generally faring worst.[10]

Despite the decisive victory and glowing predictions of future success, El Partido del Pueblo did little to change county administration. The legislative delegation gained some victories, particularly regarding Nestor Montoya's fence law, which made it a crime either to destroy a fence on land of good title or to erect one on property not owned in fee simple, but they were defeated by Catron over the abolition of the three-hundred-dollar exemption for heads of households—a severe setback to people who did not own three hundred dollars' worth of property—and the concomitant jury law which forbade anyone who had not paid taxes to sit on a jury.[11]

If county administration did not change appreciably and the legislative impact was less than earthshaking, El Partido del Pueblo did remain embroiled in the land question.

## The Land Issue

For several years, territorial officials and businessmen had petitioned Congress for a special court to settle the confused property situation in New Mexico. The People's Party supported the creation of a U.S. Court of Private Land Claims, in hopes that it would untangle land titles and end large-scale speculation. Created in 1891, the court did not meet in New Mexico until 1892. Charged with ascertaining the validity and extent of Spanish and Mexican land grants in New Mexico, Colorado, and Arizona, the court sat until 1904 and heard cases involving a total of 235,491,020 acres. Unfortunately for *mexicanos*, it viewed most claims with suspicion; at the end of its term, only 2,051,526 acres remained as grant land, with the balance classified as public domain.[12]

As the court was just beginning in 1891, and as it had no jurisdiction over grants that had been patented by Congress—the Las Vegas Grant was one—New Mexicans involved in land controversies sought other avenues.

The territorial legislature offered a possible solution in an act of February 26, 1891. This act provided for the incorporation of a grant upon petition by inhabitants, and empowered a board of trustees, elected from the precincts within the grant, to determine legitimate owners and the extent of their private holdings, and to administer the common lands and other corporate matters.[13] El Partido del Pueblo used its strength to control the membership and policies of various committees formed to investigate this possibility.

The rights of *los hombres pobres* gained support from a decision rendered by Judge O'Brien in the case of *Millhiser et al. v. José Albino Baca et al.* The Millhiser group had not quit after the 1889 decision, but continued to bring suit against grant residents in, as the *Optic* put it, an apparent attempt to bankrupt every grant inhabitant. O'Brien ruled that the law of ten years' limitation, that is, ten years of unchallenged occupancy, gave all known native New Mexican residents on the Las Vegas Grant clear title to their holdings, even in the absence of documentary proof.[14]

The decision prompted the formation of a committee which began to identify all legitimate occupants of the grant under the law of ten years' limitation. A convention in July, 1891, resolved to petition for incorporation under territorial law and drafted the machinery for choosing the board of trustees. It also passed five resolutions proposed by Félix Martínez. These reduced the minimum tenure for legitimacy to five years and provided that those who could not meet this standard would be allowed to remain until they had established title; it made the maximum amount allowed any one individual 160 acres and stipulated that the proper tribunal would determine each claimant's holdings up to this amount. The fifth resolution stated that anyone settling after the date of the meeting would be an intruder, and that no uncultivated land could be allocated without the approval of proper authority.[15]

El Partido del Pueblo controlled the convention, and its proposals reflected the impact of Las Gorras Blancas: they stressed the rights of *los hombres pobres*, including the uncultivated or common land, and devised machinery that would in theory allow grant residents self-determination. Yet the resolutions really reflected an anticorporate thrust rather than pure White-Cappism. Four of the five emphasized size of holdings and length of residence; the size was small, a victory for *los pobres*, but residence was short, thereby potentially including some Anglos. The last provision, although alluding to common land, provided for future settlement—something that Las Gorras Blancas had not fought for.

## Political Jousting

Organized violence died down. Sporadic attacks on fences or crops occurred, fights and killings with political overtones continued as part of the scheme of things, but the coordinated bands that had roamed the countryside during the previous two years were no more. Some Anglos thought that *mexicanos* had refined techniques of harassment. One complained to Governor Prince that it cost him a yearly tribute of sixty-five dollars to keep his fence upright;[16] another said that *mexicanos* boasted that they did not fear the law, as Mexican jurors would not convict their brothers.[17] But in general the victory of El Partido del Pueblo brought quiet to San Miguel County.

The opposition countered by equating the party and Los Caballeros de Labor with all lawlessness throughout the territory; by building an organization, the Sociedad de los Caballeros de Ley y Orden y Protección Mutua,[18] which competed for members in the same communities that supported the White Caps; and by putting forth *El Sol de Mayo* to rival *La Voz* for the Spanish reading public.

By the winter of 1891, Republicans blamed the White Caps for every violent incident in the territory, from the mysterious burning of the new territorial capitol building and the shooting of Territorial Senator J. A. Ancheta to collusion between administrations and bandit gangs in several counties.[19] *La Voz* denied that the White Caps existed. "*Pobres Gorras Blancas!*" exclaimed one editorial and went on to say that the name came from an isolated raid on the San Miguel courthouse some years before and had become a catchall to include all the "thieves, assassins, and usurpers" in New Mexico.[20] Yet in its continual denials of any connection between the Knights and violence, *La Voz* never failed to stress that the real villains in New Mexico were not the "vandals or masked highwaymen" but the "despotic oppressors . . . hidden technically by the law. . ."[21]

Much of San Miguel's political activity for the next three years revolved around rhetorical duels between *La Voz* and *El Sol* and recruitment competition between the Knights of Labor and the Society of Law and Order. As the clear-cut issue of fences on the common land melted into a slough of litigation, meetings, and proposals, reintroduced factions and attendant bickering punctuated with frequent switches in allegiance and individual skirmishes characterized the conflict. Both newspapers featured confessions from people who had joined the wrong organization and now saw the error of their ways; El Partido del Pueblo scored the biggest coup with the defection of Enrique Armijo, the first editor of *El Sol*.[22]

Both groups expanded their operations. Herrera bought *El Defensor del Pueblo* in June, 1891, and began to publish it in Albuquerque as the official organ of the Knights of Labor. Law and Order chapters appeared in Mora, Bernalillo, and Santa Fe counties, countered by assemblies of the Knights of Labor and local People's Party organizations. The latter, which by mid-1892 ranged from the Spanish strongholds in the north to Las Cruces on the southern Rio Grande, mirrored the San Miguel experience both in terms of their mixed support and emphasis on local considerations, and in their recognition of the themes of native control of New Mexico, hostility to Anglo economic competition, and ethnic pride.[23]

The paradox of rising group consciousness elsewhere in the territory and the reappearance of internecine feuds in San Miguel did not escape *La Voz*. "*Es necessario que obremos . . . todos como hermanos*," pleaded the paper, in order to better our condition and keep "*los extranjeros*" from dominating.[24] *Los neo-mexicanos* must stop personal and family wars, must ignore politics except during elections, and must work industriously. *Nativos* must learn English, not to replace Spanish, but to allow them to compete in the new order; New Mexicans must supplement farming and grazing with a knowledge of Anglo crafts and trades. For *La Voz*, progress was good, and technological skills, joined with political control through unity, were the ways to reach peaceful prosperity.

The national People's Party, founded on agrarian discontent and champion of the people against capitalists, inspired El Partido del Pueblo in much the same way that the national Knights of Labor encouraged Las Gorras Blancas. Beginning in the summer of 1891, peaking during the election of 1892, and continuing until 1894, El Partido del Pueblo made common rhetorical cause with the Populists on the issues of wealth, racial harmony, land, silver, and the worker. Cultural differences, racial antagonisms, and realities of power prevented a union between the two "people's" parties, however; they fought on the same side, but always as distinct armies.[25]

Land remained a continual issue, dying down and then flaring up as factions jousted for control of the grants. The Las Vegas Grant remained unsettled despite the meeting in 1891, and it would remain so until 1903. Debate centered around the definition of "community grant." Many Las Vegas businessmen, regardless of any party affiliation, argued that "community" meant the town of Las Vegas, because they wanted a settlement that would give the town control of and profit from the grant. Félix Martínez was willing to go along with this interpretation if "anglo-americans . . . would not in any way alienate the rights of hispano-americans."[26] Herrera rejected this proposal, asserting that "community" meant all of the residents of the grant, as defined in the grant document and buttressed by the Laws of the Indies, and that Las Vegas had no more land rights beyond its corporate boundaries than did the City of Denver.[27]

Concerted action had dissipated, but the wellspring of resentment remained. Thomas Catron served as its most effective focus. During the fall term of the district court, Catron employed the jury law that he had sponsored in the preceding legislature to dismiss the jurors in a case in which he was involved. Using the imperative "Sal" ("Get out"), the form used for dogs, Catron ordered the jurors from the courtroom "*con la arrogancia de un rey.*"[28] Two public meetings denounced both Catron and the jury law; an incident the following spring further enflamed most of San Miguel's *nativos* against the man.

On the night of May 29, 1892, Francisco Chaves, sheriff of Santa Fe County and grand master workman of the Knights of Labor for the territory, was killed from ambush. A rising Democratic politician who had built a strong opposition organization to the Santa Fe Ring, he had been killed by the Borrego brothers, known associates of Catron. *La Voz* lost no time in charging Catron with the murder and connecting the Law and Order Society to the assassins. Since Catron was the Republican candidate for delegate-in-Congress in the fall, the county girded for a bitter campaign.[29]

## The Election of 1892

Local personalities and the land grants had dominated the 1890 election. In 1892, Catron's shadow covered everything else. Pilloried for his enormous wealth based on land stolen from *los pobres*, his intimidation of *mexicano* jurors, and his use of harassment and assassination, Catron symbolized in San Miguel County the worst evils of Anglo encroachment; he lost by the widest margin of any candidate.[30]

El Partido del Pueblo again swept the election but, except for the delegate race, did not enjoy the superiority of 1890. Republican inroads in the 1890 areas of strength hinted that county politics were beginning to return to their old patterns.[31]

Still, El Partido del Pueblo faced the next two years with confidence. With a Democratic administration in Washington, the party leaders judged the time right for statehood—which would mean home rule for *mexicanos*. They added free silver and a wool tariff to their past programs, reflecting their adjudged self-interest among the trends affecting the nation.

Local confusion, however, contributed to the fragmentation that had begun in 1891, and national factors exacerbated it. The long depression and low purchasing power of agricultural and laboring sectors of the country's economy combined with foreign demands on U.S. gold reserves and a decline in railroad investment to produce one of the worst depressions in the nation's history. In New Mexico, the Panic of 1893 was compounded by the Wilson-Gorman tariff which placed wool, the territory's most important product, on the free list. Las Vegas businessmen refused to extend credit to *los pobres*; the Knights of Labor charged the merchants with inhumanity and an evil use of human suffering to break the back of the union.[32]

For the eighteen months after the 1892 election, factional bickering and personal animosities chipped away at *La Voz*'s dream of a united *mexicano* people, *todos como hermanos*. E. H. Salazar, son-in-law of Lorenzo López, left *La Voz* and began another paper, *El Independiente*, for no apparent reason other than personal dislike of Martínez; Carlos Rudulph, clerk of the probate court, feuded with

E. C. de Baca and earned sharp public censure from Los Caballeros de Labor.[33] Recognizing that their only hope lay in unity, Martínez supported an ethnically homogeneous mixture of Republicans and El Partido del Pueblo *políticos* for the school board in April 1894.[34] The following July brought an incident that almost united the whole *mexicano* population of the county.

### The Billy Green Disturbance

"*Encuentro Fatal*" screamed the headline of *La Voz* on Saturday, July 28; "*Tragedia Sangrienta*" echoed *El Independiente*.[35] Both stories described a series of events that had taken place the preceeding Wednesday and Thursday. Billy Green, a notorious Anglo ruffian, had shot Nestor Gallegos, one of two brothers suspected of belonging to the Vicente Silva gang and charged with the murder of Patricio Maes.[36] Green and his brother Eli had been active in attempting to earn the $300 territorial reward for the arrest of anyone suspected of belonging to the Silva gang, or Gavilla Silva. Gallegos did not die until the following day, and in the interim he swore before Justice of the Peace Pablo Ulibarrí that Green had shot him without cause. Constable José Martínez and two deputies went after Green, backed by a warrant.[37]

The killer, his brother, and a Chihuahuan named Jesús Villezea, were eating in a restaurant in West Las Vegas when the officers approached. Green promptly shot one of the deputies and barricaded himself in the kitchen. East Las Vegas Marshal T. F. Clay hurried across the Gallinas River to bring the three into the more congenial custody of the Anglo "new town"; Sheriff Lorenzo López, his deputies, and a large number of townspeople went to the aid of the constable. While the two contingents struggled for the right to make the arrests, District Attorney L. C. Fort appealed to the regular army, stationed in Las Vegas to protect the railroad. The army tipped the balance in favor of the new town, and Clay returned across the river with the Greens, leaving Villezea as a sop for the wounded pride of county authority.[38]

The incident was important because of the racial hostilities it unleashed. Both *El Independiente* and *La Voz* branded it as a conflict "*entre el americano y el mexicano*"; racial epithets denigrating the "*pueblo mexicano*" filled the air, accompanied by rocks, scuffles, and bayonet stabs.[39] The *Optic* called it an unauthorized use of the military; *mexicanos* called it race war.[40]

A mass meeting the following Monday united all *mexicano* factions behind two resolutions; Juan José Herrera's signature appeared alongside Eugenio Romero's. The first proposal was for unity. At-

tributing the gradual impoverishment of the people to political divisions among them, it resolved that all factions would unite in one party. The second resolution focused specifically on the Billy Green incident and condemned "those persons who . . . delivered speeches as a pack of seditious agitators; their insults were directed candidly against the Mexican people, and their attempts to incite the race question places them on the same level as the Greens."[41]

Tension remained high on both sides of the river for the next month. The Greens' supporters clamored for their appointments as deputy U.S. marshals, a fitting reward, remarked *El Independiente* sarcastically, for "killing two Mexicans in the same day."

E. H. Salazar. From campaign biography, *La Voz del Pueblo*, October 29, 1892.

Both papers stressed the end of past political wars, motivated by greed and jealousy, that had allowed "*el extranjero*" to take advantage of the people. "There will be no further mention of the factions of Don Eugenio or Don Lorenzo," promised *El Independiente*.[42]

News of the union in San Miguel spread throughout the territory: Guadalupe County *mexicanos* wrote that they were following their neighbors' example; from Rio Arriba County came news first of a strike against "capitalists," then of support of the united movement.[43]

Unity did not last into the month of September. Disagreements about the party platform and fights for leadership fragmented San Miguel *políticos* more sharply than ever before.[44] Eugenio Romero and Félix Martínez lined up under the banner of El Partido de Union, while Lorenzo López, E. H. Salazar, and others bolted to form El Partido Independiente. Calling each other the "*partido bastardo*," both presented strange alliances to the San Miguel electorate. The Unionistas gathered Eugenio Romero, Félix Martínez, and Juan José Herrera on one ticket; the Independientes countered with an equally confusing alignment of Lorenzo López, Miguel Salazar (prosecutor of the White Caps in 1890), and Knights of Labor officer Aniceto

"Ley y orden! La Gendarmeria de la mafia asaltando cuidadanos en la calle."
(Law and order! The gendarmerie of the mafia assaulting the citizens in the
street.") Editorial cartoon attacking the Republicans, *La Voz del Pueblo*,
November 5, 1892.

Abeytia. To further compound the issue, all candidates retained their
original affiliations for territorial offices—Romero supported Catron
for delegate, while Martínez continued to stand with Joseph.[45]
    It was an alignment that benefited only Catron, who won. In San
Miguel, the Unionistas prevailed in a hotly contested race, losing
only one place, but the county never recovered from the confusion
produced by the attempted union.[46] Politics returned to the fac-
tionalism of old that allowed the gradual impoverishment of *el
pueblo*. Martínez soon repaired to El Paso to seek his fortune; age

"La Mafia bolseando a Catron." (The Mafia riding on the coattails of Catron.) Editorial cartoon attacking the Republicans, *La Voz del Pueblo*, November 5, 1892.

and illness drove Juan José Herrera to Kansas City.[47] Herrera's brother Pablo had been killed by the ubiquitous Bill Green, and Nicanor retired to his ranch near Ojitos Frios.[48]

## Strengths and Weaknesses

The election of 1894 signaled the end of planned and coordinated resistance to Anglo American encroachment in San Miguel County.

The movement failed for two reasons: the struggle over land, the fundamental issue that welded *los hombres pobres* into effective units, changed from direct physical confrontation to drawn-out, complex litigation; and class animosities and aspirations divided *los pobres* and *políticos* too sharply for any but the most serious and direct of threats to overcome.

For the people who rode with or supported Las Gorras Blancas, land was the issue. The raids of 1889 and 1890 brought speculation to a standstill; the territorial laws providing for incorporation of grants and the creation of the U.S. Court of Private Land Claims helped to defuse the hostility produced by the arbitrary fencing of the 1880s. Abrupt, crude changes ceased, and inconsistent court decisions or subtle conspiracies shrouded the fate of the grants. On the San Miguel del Bado Grant, for example, two years of power struggles resulted in a suit before the Court of Private Land Claims. The court ruled in 1894 that the San Miguel was a community grant. Victory for the people, exclaimed *La Voz*. Final settlement, however, did not come until 1904, when, after an appeal by the federal government, the U.S. Supreme Court ruled that only 5,024 acres—the land under ditch—would be allowed. Interpreting the grant as applying only to "house lots and garden plots" ignored the concept of common pasturage and destroyed the economic utility of the land for its residents.[49]

The Las Vegas Grant remained in similar limbo. Interior Secretary John W. Noble disallowed the attempt at incorporation and ruled that Congress had patented the grant "so that the proper parties in interest could perfect their title to their lands"; Noble ordered the remainder resurveyed and opened to settlement "under the general land laws."[50] Lack of funds kept the surveyor general of New Mexico from acting, and the Las Vegas was never declared "free land." Finally, in 1903, the San Miguel delegation to the territorial legislature got a bill passed that gave the district court of San Miguel County the power to appoint and supervise a board of trustees to manage the grant. The board could issue deeds and had the power to "lease, sell or mortgage any part of said tract" at its discretion. The land not actually occupied was sold, and *los pobres* on the Las Vegas, like their neighbors on the San Miguel, retained only house lots and garden plots.[51]

*Políticos* and *los pobres* did not embrace each other wholeheartedly. Men like Félix Martínez, Nestor Montoya, and E. H. Salazar had some education and shared a vision of the future made up of equal parts liberal-democratic ideology and pure laissez-faire economics founded on a unified Hispanic population. Theirs was a movement toward "progress" with themselves in the vanguard, and with a sense of class and appropriate leadership graphically illustrated in the 1894 election: *La Voz* apologized for having Gregorio Flores, *un pobre agricultor*, on the ticket, but he was so scrupulously honest that "the people have honored him with this high distinction."[52]

If the Martínezes saw themselves as a kind of intelligentsia for the general *mexicano* population, *los pobres* saw them as *políticos*, an epithet with the same negative connotations that "politician" carries in many quarters today. With the fences down, the movement became political, and the *políticos* took over the movement. *Los hombres pobres* retreated to their homes and watched with a cynicism that proved well-founded. The sense of ethnic cohesiveness and shared outrage was there, strong enough to support the White Caps for more than a year and to inflame the county for a month after the Billy Green fiasco. But it never permanently transcended class divisions, factional alignments, or personal animosities in one volatile county.

Born in violence, the movement envisioning a united *mexicano* front against the *americano* advance ended in violence. To be sure, violence did not disappear completely. Land was still wrenched from its traditional use, and *los hombres pobres* were still hungry. In 1903, three hundred masked horsemen rode through Antonchicho before going up on a mesa northeast of the village and leveling the fence of an Anglo cattle company.[53] Singly or in groups, *los hombres pobres* persisted, at least until 1926, in cutting fences put up where none had stood before.[54] But never again did *mexicano* outrage achieve the coordinated success of the heady summer of 1890.

# CHAPTER 10

# The Sacred Right
# of Self-Preservation

El Partido del Pueblo Unido swept the 1890 and 1892 elections in San Miguel County because ambitious *políticos* like Félix Martínez, old-line *jefes* like Lorenzo López, and a handful of Anglos capitalized on the outrage of *las masas de los hombres pobres*. All four—*los ricos*, the Anglos, the new *políticos*, and *el pueblo nativo*—acted out of a sense of self-preservation, but since they saw self-preservation differently, their coalition lasted only a moment longer than the period of intense polarization in which it formed.

Efforts at self-preservation fall into three categories. In the first are efforts at physical survival, either individual or collective. The second category includes attempts to preserve a traditional way of life, particularly its economic forms and spheres of autonomy; these efforts are usually collective in one way or another. Efforts of the third type involve adjusting or adapting to change as well as survival and preserving traditions. Perceptions of clear and present dangers provoke responses of the first two types, while perceptions that mix threat and opportunity evoke responses of the third type. As with all human activity, efforts at self-preservation are easier to categorize in the abstract than in the concrete. Efforts at survival against threats less immediate than leveled rifles blend with attempts at preserving traditions; adaptations and adjustments can range from the minimum necessary to preserve the main body of traditions to efforts at assimilation and integration. Survival, preservation, and adaptation, therefore, ought to be viewed as gradations across a spectrum rather than as immutable categories. And all efforts at self-preservation start from the cultures of the threatened peoples: their socially established structures of meaning identify the threats and give shape to their goals and methods.[1]

In a broad sense, all human activity can be construed according to this three-part definition. For the purposes of this study, however, self-preservation means the active attempt by a subordinate group to maintain itself—to preserve the qualities cherished by group members for cultural or ethnic self-identification—and to survive in a world dominated by the institutions and procedures and the standards and values of others. Thus, social bandits fight for self-preservation, whereas those who try to assimilate do not, although in the broader sense their efforts are aimed at their individual self-preservation. Similarly, although groups can be threatened by many things—foreign invasion, natural catastrophe, or internal dissension, for example—this study treats neither intragroup conflicts such as fights between villages over an *acequia*'s water nor intergroup conflicts such as wars between nations as efforts at self-preservation.[2]

Subordinate peoples have often used armed protest as a means of self-preservation; they have at least as frequently employed less extreme methods. Nonviolent efforts at self-preservation include withdrawal—the use of natural barriers and the creation of social ones to minimize or eliminate contact with the dominant—and various organizations designed to cope with the fact of domination and to coordinate the unavoidable involvement with those in power.

## Self-Preservation through Politics

Any process used by a group to make decisions that affect the group as a whole is a political process, and any process used by a group to deal with its subordinate position is an effort at self-preservation through politics. The relatively widespread franchise in the United States has led many subordinate groups to try for self-preservation by organized use of the ballot box. The momentary success and ultimate failure of El Partido del Pueblo Unido illuminates some of the possibilities and a number of the problems faced by *mexicanos* in particular, and minorities in general, in using electoral politics.

### *El Partido del Pueblo Unido*
El Partido del Pueblo took the issue, the energy, and the organizational base of Las Gorras Blancas and tried to forge a political movement to protect and enhance the position of all *mexicanos* living under the Anglo American regime. The party called for ethnic solidarity, sounded themes of elementary class consciousness, and counseled some adaptation to Anglo ways as the means for survival and prosperity in a world of economic change and Anglo government.

Through *La Voz*, the party called for an end to factional bickering and pleaded for unity "all as brothers, all as members of the same family."[3] The party said it was for "the masses, in favor of the oppressed, in favor of the worker" and against "despotism and monopoly";[4] the main issue in the nation, wrote *La Voz*, was not Democrats versus Republicans or gold versus silver, but "the millionaire against the middle-class, the rancher, and the worker."[5] And *La Voz* urged all to learn English, the language of business, not to replace Spanish but in order to compete with Anglos; likewise the paper enjoined *mexicanos* to learn the crafts of the Anglo world.[6]

The new party realized its initial success not because the majority shared the vision of its guiding spirits but because the majority supported the White Caps. By embracing the White Caps' position about the common land, the party carried all White Cap precincts. In addition, the tumultuous state of San Miguel politics attracted Lorenzo López and a number of lesser *jefes*; Anglo Democrats and incipient Populists joined because they had no other political choice in the county; and two national organizations, the Knights of Labor and the People's Party, lent the county movement an aura of legitimacy.[7]

Rifts began to appear shortly after the victory in 1890 and grew in size and number until the sequence of alignments and realignments prior to the 1894 election shattered the party beyond repair. Its inability to effect change cost the party support; although it exerted some influence on the fate of the community grants, the party had no impact on the territorial legislature and little more on county administration. Ethnic hostility complicated matters. As the party raised the stridency and frequency of its appeals for ethnic solidarity, ethnic hostility increased, and *mexicanos*, who had warily accepted the Anglos' cautiously extended support at the beginning, began to actively exclude *americanos*, who in turn formed their own organizations.[8] But if appeals to ethnic solidarity increased anti-Anglo behavior, they did not increase unity among *mexicanos*; internecine personal and factional jealousies had reappeared by the spring of 1891. With fencing stopped, conflict on the grants changed from straightforward battles between *mexicano* residents and *extranjero* encroachers to a confusion of factional alliances struggling to control meetings and win lawsuits. The White Caps' successes removed the overt threat, and most *mexicanos* ceased to see violence as justifiable and necessary; with violence in disrepute, the apostles of violence like the Herrera brothers fell from favor.[9] Thus, El Partido del Pueblo peaked at its birth. After 1890, the party spent its energy trying to keep itself together. That it lasted until 1894 is a tribute to the efforts of the new *políticos*. But despite an overwhelmingly *mexicano* electorate, despite an ethnic consciousness expressed in hostility against *americanos*, and despite the rudiments of an ideology, the movement of self-preservation through organized electoral politics could not carry the county.

An organization that could not survive in one county could not expand into other areas. Although *La Voz* published accounts of *mexicano* resistance to the Maxwell Land Grant Company, no San Miguel White Caps rode to aid their neighbors in Colfax County. The chapters of Los Caballeros de Labor and the organizations of "*partidos del pueblo*" that formed in several counties gave verbal support to the idea of unity, but they never transcended local boundaries and their life spans were even briefer than that of the San Miguel organization.

Local and factional loyalties proved stronger than the idea of unity once fencing had stopped. After Las Gorras Blancas had removed the immediate threat, *mexicanos* could not agree about what to do with the land. Their attitudes toward community grants corresponded to their class; class differences also influenced other attitudes, or reservations, toward the party of unity and its programs. *Ricos* like Lorenzo López wanted to maintain and increase their wealth and power. Their wealth came from land and their power from the votes of *los pobres*. Getting *los pobres* to vote for them required perpetual courtship—the use of material rewards or the promise of attending to a matter of particular local concern. *Ricos* had no qualms about exploiting *el pueblo* or claiming tracts of common land when they could get away with it, but they did not want to have their positions weakened by *americano* newcomers. *Ricos* supported Las Gorras Blancas because the night riders spiked Anglo competition, and they joined a party that promised to keep political power in *mexicano* hands. But *ricos* did not fight for the common land as such, and they had even less interest in the kinds of social change proposed by the new *políticos*: "*Educar un muchacho es perder un buen pastor*," [10] said Solomon Luna of Valencia County, a sentiment to which both Eugenio Romero and Lorenzo López could subscribe. López joined El Partido del Pueblo to thwart Anglos and fight Romero, and he did so as a conservative who wanted to retain and manipulate traditional social relationships. His prominence in the party demonstrates the strength of those relationships in San Miguel County. *Los pobres* were also conservative: they wanted to preserve their land and their traditional way of life. After their own direct action had removed the visible and immediate danger, *los pobres* had no objection to voting for *ricos* who promised to support the community grants—*ricos* had traditionally dealt with the demands of distant governments for them—but *los pobres* had no illusions about *los ricos'* altruism. When the movement became political, the *políticos* took over the movement and *los pobres* retreated to their holdings and watched with the cynicism of long experience. The young *políticos*—the new middle class—were caught in the cynical symbiosis of the *ricos* and the *pobres*. By tempering liberal ideology with ethnic unity, the new *políticos* hoped to become the leaders of society and improve the general lot of *mexicanos*. Martínez, Salazar, and Montoya may have seen themselves as the vanguard of social progress, but to *los pobres* they were *políticos* pure and simple. For all their rhetoric in support of workers and *el pueblo nativo*, the progressives, like *los ricos*, excluded *los pobres* from party councils.[11] For their part, *los pobres* treated the progressives as they treated *los ricos*—they supported them when it suited their interests. Promises to protect common land won votes for the progressives, but bilingual competence, the merits of free trade and free silver, cooperation across cultural and ethnic lines, and the vision of sharing in the American Dream left *los pobres* unmoved. The new *políticos*, while they tried to speak for *los pobres* and certainly spoke at them, attempted to move in circles defined by *rico* and Anglo politicians. The contradictions of such a course were insurmountable, and El Partido del Pueblo disappeared from San Miguel County after the debacle of 1894.

The brief life of El Partido del Pueblo reveals the simplicity in conception and difficulty in execution inherent in using electoral politics for self-preservation. At the outset, conditions in San Miguel County seemed ideal: *mexicano* voters held a majority of more than four to one; language, custom, and appearance distinguished the two peoples; an issue had polarized the county; and the Knights of Labor and the Populists seemed to be omens that the time was right in the nation. But San Miguel was only one New Mexican county, and New Mexico at the time was a territory with even less autonomy from Washington than that enjoyed by states; even had the party lasted, its accomplishments would have been severely limited by the weight of the U.S. government as channeled through the territorial administration and the courts. The national movements that inspired optimism proved illusive; the Knights of Labor were on the point of collapse, and the Populists never got beyond third-party status and, in addition, wanted the common lands declared public domain. *Mexicano* characteristics compounded the situational problems. Nothing in the experience of *los pobres* taught them to think about people or conditions outside of their immediate world. And the restricted scope of *los pobres* was part of the general differences in class orientation among *mexicanos* that sundered the movement.

To attempt self-preservation through electoral politics means to attempt to get enough votes to be reckoned with. A consequential number of votes requires unity, and unity requires a reason to unite. Even a united minority has difficulty marshaling enough support to have an effect. But, as the history of El Partido del Pueblo shows, unity is extremely difficult to maintain.

The issue that gave birth to the party was immediate and conservative, and the new *políticos* tried to transform it into a movement for adaptive self-preservation. Because of its electoral success, however fleeting, El Partido del Pueblo stands out as a dramatic precursor to modes of self-preservation used by *mexicanos* in the twentieth century. But dramatic though it was, the San Miguel movement of 1890 to 1894 was not the only time that *mexicanos* tried organized, adaptive self-preservation before the turn of the century.

### The Nineteenth Century

Efforts at self-preservation through politics developed out of two separate *mexicano* traditions. One built upon the village organizations that coped with matters affecting the community; with some exceptions, *los pobres* created and ran organizations from this tradition, and they tended pragmatically to address local problems of immediate concern. The other kind of efforts grew out of the tradition of liberal politics that dated from Mexican independence; initially, *mexicano* progressives argued for adaptation in terms of a literal interpretation of democratic theory, but, as they experienced the realities of life in the United States, they modified their stance in favor of politics organized along ethnic lines. Efforts from the two traditions combined occasionally, although, as the history of El Partido del Pueblo indicates, they rarely produced a fruitful union.

Community land grants placed the responsibility for defense, for allocation of land and water, and for the care of the indigent on individual villages—evidence of *los pobres'* self-sufficiency that contradicts the Anglo stereotype of a childlike people who followed their *patrones* like sheep. The tradition of autonomy was most developed on New Mexican grants and among the clusters of small ranchos along the Lower Rio Grande; it is no coincidence that *mexicanos* resisted Anglo encroachment vigorously in these regions, while the absence of this tradition in California contributed to the demise of *californio* society. As the Anglo presence increased in Texas and New Mexico (and Arizona), community organizations modified. The Penitentes of New Mexico, a lay religious brotherhood devoted to protecting traditional religious practices from the attacks of Protestant zealots and the Church hierarchy, grew in membership

throughout the century. Its focal point was religious, but the brotherhood also reinforced cultural mores and influenced elections in a
judicious mixture of withdrawal and bloc voting; the Penitentes
attempted self-preservation through the minimum degree of adaptation necessary to preserve traditional ways of life.[12] The *mutualista*,
or mutual benefit society, another grass-roots organization, began to
appear in the early 1870s and became more widespread than the
Penitentes. Usually fraternal orders of working men, the *mutualistas*
served as social clubs that also provided insurance and medical benefits; they proved to be vehicles for organized self-preservation as
well.[13]

Through organizations like the Penitentes and the *mutualistas*,
*los pobres* responded to Anglo domination by attempting to preserve their traditions in ways derived from the villages. *Ricos* and
the incipient middle class usually chose adaptation, a response
whose roots predate the conquest. While economic and ideological
motives were interwoven in various proportions, *mexicanos* generally wanted to adapt to take advantage either of American commerce
or of politics under the U.S. Constitution. The new *políticos* were the
heirs of the latter, and the writings of Francisco P. Ramírez, publisher
of *El Clamor Público* in Los Angeles between 1856 and 1860, typify
the early conceptualizations of self-preservation through adaptation.[14] Ramírez defended *californios* against denigrating Anglo descriptions, published detailed accounts of Anglo brutality towards
*mexicanos*, and criticized *americanos* for not living up to the ideal
expressed in their constitution. But Ramírez's solutions were for
*mexicanos* to learn English, become adept at "useful" trades, and
participate "intelligently" in the electoral process. Ramírez never
advocated an ethnically organized political movement and was himself a partisan Republican who criticized his fellows for their support of the Democrats. By the mid-eighties, many *mexicanos* saw organization as the only way to participate in politics intelligently.
New Mexico Governor Ross discovered, in 1886, a secret organization among native New Mexicans devoted to ridding New Mexico of
"corrupt federal and local officials, lawyers and others formed into
rings or cliques . . . and monopolies."[15] Spanish-language newspaper editors also took steps toward organization: representatives of
seven papers met at Las Vegas in 1892 and formed La Prensa Asociada Hispano-Americana; its goal was to unite Spanish American
"periodicals, writers and poets" across the United States into an association designed to preserve the heritage and protect the rights of
all Hispanic peoples in the country.[16]

By the 1890s, many Spanish newspapers applauded any *mexi-*

*cano* organization and labeled as fools all who called them unnecessary on the grounds that "we are all American citizens." [17]
When the Sociedad Filantrópica Latino-Americano, a *mutualista*
that regarded the "persecution" of one member as an attack on all,[18]
formed in Albuquerque, *El Ciudadano* of El Paso exclaimed that
now was the time for *"neo-mexicanos"* in Texas, New Mexico, Colorado, Arizona, and California to unite in a great army and obtain the
rights due them under a democracy.[19] And when *mexicanos* in Tucson founded La Alianza Hispano-Americana, the army envisioned
by *El Ciudadano* seemed almost ready to march. Created to "protect
and fight for the rights of Spanish Americans," La Alianza numbered
twenty-two chapters in Arizona, New Mexico, and Texas by 1906,
and by 1929 it claimed fifteen thousand members in chapters from
San Diego to Brownsville and from Tucson to Chicago.[20]

By the end of the century, a growing number of educated *mexicanos* viewed organization as the only way to achieve self-preservation and enjoy the self-determination promised in Anglo political
theory; their horizons, in other words, extended beyond their immediate locales. *Los pobres* also learned the value of organizing to combat Anglo domination, but their modification and development of
organizations was not accompanied by expansion of horizons. Since
perceived threats took different guises at different times and in different places in the Southwest, *mexicanos* as a whole never arose in
concerted action; since the progressives' unifying vision of self-preservation through adaptation held no appeal for *los hombres pobres*,
liaisons between the two groups were tentative at best. A number of
things contributed, but the basic factor that prevented the formation
of a united army of *mexicanos* marching for first-class citizenship
was the same one that stopped El Partido del Pueblo from carrying
New Mexico: the incompatibility of regional and class orientations
within the same cultural group.

Progressives and *los pobres* did cooperate effectively on occasion. The Miguel Hidalgo Workers' Society of San Antonio began the
fund raising for Gregorio Cortez's defense, and Pablo Cruz, editor
and publisher of San Antonio's *El Regidor*, expanded from this base
to coordinate a campaign that raised money from both sides of the
Rio Grande.[21] *Mexicano* copper miners in the Clifton-Morenci district of Arizona struck in 1903 and again in 1915; in both strikes,
*mutualistas* provided the organizational structure and material support.[22] On the Lower Rio Grande, the first fifteen years of the twentieth century saw rising tensions between Anglo and *mexicano* that
culminated in the raids by *los sediciosos*. But earlier, in 1911, the
tensions had led to the Congreso Mexicanista, a meeting of represen-

tatives from *mutualistas* across South Texas that condemned unpunished lynchings, police brutality, school segregation, and racism. Urging all, whether Mexican nationals or American citizens, to
form "*ligas mexicanistas*" so that "once united, with the help of the
press, . . . they will be able to strike back at the hatred of some bad
sons of Uncle Sam who believe themselves better than Mexicans because of the magic that surrounds the word *white*,"[23] the congress
showed the traditional Border indifference to the international boundary, an attitude that political efforts at self-preservation were forced
to change in the next decade.

### The Twentieth Century

When viewed in terms of *mexicano* efforts at self-preservation
through politics, the twentieth century divides into three eras: before World War I, from the end of the war to the election of John F.
Kennedy, and after 1960. The first era brought pioneering efforts at
self-preservation to an end and therefore belongs with the preceding
century. The second was a period of expansion and refinement of the
two strategies that began out of nineteenth-century traditions: middle-class progressives intensified their drive toward adaptation by
forming pressure groups and political organizations, while *los pobres* employed community-derived organizations either to combat
change or to cope with specific problems; both tacks had to adjust to
changing conditions in the country, which for *mexicanos* included
increased migration from Mexico, urbanization, and a rise in aggressive nativism by Anglo Americans. The present era is marked by a
variety of attempts to overcome the historic regional and class distinctions that have plagued *mexicano* unity.

Large-scale migration from Mexico and urbanization magnified
divisions among *mexicanos* just as the idea of strength through
unity began to gain some general currency. Migration had occurred
throughout the nineteenth century, but enclosure of the common
lands by the *científicos* of the Díaz regime, the dislocations of the
Mexican Revolution, and the demand for labor in mines and on the
railroads and commercial farms of the United States attracted a large
and continuing influx of Mexican laborers that slowed only briefly
during the repatriation program of the Depression years.[24] Mexican
migrants swelled the number of *mexicano* residents in the country,
but native *mexicanos* did not accept them readily, and the migrants,
for their part, viewed themselves as temporary sojourners north of
the Border. In addition, the newcomers competed for jobs with the
natives, and their alien status made it easy for Anglos to brand all
*mexicanos* as foreigners and deny them the rights of citizens. Land

loss and the subsequent death of traditional communities drove *mexicanos* to barrios and changed them from a self-sufficient peasantry to an agrarian or industrial proletariat.[25] And, at the same time that migration and urbanization changed the shape of the *mexicano* world, they were threatened by an outburst of racist, anti-Catholic, and antiradical nativism that swept the country and produced among other things the Ku Klux Klan of the twenties and the immigration quotas based on national origin passed by Congress in 1924.[26]

Migration, urbanization, and nativism forced *mexicano* efforts at self-preservation to include some kind of adaptation, but the differences evident in the nineteenth century persisted: middle-class progressives organized to apply social and political pressure; *los pobres* built upon the *mutualista* and concentrated primarily on labor issues. After World War I, progressives founded organizations like La Orden de Hijos de America and its successor, the League of United Latin American Citizens (LULAC), which stressed American citizenship, advocated assimilation at least to the extent of learning English and modern trades, and aimed for integration through moral persuasion and court action.[27] LULAC's founders cast their lot with the United States; because of the viciousness of the Texas Ranger responses to *los sediciosos* coupled with the rise in Mexican migrants and the virulence of nativism in the twenties, LULAC concluded that self-preservation north of the Border depended upon becoming good Americans. Organizations that appeared after World War II, like the American G.I. Forum, the Unity Leagues, and the Community Service Organization, adopted more aggressive political stances than had their predecessors, but their programs and goals also emphasized integration and first-class citizenship. *Los pobres*, on the other hand, attended to immediate problems. Using the organizational form of the *mutualista*, as they had in the Clifton-Morenci district, *mexicanos* struck in a number of industries across the Southwest in a series of efforts at self-preservation exemplified by the Cantaloupe Strike of 1929, the Berry Strike of 1933, the Pecan Shellers' Strike in 1938, and the De Gregorio Strike of 1947. Strikes, however, address the problems caused by a particular employer or faced by workers in a specific industry; they have no necessary correlation to issues of citizenship or the concerns of a particular ethnic group, and, furthermore, strikes tend to be controversial and linked with political radicals. The progressives saw the strikes as a hindrance to their goals, while *los pobres* found integration too slow and abstract to be taken seriously; progressives and *los pobres* worked for self-preservation separately for most of the century.

John F. Kennedy's narrow presidential victory in 1960 and the increased visibility of the civil rights movement inaugurated an era of new approaches to the problem of unifying *mexicanos*. The impact of Viva Kennedy clubs in the election underlined the effect a unified minority could have on a close race; *mexicano* politicians recognized the potential in being able to tip the balance and began to organize in ways designed to win concessions from the two parties and from bureaucracies on local, state, and national levels.[28] The victory of an all-*mexicano* slate in the municipal elections of 1963 in Crystal City, Texas, pointed to another way *mexicanos* could use electoral politics; as envisioned by El Partido de la Raza Unida, by organizing along ethnic lines in areas where they were a majority, *mexicanos* could control their local governments and demonstrate enough strength in state and national elections to force *americanos* to deal with them.[29] Both political approaches depend upon close elections and a unified electorate with which to make the difference, but the first follows the integrative path and takes place in the national arena of progressive *políticos*, while the second proceeds from a regional independence unconcerned with integration that is more characteristic of *los pobres*. The two approaches, however, compete for the same constituency. Other movements appeared during the sixties as well. César Chávez and the United Farm Workers carried the traditions of *mutualista*-based labor activity to national prominence; Reies López Tijerina led a movement in New Mexico to regain and revitalize community land grants that harkened back to Las Gorras Blancas; and Rodolfo Gonzales spoke of a cultural nationalism that included a vision of the nation of Aztlán reminiscent of the Republic of the Rio Grande and the Plan de San Diego. But Chávez leads a union concerned primarily with working conditions in a specific industry, not with ethnic solidarity; Tijerina's land grant movement has little appeal for *mexicanos* long removed from their ancestral holdings; La Raza Unida does not win adherents where *mexicanos* are in a minority or from those with a less militant stance; and cultural nationalism, however appealing emotionally, is difficult to put into practice. In varying degrees, the recent movements try to unify *mexicanos* in efforts at self-preservation, and, to the extent of the size of their memberships and the scope of the arenas in which they operate, each has increased unity. But regional and class orientations still divide the *mexicano* population.

Mexicanos have not yet achieved a unity sufficient to end Anglo domination, but this does not mean that they will not in the future. As was not the case earlier, a large and growing number of *mexicanos* have a command of technology and a grasp of legal, governmental, and fiscal procedures; in other words, many *mexicanos* know the rules and tactics of the game, and more are learning every day. The shared experience of discrimination and the greater ease of communication through the media and in other ways offer the possibility of mexicanos developing a group consciousness similar to working-class consciousness in nineteenth-century England.[30] Population projections indicate that Spanish-speaking peoples as a whole will form the largest minority in the country by the 1980s; if they perceive themselves as having common problems and common goals, Hispanics may well be the political movement of the future in a union foreshadowed by La Prensa Asociada Hispano-Americana.[31] And, to pick but one from a number of imponderables, oil-rich Mexico may soon be in a position to demand better treatment for persons of Hispanic descent residing in the United States rather than, as in the past, having to rely on moral suasion.

### Cultural Pluralism and National Unity

Each mexicano effort at self-preservation is inseparable from its historical and cultural setting; in this sense, each is unique. But just as each effort represents one way that mexicanos responded to common problems created by Anglo American domination, so too does the sum of their efforts represent one people's response to problems shared by every cultural or ethnic minority in the United States. All minorities must cope with the fact of Anglo domination; that is what being a minority in the United States means. Unity is central to all responses that aim at ethnic self-preservation, and unity focuses these efforts from two directions: for each group, self-preservation includes trying to transcend class and regional differences, particularly those that affect perceptions of the threat from and the attractions of the Anglo world; for the nation, each effort at self-preservation threatens national unity. As the strife in northern Ireland and the civil wars in emerging nations indicate, the tensions between unity and diversity afflict pluralistic nations around the world, and, to one degree or another, cultural pluralism has persistently challenged the unity of the United States.

Anglos control the United States because Anglos founded the nation and established the formal codes and informal procedures for government. Foreign immigration and territorial expansion, especially during the nineteenth century, steadily reduced Anglo numerical superiority, but Anglos still dominate, in part because they respond to cultural pluralism through a range marked by nativism at one extreme and integration at the other, and in part because ethnic minorities have yet to unite and change the rules of the game. Most minorities came from traditions that did not prepare them for thinking and acting in national terms or for making alliances with cultural groups different from their own—ethnic minorities described various forms of *Gemeinschaft* arrayed against the Anglo *Gesellschaft*.[32] With their preindustrial sense of community and their antipathy toward each other, ethnic minorities reacted to life in the United States in terms established by Anglos; they withdrew from, fought over, or adapted to emanations from the Anglo world. Anglos responded to the new residents either with discrimination or by allowing opportunities to learn and participate by degrees. Race riots, housing and employment restrictions, and the like intensified hostility between the dominant and various subordinate groups, while naturalized citizenship, opportunities for education and social mobility, voting rights, and so forth brought many ethnics closer to the mainstream, thereby muting their hostility toward those in power. Nativists and integrationists differed about the way to maintain and enhance national unity but not about the threat to it posed by cultural diversity; both wanted national homogeneity according to Anglo American governmental and social precepts.

Territorial minorities have shown a consistent reluctance to assimilate and a consistent preference for minimal defensive adaptation. Beginning in the 1960s, voices from almost all ethnic minorities in the country—black, brown, red, and yellow power advocates and representatives from the PIGS, Michael Novak's acronym for "white" ethnics—spoke out against the melting pot ideal of integration and assimilation.[33] Spurred by the realization that antidiscrimination statutes alone were inadequate to provide equality and by a deep-seated resentment against Anglos resulting from the accumulation of insults and dashed hopes over the generations, representatives of virtually all minorities announced not only that the melting pot had not worked, but that it shouldn't even if it could. The new militants asserted that loss of heritage was too high a price to pay for full citizenship and furthermore pointed out that there is nothing in democratic theory that says that they should have to; their charges have expanded the boundaries of the debate over national unity. In the decades before the 1960s, the issue was drawn in Anglo terms of exclusion versus integration; now it includes considerations of ways to preserve cultural traits and encourage diversity.[34]

It is far too early to determine the effect that ethnic pride and cultural affirmation will have on unity for self-preservation. Political ideologies and regional identifications, issues like women's rights and school integration, and considerations of class and occupation cut across cultural lines and provide competing foci for organization. But a number of ethnic groups are now saying that they are

Americans, that they neither can nor want to leave the country, but they neither can nor want to relinquish their heritage any more than Anglos have relinquished theirs.[35] Sentiments of cultural pride are relatively amorphous and unfocused, but they are extremely deep-seated. That so many groups should express them so vehemently after decades in the United States shows the vitality of feelings of pride, and the frequency of politics so organized in the third world and in Europe testifies to their power.

The tensions between cultural or primordial associations inherent in pluralistic societies can be the major determinants of political behavior. But the history of internal conflict, both past and present, both domestic and worldwide, is largely one of violence. This study began by examining the violence between *mexicano* and *americano* during the nineteenth century, and it is fitting to return to a discussion of violence in conclusion.

## Violence

From the Treaty of Guadalupe Hidalgo until well after the turn of the century, *mexicanos* resisted Anglo domination with violence. Violent efforts at self-preservation ranged from the individual outbursts of social bandits to planned and coordinated uprisings by groups like Las Gorras Blancas, but whatever their form, all incidents originated from and were carried out by *los pobres*. All incidents, moreover, aimed at preserving traditional ways of life, all drew upon the repertoire of *los pobres* for their organizations and tactics, and all tried to redress specific grievances in immediate locales. Thus, although *mexicanos* across the Southwest shared a hostility toward Anglos and a willingness to use violence, their common resentment found expression in independent and isolated revolts. The separate, local nature of the revolts kept them from having anything more than a delaying effect, but the fact that *mexicanos* in California, Texas, and New Mexico resisted violently demonstrated their dissatisfaction with the Anglo regime and their active commitment to doing something about it.

When people decide to use violence, particularly within the confines of their own neighborhoods, they are choosing an extreme response to a situation: violence carries with it the obvious danger of death and destruction. In broad terms, a decision to use violence results from combining the perception of a severe threat with the perception that violent action promises to be successful.[36] Perceptions of the severity of the threat are influenced, among other things, by which aspects of life are threatened and how many people are affected. Perceptions about the utility of violence are influenced in part by the value a people place on physical courage, their experiences with violence, the strategic possibilities of the battlegrounds, and their perceived strength relative to that of their enemy. These perceptual and traditional criteria help them decide whether to use violence and, if so, what kind and how much. Just as some societies are more habitually violent than others, some rebellions are more sweepingly violent than others. In general, los pobres used limited, controlled violence, and the reason for their restraint lies in the way they saw the world.

Their attitudes and experiences, from the importance of courage and the defense of one's honor to Indian raids and foreign invasions, put violence in the front rank of life's possibilities for los pobres. Violence continued as a real possibility under U.S. rule for a number of reasons, not the least of which was that los ricos, their traditional mediators with the state, maneuvered in the new order for their own purposes and thereby became part of the problem; los pobres realized that they would have to take care of serious matters themselves. Serious matters included threats to land or life, and mexicanos responded by drawing upon their experience in armed defense. Local conditions determined particular forms—massive Anglo immigration and a disorganized society limited resistance in California to an epidemic of banditry, while the slow influx of Anglos among the established communities of New Mexico and the Border produced organized resistance movements in those regions—but all violent efforts at self-preservation were conservative, and therein lay at once their strengths and their weaknesses.

Conservatism meant that ideological disputes did not splinter los pobres: they could agree about the goal of preserving traditional ways of life. But their preservationist orientation prevented the development of aggressive tactics for adjusting to changing conditions. The preservationist orientation, moreover, meant that action was confined to the traditional arenas of immediate localities. This emphasis on home areas, on the patria chica, had several advantages: it made the conflict clear—you knew what you were fighting for—and it involved neighbors using familiar organizations operating on well-known terrain. But the loyalty to place inhibited attempts to join with mexicanos elsewhere toward a common goal, and it limited the supply of supporters, firearms, and the like to the resources of one or two villages. More importantly, the world view of los pobres could not fathom a nation or society as large and as strong as the United States, and the tactics they used point out this lack of comprehension. In all cases, violent resistance attacked selected targets and specific individuals—fences, buildings, crops, evil persons, or the rich. Limiting attacks to those thought responsible for problems, or to things that symbolize them, seems to be characteristic of communities that function with traditional, face-to-face frames of reference, while sweeping, impersonal responses appear more characteristic of modern nations; Anglos, whose world view developed in the context of aggressive nationalism, constantly saw the beginnings of bloody revolution in the strategic violence of *los pobres*, a contrast that underlines this difference. In some circumstances social turmoil can be so extensive that traditional societies lose all control and engage in an orgy of bloodletting, but this never happened among *mexicanos* in the United States.[37] *Mexicanos* did not adopt the modern perspectives of their opponents either: the Plan de San Diego, with its command to kill all males over sixteen, looks like an exception, but there is no evidence that *los sediciosos* actually attacked anything but property or fighting men.

The history of *mexicano* violent efforts at self-preservation is that of an agrarian, self-sufficient people clustered in isolated communities doing battle with the visible manifestations of a huge nation which they could neither see nor conceive of. In terms of what they could see and what they knew how to do, their efforts made sense and were effective until Anglos changed the situation either by retreating to the courts, as in New Mexico, or sending in the army, as on the Border. *Mexicanos* had the same fundamental weakness of all peasant communities in conflict with modern societies. As Eric Hobsbawm puts it, peasants have a low sense of "classness" and have only two frames of reference, "the universe . . . [and] their locality."[38] The restricted framework for action means that revolts in peasant societies are either the localized rebellions that Ted Robert Gurr defines, with riots and strikes, as Turmoil,[39] or social banditry. Social banditry, the symbolically important "programme of self-help," appeared across the Southwest, but bandits form only a miniscule part of the population—one-tenth of one percent is a generous estimate under "normal" oppression according to Hobsbawm—and banditry is not an effective way to redress grievances or stop change.[40] During severe dislocations like natural catastrophes or invasions, banditry can increase to epidemic proportions, and if other conditions in the society are in sufficient disarray, bandits can form the military arm of a revolution, as happened in the north of Mexico under Pancho Villa.[41] California bandits, however, reacted in a brief flurry of violence against a stable and growing society. Local or community rebellions can also play important roles in national revolutions, as Emiliano Zapata's Army of the South demonstrated in the Mexican Revolution.[42] But general social dislocation, governmental instability, and a concentrated, numerous, and committed peasantry must coincide for this to happen. Individually, the villages of New Mexico and of the Lower Border were as committed and as capable as those that Zapata brought together in Morelos, but their traditional orientation toward local autonomy and the objective fact of distance prevented them from uniting. And, in the United States, they faced a stable and powerful opponent.

Social elasticity, a product of democratic theory practiced in a situation of plenty, has kept the United States free from social revolution for two centuries. Internal violence has been commonplace in U.S. history, but it has not been general. Violence has been directed against "private" industries or "deviant" groups; it has appeared as outbursts of general frustration or as isolated acts of terrorism; but rarely has violence aimed at institutions of government.[43] Differences of region, occupation, and culture fragmented potential insurgents initially, enabling the government to weather frequent peripheral violence; material abundance allowed those in power to make strategic concessions, without yielding their central position, when tensions got too high.[44] The concessions made possible by abundance created enough social elasticity to mute the hostility produced by nativism and inhibit the development of a class consciousness that could cross cultural, regional, or occupational lines. Insurgency based on class conflict had little appeal for people chasing the American Dream or divided by culture, and rebellions founded on cultural affiliations had no attraction for anyone not part of the primordial group. Thus, to date, any group attempting social change through violence has found itself in potential combat with the whole of U.S. society. By the end of the second decade of the twentieth century, mexicanos recognized this and abandoned violent efforts at self-preservation.

To say that mexicanos abandoned violent efforts at self-preservation is a historian's generalization that is true in so far as it compares two eras; the assertion does not mean that violence has been absent during the recent past and does not necessarily mean that violence will not figure prominently in the future. Individual mexicanos who will "break before they bend" have continued to rebel like their social-bandit predecessors. Violence has accompanied strikes and demonstrations throughout the century. Fence cutting, barn burning, and occasional gunfights have continued as acceptable ways to punish evil persons and express discontent in New Mexico; Tijerina's courthouse raid in Tierra Amarilla in 1966 testi-

fies that organized violent resistance lives in the Land of Enchant-
ment.[45] And, as *mexicanos* become more urbanized and more politically aware, forms of violent protest that range from the urban
equivalent of social bandits to planned and coordinated terrorism
and guerrilla attacks are conceivable. Certainly a world that has witnessed the raid on the Israeli athletes during the 1972 Olympics or
the epidemic of knee-capping and kidnapping in Europe and South
America cannot dismiss violence as a relic of the past.

Speculations about the future aside, *mexicanos* succumbed to
Anglo domination because they did not have the numbers, the tools,
or the conceptual framework with which to fight a modern nation.
Yet it is intriguing to wonder about what might have been. If the perceived threat in New Mexico had been sharp enough to unite all native New Mexicans against the Anglos, could they have exploited
the opportunities of representative government to their own benefit?
But that is not what happened. One can argue that modernity was
inevitable and good, that no one wants to forego the blessings of
modern medicine or the fruits of technology, and that to look backward to a pastoral Golden Age is romantic nonsense. One can argue
that if loss of freedom because of conquest is the issue, sympathy
ought more properly to lie with Native Americans, for *mexicanos* are
the heirs of earlier conquerors. One can argue that cultural diversity
is an impractical ideal, given the reality of modern nations, or that
cultural conflicts are diversions that cloud the "true" issue of class
struggle. But whatever the validity of the above arguments, the wish
to be free *in one's own terms* is universal. And the fact remains that
most *mexicanos* in the United States lost the freedom to live the way
they wanted to live during the nineteenth century.

## Major Territorial Offices

### Federal Appointments

Governor                        Registrars of the Land Offices
Secretary of the Territory      Receivers of the Land Offices
U.S. Attorney                   Indian Agents
U.S. Marshal                    Postmasters
U.S. District Judges            Collector of Internal Revenue
  (also served as territorial
  district judges)

### Territorial Appointments

Solicitor General               Warden of the Territorial Penitentiary
Adjutant General                Cattle Sanitary Boards
District Attorneys              Sheep Sanitary Boards
Auditor                         Notaries Public
Treasurer                       Regents and Trustees of Territorial
Librarian                         Institutions
Superintendent of Public        Coal Oil Inspector
  Instruction (after 1891)

### Elective Offices

Territory            Delegate-in-Congress

Electoral Districts  Members of the Council
                     Members of the Assembly

County               County Commissioners (3)
                     Probate Judge
                     Clerk of the Probate Court
                     Sheriff
                     Assessor
                     Treasurer
                     Surveyor
                     School Superintendent
                     Coroner
                     River Commissioners (in some counties)

Municipal            Mayor
                     Alderman
                     Marshal

Precinct             Justice of the Peace
                     Constable

Source: U.S. Department of the Interior, *Appointment Papers: Territory of New Mexico, 1850–1907.*

## Settlement on the Maxwell Land Grant, 1887

| Location | Homesites Mexicano | Americano | Total | Value of Improvements Mexicano High | Low | Avg. | Americano High | Low | Avg. |
|---|---|---|---|---|---|---|---|---|---|
| 1. Largo Creek | 5 | 7 | 12 | 800 | 200 | 500 | 1,000 | 45 | 385 |
| 2. South Fork | 33 | 0 | 33 | 1,327 | 15 | 205 | | | |
| 3. Valley of San Francisco | 27 | 0 | 27 | 1,564 | 20 | 155 | | | |
| 4. Middle Fork | 18 | 0 | 18 | 575 | 10 | 85 | | | |
| 5. Stonewall Valley | 4 | 18 | 22 | 324 | 25 | 162 | 2,150 | 100 | 737 |
| 6. Back of the Wall | 0 | 6 | 6 | | | | 800 | 300 | 541 |
| 7. Head of Cañon | 0 | 2 | 2 | | | | 300 | 150 | 225 |
| 8. Vermejo | 68 | 32 | 100 | 800 | 10 | 166 | 2,000 | 50 | 511 |
| 9. Rito Bernal | 2 | 0 | 2 | 30 | 20 | 25 | | | |
| 10. Rito Leandro | 9 | 0 | 9 | 100 | 25 | 36 | | | |
| 11. Rito Piedra | 1 | 0 | 1 | 300 | | | | | |
| 12. Castle Rock | 0 | 1 | 1 | | | | 400 | | |
| 13. Vermejo Park | 0 | 9 | 9 | | | | 600 | 300 | 425 |
| 14. Caliente | 0 | 10 | 10 | | | | 500 | 100 | 370 |
| 15. Dry Cañon | 0 | 1 | 1 | | | | 100 | | |
| 16. Crow Creek | 0 | 2 | 2 | | | | 400 | 400 | 400 |
| 17. Van Bremer | 0 | 2 | 2 | | | | 600 | 125 | 365 |
| 18. Salyer's Cañon | 1 | 6 | 7 | no information | | | no information | | |
| 19. Ponil | 44 | 2 | 46 | 750 | 20 | 162 | 250 | 75 | 160 |
| 20. North Ponil | 8 | 1 | 9 | 350 | 25 | 120 | 100 | | |
| 21. Ponil Park | 0 | 13 | 13 | | | | 500 | 125 | 336 |
| 22. Cerrososo | 0 | 4 | 4 | | | | 600 | 150 | 324 |
| 23. South Ponil | 14 | 6 | 20 | 600 | 30 | 120 | 200 | 25 | 140 |
| 24. Ute Creek | 0 | 13 | 13 | | | | 700 | 60 | 230 |
| 25. Moreno Valley | 0 | 8 | 8 | | | | 800 | 40 | 230 |
| 26. Cienega | 0 | 5 | 5 | | | | 1,000 | 75 | 305 |
| 27. Willow Gulch | 0 | 2 | 2 | | | | 900 | 250 | 575 |
| 28. Comanche Creek | 0 | 5 | 5 | | | | 800 | 20 | 282 |
| 29. Wet Gulch | 1 | 0 | 1 | 100 | | | | | |
| 30. Cimarron | 23 | 2 | 25 | 300 | 20 | 121 | 250 | 75 | 160 |
| 31. Crow Meadows | 0 | 1 | 1 | | | | 500 | | |
| 32. Crow Cañon | 0 | 1 | 1 | | | | no information | | |
| 33. Red River[b] | 0 | 32 | 32 | | | | 1,500 | 200 | 700 |
| 34. Sugarite[b] | 0 | 34 | 34 | | | | 700 | 25 | 273 |
| 35. Dillon Cañon | 1 | 4 | 5 | 300 | | | 300 | | |
| 36. Upper Dillon Cañon | 0 | 1 | 1 | | | | no information | | |
| 37. Eagle's Tail | 0 | 1 | 1 | | | | no information | | |
| 38. Garner's Cañon | 0 | 1 | 1 | | | | no information | | |
| 39. Lower Dillon Cañon | 0 | 8 | 8 | | | | 200 | 100 | 180 |
| 40. Dutchman's Cañon | 0 | 1 | 1 | | | | no information | | |
| 41. Brown's Pocket | 0 | 1 | 1 | | | | no information | | |
| 42. Big Hollow | 0 | 1 | 1 | | | | no information | | |
| 43. Una de Gato and Old Man's Cañon | 0 | 1 | 1 | | | | no information | | |
| 44. Uraca | 0 | 1 | 1 | | | | 600 | 75 | 281 |
| 45. Upper Red River | 0 | 4 | 4 | | | | 1,500 | | |
| 46. Cole Cañon | 0 | 1 | 1 | | | | 500 | | |
| 47. Mouth Cottonwood Cañon | 0 | 1 | 1 | | | | 100 | | |
| 48. Brush Creek | 0 | 1 | 1 | | | | 800 | | |
| 49. Seely Cañon | 0 | 1 | 1 | | | | 500 | 400 | 450 |
| 50. Chicken Creek | 0 | 3 | 3 | | | | 100 | | |
| 51. Shawnee Creek | 0 | 1 | 1 | | | | 300 | | |
| 52. Head of Red River | 0 | 1 | 1 | | | | | | |

[a]First settler means the first person recorded as living in the area, not necessarily the one with the longest period of occupancy at the time of enumeration.
[b]Many individuals were listed as owning property at Red River and Sugarite, but the holdings were counted separately. In addition, it is not clear how many people actually lived in these two areas, so they were omitted from the map.

| Period of Occupancy (in years) | | | | | | | |
|---|---|---|---|---|---|---|---|
| Mexicano | | | | Americano | | | |
| 1st Settler[a] | High | Low | Avg. | 1st Settler[a] | High | Low | Avg. |
| 1864 | 10 | 1 | 5½ | 1881 | 5 | 1 | 3 |
| 1868 | 18 | ½ | 11 | | | | |
| 1865 | 20 | 2 | 13½ | | | | |
| 1866 | 20 | 1 | 8½ | | | | |
| 1868 | 10 | 2 | 5 | 1866 | 16 | 1 | 9 |
| | | | | 1872 | 12 | 4 | 6· |
| | | | | 1876 | 10 | 5 | 7½ |
| 1870 | 16 | 2 | 8 | 1872 | 10 | 2 | 5 |
| | no information | | | | | | |
| 1872 | 14 | 5 | 9 | | | | |
| 1872 | 8 | | | | no information | | |
| | | | | 1873 | 12 | 3 | 7½ |
| | | | | 1874 | 12 | 4 | 10½ |
| | | | | 1882 | 4 | | |
| | | | | 1883 | 3 | 3 | 3 |
| | | | | 1871 | 15 | 3 | 9 |
| | | | | | no information | | |
| | no information | | | 1879 | 7 | 3 | 5 |
| 1866 | 20 | 1 | 8 | 1874 | 12 | | |
| 1875 | 10 | 1 | 5½ | | | | |
| | | | | 1872 | 8 | 2 | 4½ |
| | | | | 1872 | 4 | 2 | 3 |
| 1878 | 7 | 2 | 4½ | 1882 | 4 | 1 | 3 |
| | | | | 1868 | 14 | 1 | 7 |
| | | | | 1873 | 12 | 3 | 7 |
| | | | | 1868 | 14 | 5 | 7 |
| | | | | 1869 | 10 | no information | |
| | | | | 1870 | 16 | 8 | 11 |
| 1868 | 18 | | | | | | |
| 1872 | 14 | 2 | 10 | 1872 | 14 | 2 | 7 |
| | | | | | no information | | |
| | | | | | no information | | |
| | | | | | no information | | |
| | | | | | no information | | |
| | | | | | no information | | |
| | | | | | no information | | |
| | | | | | no information | | |
| | | | | | no information | | |
| | no information | | | | no information | | |
| | | | | | no information | | |
| | | | | | no information | | |
| | | | | | no information | | |

Source: Maxwell Land Grant Settlers Book, March 1887, Maxwell Land Grant Collection, University of New Mexico Library.

## Land Grants

### I. Petition

To the Lieutenant Colonel and Civil and Military Governor:

I, Lorenzo Márquez, resident of this town of Santa Fe, for myself and in the name of fifty-one men, accompanying me, appear before your Excellency and state that, in consideration of having a very large family, as well myself as those accompanying me, though we have some land in this town it is not sufficient for our support, on account of its smallness and the great scarcity of water, which owing to the great number of people we cannot all enjoy, wherefore we have entered a tract of land on the Rio Pecos, vacant and unsettled, at the place commonly called El Vado, and where there is room enough not only for us, the fifty-one who ask it, but also for everyone in the province not supplied, and its boundaries are on the north of the Rio de la Vaca from the place called the Rancheria to the Agua Caliente, on the south the Cañon Blanco, on the east La Cuesta with the little hills of Bernal, and on the west the place commonly called the Gusano—which tract we ask be granted us in the name of our Sovereign, whom may God preserve, and among these fifty-one men petitioning are thirteen Indians, and among them all there are twenty-five fire-arms, and they are all the same persons who appear in the subjoined list, which I present in due form, and we unanimously and harmoniously as one person do promise to enclose ourselves in a plaza well fortified with bulwarks and towers, and to exert ourselves to supply all the fire-arms and ammunition that it may be possible for us to procure. And as we trust in a compliance with our petition we request and pray that your Excellency be pleased to direct that we be placed in possession, in the Name of his Royal Majesty our Sovereign, whom may God preserve, and we declare in full legal form that we do not act with dissimulation.

Lorenzo Márquez
For himself and the Petitioners

### II. Decree

At the town of Santa Fe, Capital of this Kingdom of New Mexico, on the twenty-fifth day of the month of November, One Thousand Seven Hundred and Ninety-four, I, Lieutenant-Colonel Fernando Chacón, Knight of the Order of Santiago, Civil and Military Governor of said Kingdom, Sub-Inspector of the regular troops therein and Inspector of the militia thereof, for His Majesty (whom may God preserve) having seen the foregoing document and petition of Lorenzo Márquez for himself and in the name of fifty-one men, should and did direct the principal Alcalde of this town, Antonio José Ortiz, to execute said grant as requested by the petitioners, so that they and their children and successors may have, hold and possess the same in the name of His Majesty, observing at the same time the conditions and requisites required in such cases to be observed, and especially that relative to not injuring third parties. Thus I provided, ordered and signed with the witnesses in my attendance, with whom I act for want of a royal or public notary of which there is none in the said Kingdom, and upon this common paper, there being none of any seal—to which I certify.

Fernando Chacón

On the twenty-sixth of the month of November, One Thousand Seven Hundred and Ninety-four, I, Antonio José Ortiz, Captain in the militia and principal alcalde of the town of Santa Fe, in pursuance of the order of Lieutenant Colonel Fernando Chacón, Knight of the Order of Santiago and civil and military Governor of this Kingdom, before proceeding to the site of El Vado, I, said principal alcalde in company with two witnesses who were Xavier Ortiz and Domingo Santistevan, the fifty-two petitioners being present, caused them to comprehend the petition they had made, and informed them that to receive the grant they would have to observe and fulfill in full form of law the following conditions:

First—That the tract aforesaid has to be in common, not only in regard to themselves but also to all settlers who may join them in the future.

Second—That with respect to the dangers of the place they shall have to keep themselves equipped with fire-arms and bows and arrows in which they shall be inspected as well at the time of settling as at any time the alcalde in office may deem proper, provided that after two years settlement all the arms they have must be fire-arms, under the penalty that all who do not comply with the requirement shall be sent out of the settlement.

Third—That the plaza they may construct shall be according as they expressed in their petition, and in the meantime they shall reside in the Pueblo of Pecos where there are sufficient accommodations for the aforesaid fifty-two families.

Fourth—That to the alcalde in office in said pueblo they shall set apart a small separate piece of land for him to cultivate for himself at his will, without their children or successors making any objection thereto, and the same for his successor in office.

Fifth—That the construction of their Plaza as well as the opening of ditches, and all other work that may be deemed proper for the common welfare shall be performed by the community with that union which in their government they must preserve.

And when this was heard and understood by each and all of the aforementioned persons, they accordingly unanimously responded that they understood and heeded what was communicated to them. Wherefore, I took them by the hand and announced in clear and intelligible words that in the name of His Majesty (God preserve Him) and without prejudice to the Royal interest or that of any third party. I led them over said lands, and they plucked up grass, cast stones and shouted "Long Live the King," taking possession of said land quietly and peaceably, without any objection; pointing out to them the boundaries, which are, in the North the Rio de la Vaca from the place called the Rancheria to the Agua Caliente, on the South the Cañon Blanco, on the East La Cuesta with the little hills of Bernal, and on the West, the place commonly called the Gusano, notifying them that the pastures and watering places are in common.

And that in all time it may so appear, I, acting by appointment, for want of a notary, there being none in this jurisdiction, signed this with my attending witnesses, with whom I act, to which I certify.

Antonio José Ortiz

### III. The San Miguel Del Bado Grant

At this place, San Miguel del Bado, *del Rio de Pecos*, jurisdiction of the Capital town of Santa Fe, New Mexico, on the twelfth day of March, in the present year, One Thousand Eight Hundred and Three, I, Pedro Bautista Pino, Justice of the Second Note of the Town of Santa Fe and its jurisdiction by verbal order of Colonel Fernando Chacón, Governor of this Province, have proceeded to this said settlement for the purpose of distributing the lands which are under cultivation, to all the individuals who occupy said settlement, and having examined the aforesaid cultivated land, I measured the whole of it from North and South and then proceeded to lay off and divide the several portions with the concurrence of all the parties interested, until the matter was placed in order, according to the means myself and the parties interested deemed the best adopted to the purpose, in order that all should be satisfied with their possessions although said land is very much broken on account of the many bends in the river, and after the portions were equally divided in the best manner possible, I caused them to draw lots, and each individual drew his portion and the number of varas contained in each one portion was set down, as will appear from the accompanying list, which contains the number of individuals who reside in this precinct, amounting to the number of fifty-eight families, between whom all the land was divided, excepting only the portion appertaining to the Justice of the Precinct, as appears by the possession given by the said Governor, and another surplus portion which by the consent of all is set aside for the benefit of the blessed souls in Purgatory, on condition that the products are to be applied annually to the payment of free masses, the certificates for which are to be delivered to the Alcalde in the office of said jurisdiction. And after having made the distribution I proceeded to mark out the boundaries of said tract from North to South, being on the North a hill situated at the edge of the river above the mouth of the ditch which irrigates said lands, and on the South the point of the hill of Pueblo and the valley called Temporales, a large portion of land remaining to the South, which is very necessary for the inhabitants of this town who may require more land to cultivate, which shall be done by the consent of the Justice of said town, who is charged with the care and trust of this matter, giving to each one of those contained in the list the amount he may require and can cultivate, and after having completed all the foregoing I caused them all to be collected together and notified them that they must each immediately erect mounds of stone on the boundaries of their land so as to avoid disputes, and I also notified them that no one was privileged to sell or dispose of their land until the expiration of ten years from this date, as directed by said Governor who, if he is so pleased, will certify his proper approval at the foot of this document, of which a copy shall remain in this town and the original be deposited in the Archives where it properly belongs.

Pedro Bautista Pino<br>(By order of the Governor)

By virtue of what has been done by Pedro Pino,.senior Justice of the Second Note of this capital town of Santa Fe, concerning the distribution of lands made in the name of His Majesty to the residents of the new town of El Vado known as San Miguel, I declare the aforementioned residents of El Vado the lawful owners thereof, approving and confirming the possession given by said Senior Justice Pedro Pino, and in order that it may so appear in all time, I signed this at Santa Fe, New Mexico, on the third day of March, One Thousand Eight Hundred and Three.

Fernando Chacón

Source: Bureau of Land Management, Santa Fe, *Papers Relating to Land Grants in the Office of the Surveyor General of New Mexico*, Microfilm Publication of the University of New Mexico Library, Reel 14; Leonard, *Role of the Land Grant*, pp. 167–179.

Table C-1. **Major Land Grants in the San Miguel Region**

| Grant | Granted | Acreage (Estimated) |
|---|---|---|
| Grants patented by Congress (as of 1884) | | |
| 1. Mora Grant | 1835 (Mexican, Community) | 827,621 |
| 2. Perea Grant (Los Esteros) | 1825 (Mexican) | 17,712 |
| 3. Pablo Montoya Grant | 1824 (Mexican) | 655,468 |
| 4. Antonchico Grant | 1822 (Mexican, Community) | 383,856 |
| 5. Preston Beck Grant (Juan E. Pino) | 1823 (Mexican) | 318,699 |
| Grants confirmed but pending (not sent to Congress, 1884) | | |
| 1. Tecolote Grant | 1824 (Mexican, Community) | 20,636 |
| 2. Agua Negra Grant | 1824 (Mexican) | 17,361 |
| 3. Cañon de Pecos Grant | 1815 (Spanish, Community) | 574 |
| 4. Las Vegas Grant | 1835 (Mexican, Community) | 496,446 |
| 5. Baca Location No. 2[a] | 1860 (U.S.) | 99,289 |
| Grants reported to Congress and awaiting action (as of 1884) | | |
| 1. Añil Spring Grant | 1838 (Mexican) | 69,445 |
| 2. Angustura Tract | 1843 (Mexican) | 2,319 |
| 3. San Miguel del Bado Grant | 1794 (Spanish, Community) | 315,300 |
| 4. Gervacio Nolan Grant | 1845 (Mexican) | 575,968 |

[a]The Las Vegas Grant was first awarded to Luis María Cabeza de Baca and his seventeen sons in 1823. Attacks by Indians drove the de Bacas from the area. The tract was re-awarded to Juan de Dios Maese et al. in 1835. Congress ruled, in 1860, that both were valid grants, confirming the Las Vegas Grant to the community and allowing the de Baca heirs to choose an equal acreage located in square bodies not exceeding five in number. See Map 7 for site of Baca No. 2.

Source: Thomas Donaldson, "The Public Domain," House Miscellaneous Documents, 45th, 47th Congress, 2nd Session, 19, 1152–1154.

## Nuestra Platforma

Not wishing to be misunderstood, we hereby make this our declaration.

Our purpose is to protect the rights and interests of the people in general; especially those of the helpless classes.

We want the Las Vegas Grant settled to the benefit of all concerned, and this we hold is the entire community within the grant.

We want no "land grabbers" or obstructionists of any sort to interfere. We will watch them.

We are not down on lawyers as a class, but the usual knavery and unfair treatment of the people must be stopped.

Our judiciary hereafter must understand that we will sustain it only when "Justice" is its watchword.

The practice of "double-dealing" must cease.

There is a wide difference between New Mexico's "law" and "justice." And justice is God's law, and that we must have at all hazards.

We are down on race issues, and will watch race agitators. We are all human brethren, under the same glorious flag.

We favor irrigation enterprises, but will fight any scheme that tends to monopolize the supply of water courses to the detriment of residents living on lands watered by the same streams.

We favor all enterprises, but object to corrupt methods to further the same.

We do not care how much you get so long as you do it fairly and honestly.

The People are suffering from the effects of partisan "bossism" and these bosses had better quietly hold their peace. The people have been persecuted and hacked about in every which way to satisfy their caprice. If they persist in their usual methods retribution will be their reward.

We are watching "political informers."

We have no grudge against any person in particular, but we are the enemies of bulldozers and tyrants.

We must have a free ballot and a fair count, and the will of the majority shall be respected.

Intimidation and the "indictment" plan have no further fears for us. If the old system should continue, death would be a relief to our sufferings. And for our rights our lives are the least we can pledge.

If the fact that we are law abiding citizens is questioned, come out to our homes and see the hunger and desolation we are suffering; and "this" is the result of the deceitful and corrupt methods of "bossism."

Be fair and just and we are with you, do otherwise and take the consequences.

The White Caps, 1,500 Strong and Growing Daily

Source: Prince Papers, New Mexico State Records Center and Archives.

## Attacks by Las Gorras Blancas

| 1889 | April | Rawlins and Quarrell, San Gerónimo |
|---|---|---|
| | May | Agua Sarca |
| | | Bernal, general fence cutting and some killings |
| | | San Gerónimo |
| | | Edward Hobart, Las Vegas Hot Springs |
| | June | Rawlins and Quarrell, twice, San Gerónimo |
| | | José Y. Luhan, San Ignacio |
| | | W. C. Wright, warned, Fulton |
| | | J. B. Snouffer, warned, and house burned, Fulton |
| | July | José Y. Luhan, twice, San Ignacio |
| | | Gregorio Varela, San Gerónimo |
| | August | Lorenzo Lopez, near Romeroville |
| | | J. W. Lynch, near Romeroville |
| | | J. Placido Romero, Peralta |
| | November | Station Agent, Rowe |
| | | Section Hands, warned, Bernal |
| | | Nightride through Las Vegas |
| | | Severino Trujillo, Guadalupita |
| | December | Demonstration, Las Vegas |
| | | W. C. Wright, Fulton |
| | | J. B. Snouffer, Fulton |
| 1890 | February | Severino Trujillo, twice, Guadalupita |
| | March | Eugenio Romero, ties cut; platform distributed, Las Vegas |
| | | F. Le Duc, Las Vegas Hot Springs |
| | | Railroad bridge, Las Vegas Hot Springs |
| | | Gordon's Planing Mill, Las Vegas Hot Springs |
| | | Glorietta |
| | | Cow Creek |
| | | Upper Pecos, reports of activity |
| | | Chaperito |
| | April | Notices posted setting wage scales and hauling rates |
| | | Teamsters ordered to strike |
| | | Alberti, Las Vegas Hot Springs |
| | | Las Vegas Electric Light Company, poles cut |
| | May | Acquittal of accused fence cutters, Las Vegas |
| | | José Y. Luhan, sawmill, San Ignacio |
| | June | Eduardo Martínez, twice, Antonchico |
| | | Jose Sanchez, twice, Antonchico |
| | | Candelario Rael, twice, Antonchico |
| | | Three others, once, Antonchico |
| | | L. C. Fort, twice, near Las Vegas |
| | | G. V. Scott, southwest of Las Vegas |
| | | O. A. Hadley, Wagon Mound, Mora County |
| | | Wheeler Pasture, five miles east of Las Vegas |
| | | Three railroad bridges burned |
| | July | Wilson Waddingham, near Romeroville |
| | | Eugenio Romero, two miles east of Las Vegas |
| | | Charles Blanchard, two miles east of Las Vegas |

## Attacks by Las Gorras Blancas (continued)

|          |           |                                                        |
|----------|-----------|--------------------------------------------------------|
|          |           | Frank Manzanares, two miles east of Las Vegas          |
|          |           | Lorenzo Lopez (this time he took fences down)          |
|          |           | Wheeler Pasture, five miles east of Las Vegas          |
|          |           | Two other fences cut near Wheeler Pasture              |
|          |           | La Concepción, report of attacks                       |
|          |           | Julian Sandoval, San Miguel                            |
|          |           | Félix Martínez, near Las Vegas                         |
|          |           | Section hands ordered to strike, Fulton                |
|          |           | Section hands ordered to strike, Rowe                  |
|          | August    | Gallesteo, Santa Fe Co., report of White Caps          |
|          |           | Bernalillo County, report of White Caps                |
|          |           | Mrs. Joseph Bernard, Trementina                        |
|          |           | Mrs. M. A. Hummell, Conchas                            |
|          |           | Severino Trujillo, Guadalupita                         |
|          |           | Phoenix Farm and Ranch Company, Mora County            |
|          | September | Mahlon Harrold                                         |
|          |           | Phoenix Ranch                                          |
| 1891     | November  | J. S. Nelson, Isperenza                                |
|          | December  | J. S. Nelson, twice, Isperenza                         |
|          |           | Miss Hannah Carr, Isperenza                            |
| 1892     | Spring    | S. A. Clark, several times                             |

Source: Prince Papers, New Mexico State Records Center and Archives.

## San Miguel Election Returns

Table F-1. **Totals, 1890**

| | | |
|---|---|---|
| Delegate | Mariano Otero (R) | 1,903 |
| | Antonio Joseph (D-PdelP) | 3,387 |
| Council | J. H. Ward (R) | 2,203 |
| | H. Vigil (PdelP) | 3,142 |
| | Felipe Sánchez (R) | 2,130 |
| | T. B. Mills (PdelP) | 2,994 |
| House | B. F. Forsythe (R) | 2,139 |
| | García (PdelP) | 3,119 |
| | Antonio Lucero (R) | 2,257 |
| | Nestor Montoya (PdelP) | 3,057 |
| | Leandro Gallegos (R) | 2,166 |
| | Pablo Herrera (PdelP) | 2,923 |
| | Blas Ortega (R) | 2,074 |
| | Pablo Aragón (PdelP) | 3,089 |
| County Commissioners | José Y. Esquibel (R) | 2,249 |
| | John Shank (PdelP) | 2,999 |
| | Placido Sandoval (R) | 2,259 |
| | Montoya (PdelP) | 3,023 |
| | Pascual Baca | 2,110 |
| | Solano | 3,132 |
| Sheriff | Eugenio Romero (R) | 2,188 |
| | José L. López (PdelP) | 3,081 |
| Probate Judge | Ramón Ulibarrí (R) | 2,019 |
| | Dionicio Martínez (PdelP) | 3,238 |
| Assessor | Felipe López (R) | 2,221 |
| | N. Segura (PdelP) | 3,023 |
| Clerk of Probate Court | Gonzales (R) | 2,286 |
| | R. F. Hardy (PdelP) | 2,955 |
| Treasurer | Barela (R) | 2,181 |
| | Tafoya (PdelP) | 3,080 |
| School Superintendent | Dr. John Pettijohn (R) | 1,990 |
| | Carlos Rudulph (PdelP) | 3,288 |
| Coroner | D. Otero (R) | 2,201 |
| | José Valdez (PdelP) | 3,036 |

R: Republican
D: Democrat
PdelP: Partido del Pueblo
Source: *Las Vegas Daily Optic*, November 13, 1890.

Table F-2. **Precinct Returns, 1890**

| Precinct Number | Precinct | Population | Average Total Vote | Party | Average Margin |
|---|---|---|---|---|---|
| 1 | San Miguel | 475 | 109 | PdelP | 85 |
| 2 | La Cuesta | 462 | 136 | PdelP | 36 |
| 3 | Antonchico | 519 | 102 | R | 15 |
| 4 | Tecolote | 525 | 128 | PdelP | 48 |
| 5 | Las Vegas | 1,349 | 320 | PdelP | 55 |
| 6 | La Concepción | 217 | 53 | PdelP | 9 |
| 7 | Los Alamos | 300 | 72 | R | 17 |
| 8 | Pecos | 673 | 155 | R | 9 |
| 9 | Upper Las Vegas | 576 | 85 | PdelP | 22 |
| 10 | Chaperito | 346 | 84 | PdelP | 26 |
| 11 | San Geronimo | 749 | 158 | R | 50 |
| 12 | Rowe | 315 | 64 | R | 2 |
| 13 | Rincon | 225 | 67 | PdelP | 17 |
| 14 | Sapello | 404 | 70 | PdelP | 25 |
| 15 | Manuelitas | 305 | 75 | PdelP | 51 |
| 16 | La Junta | 241 | 49 | R | 23 |
| 17 | Puerta de Luna | 318 | 62 | PdelP | 38 |
| 18[a] | San Lorenzo | 300 | 50 | R | 19 |
| 19 | Las Colinas Abajo | 479 | 93 | PdelP | 45 |
| 20[a] | Joya Largo | 133 | 28 | PdelP | 28 |
| 21 | Santa Rosa | 217 | 30 | Split[b] | |
| 22 | Sabinosa | 199 | 57 | Split | |
| 23 | San José | 483 | 105 | PdelP | 75 |
| 24 | La Liendre | 388 | 103 | PdelP | 18 |
| 25 | Peñasco Blanco | 181 | 42 | PdelP | 6 |
| 26 | Las Vegas | 1,036 | 240 | R | 60 |
| 27 | Ft. Sumner | 285 | 40 | Split | |
| 28 | Cabra Springs | 178 | 29 | Split | |
| 29 | East Las Vegas | 2,312 | 505 | R | 100 |
| 30 | Cañoncito | 296 | 56 | PdelP | 20 |
| 31 | Puertocito | 193 | 83 | PdelP | 37 |
| 32 | El Pueblo | 296 | 78 | PdelP | 14 |
| 33 | Los Vigiles | 215 | 77 | PdelP | 9 |
| 34 | Las Mulas | 204 | 53 | PdelP | 37 |
| 35 | Las Gallinas | 347 | 84 | Split | |
| 36 | Peña Blanca | 324 | 59 | PdelP | 20 |
| 37 | El Cerrito | 331 | 76 | PdelP | 30 |
| 38 | Los Torres | 496 | 94 | PdelP | 6 |
| 39 | Antonchico Arriba | 381 | 75 | PdelP | 7 |
| 40 | Bernal | 193 | 43 | PdelP | 43 |

| Precinct Number | Precinct | Population | Average Total Vote | Party | Average Margin |
|---|---|---|---|---|---|
| 41 | Liberty | 306 | 39 | R | 5 |
| 42 | Puerto de Luna | 558 | 115 | PdelP | 96 |
| 43 | Los Fuertes | 262 | 57 | PdelP | 23 |
| 44 | Ojitos Frios | 366 | 65 | PdelP | 59 |
| 45 | Cañada de Aguilar | 330 | 89 | PdelP | 25 |
| 46 | Bado de Juan Pais | 305 | 88 | PdelP | 84 |
| 47 | Las Vegas Hot Springs | 257 | 37 | R | 3 |
| 48 | El Llano | 235 | 45 | PdelP | 21 |
| 49 | Los Esteritos | 156 | 32 | PdelP | 12 |
| 50 | Arroyo de los Yutahs Abajo | 410 | 70 | R | 6 |
| 51 | Las Dispensas | 348 | 83 | Split | |
| 52 | Alamito Rio Colorado | 192 | 57 | PdelP | 31 |
| 53 | Alamo Gordo | 518 | 80 | Split | |
| 54 | Las Colinas Arriba | 284 | 55 | PdelP | 31 |
| 55 | Trementina | 288 | 54 | PdelP | 25 |
| 56 | Agua Sarca | 278 | 68 | PdelP | 16 |
| 57 | Cañon Largo | 286 | 70 | Split | |
| 58 | Romeroville | 326 | 42 | PdelP | 8 |
| 59 | Endee | 392 | 22 | R | 22 |
| 60 | Arroyo de los Yutahs | 302 | 57 | R | 40 |
| 61[a] | El Emplazado | 339 | 69 | PdelP | 13 |
| 62 | La Manga | ? | 48 | PdelP | 30 |
| 63 | San Pablo | ? | 49 | PdelP | 43 |

[a]Could not locate these precincts, and they are not included in Map 7, or in the rest of the tables for 1890.
[b]A precinct was categorized as split if the losing ticket in the precinct won four or more offices.
Source: *Las Vegas Daily Optic*, November 13, 1890.

Table F-3. **Returns by Land Grant, 1890**

| | Average Margin |
|---|---|
| *Strong Partido del Pueblo Precincts (60% or more)* | |
| *Antonchico Grant (7 precincts total)* | |
| No. 19. Las Colinas Abajo | 45 |
| No. 46. Bado de Juan Pais | 84 |
| No. 48. El Llano | 21 |
| No. 49. Los Esteritos | 12 |
| *Las Vegas Grant (16 precincts total, not counting Las Vegas)* | |
| No. 13. Rincon | 17 |
| No. 14. Sapello | 25 |
| No. 31. Puertocito | 37 |
| No. 43. Los Fuertes | 23 |
| No. 45. El Aguilar | 25 |
| No. 62. La Manga | 30 |
| *San Miguel del Bado Grant (9 precincts total)* | |
| No. 1. San Miguel | 85 |
| No. 2. La Cuesta | 36 |
| No. 23. San José | 75 |
| No. 34. Las Mulas | 37 |
| No. 37. El Cerrito | 20 |
| No. 40. Bernal | 43 |
| No. 54. Las Colinas Arriba | 31 |
| No. 63. San Pablo | 43 |
| *Tecolote Grant (2 precincts total)* | |
| No. 4. Tecolote | 48 |
| No. 44. Ojitos Frios | 59 |
| *Mora Grant (4 precincts total)* | |
| No. 15. Manuelitas | 50 |
| No. 30. Cañon de Manuelitas | 20 |
| No. 36. Peña Blanca | 20 |
| *Ortiz Grant (2 precincts total)* | |

| | Average Margin |
|---|---|
| *Republican Precincts (50–60%)* | |
| *Antonchico Grant (7 precincts)* | |
| No. 3. Antonchico | 15 |
| *Las Vegas Grant (16 precincts)* | |
| No. 7. Los Alamos | 17 |
| No. 47. Las Vegas Hot Springs | 3 |
| *Pecos Grant (2 precincts)* | |
| No. 8. Pecos | 9 |
| No. 12. Rowe | 2 |
| *No Grant* | |
| No. 41. Liberty | 5 |
| No. 50. Arroyo de los Yutahs | 6 |
| Total: 7 precincts | |
| 5 of 44 grant precincts | |
| 2 of 12 no grant precincts | |
| *Strong Republican Precincts (60% or more)* | |
| *Antonchico Grant (7 precincts)* | |
| No. 16. La Junta de los Pecos | 23 |
| *Las Vegas Grant (16 precincts)* | |
| No. 11. San Geronimo | 50 |
| *No Grant* | |
| No. 59. Endee | 22 |
| No. 60. Arroyo de los Yutahs Abajo | 40 |
| Total: 4 precincts | |
| 2 of 44 grant precincts | |
| 2 of 12 no grant precincts | |
| Republican Total: 11 precincts | |
| 7 of 44 grant precincts | |
| 4 of 12 no grant precincts | |

No. 52. Alamito Rio Colorado .......................... 31
No Grant
No. 17. Puerta de Luna ................................. 38
No. 42. Puerto de Luna ................................. 96
No. 55. Trementina ..................................... 25
    Total: 28 precincts
        25 of 44 grant precincts
        3 of 12 no grant precincts

*Partido del Pueblo Precincts (50–60%)*

*Antonchico Grant (7 precincts)*
No. 37. Antonchico Arriba .............................. 7
*Las Vegas Grant (16 precincts)*
No. 6. La Concepción ................................... 6
No. 24. La Liendre ..................................... 18
No. 33. Los Vigiles .................................... 9
No. 56. Agua Sarca ..................................... 16
No. 58. Romeroville .................................... 8
*San Miguel del Bado (9 precincts)*
No. 32. Pueblo ......................................... 14
*Mora Grant (4 precincts)*
No. 25. Peñasco Blanco ................................. 6
*Ortiz Grant (2 precincts)*
No. 38. Los Torres ..................................... 6
No Grant
    0
Total:  9 precincts
    **9 of 44 grant precincts**
**Partido del Pueblo Total: 34 of 44 grant precincts**
    **3 of 12 no grant precincts**

*No Grant*
No. 21. Santa Rosa
No. 22. Sabinosa
No. 37. Cañon Largo
No. 27. Ft. Sumner
No. 53. Alamo Gordo
*Las Vegas Grant (16 precincts)*
No. 35. Las Gallinas
No. 51. Las Dispensas
*Beck Grant (1 precinct)*
No. 28. Cabra Springs
*Las Vegas Precincts*
No. 5. South Las Vegas (PdelP) ........................ 55
No. 9. Upper Las Vegas (PdelP) ........................ 22
No. 26. North Las Vegas (R) ........................... 60
No. 29. East Las Vegas (R) ............................ 100

*Source: Las Vegas Daily Optic, November 13, 1890.*

Table F-4. **Smaller Geographic Groupings, 1890**

| | Average Margin |
|---|---|
| *Upper Pecos and Rio Vaca* | |
| No. 8. Pecos (R) | 9 |
| No. 12. Rowe (R) | 2 |
| No. 34. Las Mulas (PdelP) | 37 |
| No. 54. Las Colinas Arriba (PdelP) | 31 |
| *San Miguel Area* | |
| No. 1. San Miguel (PdelP) | 83 |
| No. 23. San José (PdelP) | 75 |
| No. 32. El Pueblo (PdelP) | 14 |
| No. 40. Bernal (PdelP) | 43 |
| *La Cuesta Region* | |
| No. 2. La Cuesta (PdelP) | 36 |
| No. 37. El Cerrito (PdelP) | 30 |
| *Antonchico Region* | |
| No. 3. Antonchico (R) | 15 |
| No. 39. Antonchico Arriba (PdelP) | 7 |
| No. 46. Bado de Juan Pais (PdelP) | 84 |
| No. 48. El Llano (PdelP) | 21 |
| No. 49. Los Esteritos (PdelP) | 12 |
| No. 16. La Junta (R) | 23 |
| *Lower Pecos* | |
| No. 19. Las Colinas Abajo (PdelP) | 45 |
| No. 17. Puerta de Luna (PdelP) | 38 |
| No. 42. Puerto de Luna (PdelP) | 96 |
| No. 21. Santa Rosa (Split) | |
| No. 27. Ft. Sumner (Split) | |
| *Gallinas below Las Vegas* | |
| No. 43. Los Fuertes (PdelP) | 23 |
| No. 6. La Concepción (PdelP) | 6 |
| No. 45. Aguilar (PdelP) | 25 |
| No. 24. La Liendre (PdelP) | 18 |
| No. 10. Chaperito (PdelP) | 35 |
| No. 38. Los Torres (PdelP) | 6 |
| *Las Vegas Grant, Southwest* | |
| No. 31. Puertocito (PdelP) | 37 |
| No. 56. Agua Sarca (PdelP) | 16 |
| No. 58. Romeroville (PdelP) | 8 |
| No. 62. La Manga (PdelP) | 30 |
| *Tecolote River* | |
| No. 11. San Geronimo (R) | 50 |
| No. 4. Tecolote (PdelP) | 48 |
| No. 44. Ojitos Frios (PdelP) | 59 |
| No. 63. San Pablo (PdelP) | 43 |

|                                              | Average Margin |
| -------------------------------------------- | :------------: |
| *Gallinas Northwest*                         |                |
| No. 33. Los Vigiles (PdelP)                  |       9        |
| No. 47. Hot Springs (R)                      |       3        |
| No. 35. Las Gallinas (Split)                 |                |
| No. 51. Las Dispensas (Split)                |                |
| *Sapello River Region*                       |                |
| No.  7. Los Alamos (R)                       |       17       |
| No. 13. Rincon (PdelP)                       |       17       |
| No. 14. Sapello (PdelP)                      |       25       |
| No. 15. Manuelitas (PdelP)                   |       50       |
| No. 25. Peñasco Blanco (PdelP)               |       6        |
| No. 30. Cañoncito (PdelP)                    |       20       |
| No. 36. Peña Blanca (PdelP)                  |       20       |
| *Northeast*                                  |                |
| No. 22. Sabinosa                             |                |
| No. 57. Cañon Largo (Split)                  |                |
| *Ute Creek*                                  |                |
| No. 50. Arroyo de los Yutahs Abajo (R)       |       6        |
| No. 60. Arroyo de los Yutahs (R)             |       40       |
| *Scattered*                                  |                |
| No. 28. Cabra Springs (Split)                |                |
| No. 41. Liberty (R)                          |       5        |
| No. 53. Alamo Gordo (Split)                  |                |
| No. 52. Alamito Rio Colorado (PdelP)         |       31       |
| No. 55. Trementina (PdelP)                   |       25       |
| No. 59. Endee (R)                            |       22       |

Source: *Las Vegas Daily Optic*, November 13, 1890.

Table F-5. **Election, 1892**

| Precinct Number | Precinct | Population | Vote | Party | Margin | 1890 Party | Margin |
|---|---|---|---|---|---|---|---|
| 1 | San Miguel | 475 | 121 | PdelP | 81 | PdelP | 85 |
| 2 | La Cuesta | 462 | 138 | R | 12 | PdelP | 36 |
| 3 | Antonchico—part of Guadalupe County | | | | | | |
| 4 | Tecolote | 525 | 130 | PdelP | 20 | PdelP | 48 |
| 5[a] | Las Vegas | | 139 | R | 35 | PdelP | 55 |
| 6 | La Concepción | 217 | 55 | R | 15 | PdelP | 9 |
| 7 | Los Alamos | 300 | 53 | PdelP | 11 | R | 17 |
| 8 | Pecos | 673 | 160 | R | 42 | R | 9 |
| 9 | Upper Las Vegas | 576 | 94 | PdelP | 21 | PdelP | 22 |
| 10 | Chaperito | 346 | 69 | Split | | PdelP | 26 |
| 11 | San Geronimo | 749 | 148 | R | 52 | R | 50 |
| 12 | Rowe | 315 | 75 | R | 31 | R | 2 |
| 13 | Rincon | 225 | 64 | PdelP | 10 | PdelP | 17 |
| 14 | Sapello | 404 | 77 | R | 5 | PdelP | 25 |
| 15 | Manuelitas | 305 | 66 | PdelP | 42 | PdelP | 50 |
| 16 | La Junta—part of Guadalupe County | | | | | | |
| 17 | Puerto de Luna—part of Guadalupe County | | | | | | |
| 18 | San Lorenzo | 300 | 44 | R | 2 | R | 19 |
| 19 | Las Colinas Abajo—part of Guadalupe County | | | | | | |
| 20 | Joya Largo | 133 | 26 | PdelP | 24 | PdelP | 28 |
| 21 | Santa Rosa—part of Guadalupe County | | | | | | |
| 22 | Sabinosa | 199 | 50 | PdelP | 14 | Split | |
| 23 | San José | 483 | 104 | PdelP | 22 | PdelP | 75 |
| 24 | La Liendre | 388 | 95 | PdelP | 8 | PdelP | 18 |
| 25 | Peñasco Blanco | 181 | 38 | PdelP | 3 | PdelP | 6 |
| 26[a] | Las Vegas | | 180 | PdelP | 18 | R | 60 |
| 27 | Ft. Sumner—part of Guadalupe County | | | | | | |
| 28 | Cabra Springs | 178 | 24 | R | 6 | Split | |
| 29 | East Las Vegas | 2,312 | 500 | Split | | R | 100 |
| 30 | Cañoncito | 296 | 68 | R | 30 | PdelP | 20 |
| 31 | Puertocito | 193 | 98 | PdelP | 24 | PdelP | 37 |
| 32 | El Pueblo | 296 | 85 | PdelP | 7 | PdelP | 14 |
| 33 | Las Vigiles | 215 | 58 | R | 5 | PdelP | 9 |
| 34 | Las Mulas | 204 | 49 | PdelP | 27 | PdelP | 37 |
| 35 | Las Gallinas | 347 | 89 | Split | | Split | |

| Precinct Number | Precinct | Population | Vote | Party | Margin | 1890 Party | Margin |
|---|---|---|---|---|---|---|---|
| 36 | Peña Blanca | 324 | 72 | PdelP | 10 | PdelP | 20 |
| 37 | El Cerrito | 331 | 83 | PdelP | 7 | PdelP | 30 |
| 38 | Los Torres | 496 | 68 | R | 2 | PdelP | 6 |
| 39[b] | Tecolotito | | 30 | PdelP | 22 | [PdelP | 7] |
| 40 | Bernal | 193 | 47 | PdelP | 46 | PdelP | 43 |
| 41 | Liberty | 306 | No Return | | | R | 5 |
| 42 | Puerta de Luna—part of Guadalupe County | | | | | | |
| 43[c] | San Augustín | 262 | 49 | PdelP | 21 | PdelP | 23 |
| 44 | Ojitos Frios | 366 | 78 | PdelP | 62 | PdelP | 59 |
| 45 | Aguilar | 330 | 68 | PdelP | 9 | PdelP | 25 |
| 46 | Bado de Juan Pais—part of Guadalupe County | | | | | | |
| 47 | Las Vegas Hot Springs | 257 | 31 | R | 17 | R | 3 |
| 48 | El Llano—part of Guadalupe County | | | | | | |
| 49 | Los Estentes—part of Guadalupe County | | | | | | |
| 50 | Arroyo de los Yutahs Abajo | 410 | 34 | PdelP | 34 | R | 6 |
| 51 | Las Dispensas | 348 | 70 | PdelP | 40 | Split | |
| 52 | Alamito Rio Colo. | 192 | 56 | PdelP | 12 | PdelP | 31 |
| 53 | Alamo Gordo—part of Guadalupe County | | | | | | |
| 54 | Las Colinas Arriba | 284 | 57 | PdelP | 31 | PdelP | 31 |
| 55 | Trementina | 288 | 57 | PdelP | 23 | PdelP | 25 |
| 56 | Agua Sarca | 278 | 66 | PdelP | 38 | PdelP | 16 |
| 57 | Cañon Largo | 286 | 59 | PdelP | 5 | Split | |
| 58 | Romeroville | 326 | 45 | R | 17 | PdelP | 8 |
| 59 | Endee—part of Guadalupe County | | | | | | |
| 60 | Arroyo de los Yutahs | 302 | 39 | PdelP | 20 | R | 40 |
| 61 | Emplazado | 339 | 71 | PdelP | 19 | PdelP | 13 |
| 62 | La Manga | ? | 44 | PdelP | 20 | PdelP | 30 |
| 63 | San Pablo | ? | 45 | PdelP | 27 | PdelP | 43 |
| 64[a] | Las Vegas | ? | 204 | PdelP | 35 | New | |
| 65 | Guadalupe | ? | 56 | PdelP | 6 | New | |

[a]Precinct No. 64 created out of parts of Precincts No. 5 and No. 26.
[b]In 1890 Precinct No. 39 encompassed both Antonchico Arriba and Tecolote. With new county lines, only Tecolotito remained of Precinct No. 39.
[c]The villages of San Augustín and Los Fuertes made up Precinct No. 43.

Source: *La Voz del Pueblo*, November 12, 1892.

Table F-6. **Totals, 1892**

| Office | Candidate | Votes |
|---|---|---|
| Delegate | Thomas Catron (R) | 1,765 |
| | Antonio Joseph (D, PdelP) | 2,629 |
| Council | S. T. Kline (R) | 1,938 |
| | Félix Martínez (PdelP) | 2,480 |
| | Tomás C. de Baca (R) | 1,941 |
| | John D. W. Veeder (PdelP) | 2,421 |
| House[a] | E. L. Hamblin (R) | 1,912 |
| | J. J. McMullen (D, PdelP) | 2,477 |
| | Toribio Sánchez (R) | 1,949 |
| | José Ramón Maestas (PdelP) | 2,445 |
| | Atanacio Roibal (R) | 1,932 |
| | Tomás González (PdelP) | 2,446 |
| County Commissioners | Félix Esquibel (R) | 1,933 |
| | Aniceto C. Abeytia (PdelP) | 2,450 |
| | Francisco C. de Baca (R) | 1,955 |
| | Leandro Lucero (PdelP) | 2,425 |
| | J. D. McDonald (R) | 1,938 |
| | T. W. Hayward (D, PdelP) | 2,423 |
| Sheriff | Eugenio Romero (R) | 1,963 |
| | Lorenzo López (PdelP) | 2,429 |
| Probate Judge | Plácido Sandoval (R) | 2,086 |
| | Juan José Herrera (PdelP) | 2,284 |
| Assessor | O. L. Houghton (R) | 1,938 |
| | John Pace (D, PdelP) | 2,449 |
| Clerk of Probate Court | Pablo Jarramillo (R) | 1,871 |
| | Carlos Rudulph (PdelP) | 2,503 |
| Treasurer | Lamberto Rivera (R) | 1,938 |
| | Jesús María Tafoya (PdelP) | 2,467 |
| School Superintendent | Gregorio Barela (R) | 1,967 |
| | E. H. Salazar (PdelP) | 2,446 |
| Surveyor[b] | Anselmo González (R) | 2,008 |
| | R. B. Rice (PdelP) | 2,385 |
| Coroner | Amador Ulibarrí (R) | 1,956 |
| | José P. Mares (PdelP) | 2,432 |

[a]Lost one House seat to newly-formed Guadalupe County.
[b]New county office created in 1891.
Source: *La Voz del Pueblo*, November 12, 1892.

## Some Las Vegas *Políticos*

| Name | Occupation[a] | Assessed Property[b] | Party Offices[c] | Knights of Labor Offices[d] | 1894[e] |
|---|---|---|---|---|---|
| Félix Martínez | M,RE,N | $4,895 | C,1892 O,TDC,EC,CP,TD | | U |
| Lorenzo López | G | $1,600 ($28,150)[f] | S,1892 O,EC | | I |
| José L. López | G | $5,875 | S,1890 O,EC | ST,DO,1892 | I |
| Enrique H. Salazar | N | | Sch,1892 O,TD | EC | I |
| Ezequiel C. de Baca | N | | CP,TD | S,T | U |
| Aniceto C. Abeytia | M | $3,150 | CC,1892 CP,EC | MW (2) | I |
| Jesús María Tafoya | | $ 655 | T,1890,1892 TD | T | I |
| Jesús M. H. Alarid | T | | CP | EC,T,S | I |
| Enrique Armijo | M | $ 56 | CP,TD | | I |
| Juan José Herrera | | $ 298 | PJ,1892 O,EC | DO,1888,1892 | U |
| F. A. Blake | | | O | ND,MWT | I |
| R. B. Rice | S | | CS,1892 D | | I |
| T. B. Mills | RE | | C,1892 O,TD | | P |
| John D. W. Veeder | L | $4,700 | C,1892 O,TD,EC | | U |
| Rox Hardy | | $1,565 | PJ,1890 | EC | |
| Eugenio Romero | M,G | $30,015 | R | | U |
| Pablo Ulibarrí | G | | R | | I |
| Antonio Cajal | M | | R | | U |
| Manuel C. de Baca | L | | R | | I |
| Miguel Salazar | L | $2,225 | R | | I |

[a]M: Merchant; RE: Real Estate Broker; N: Newspaperman; G: Grazier; T: Teacher; S: Surveyor; L: Lawyer.
[b]From Assessment Rolls, San Miguel County, 1890, in New Mexico State Records Center and Archives, Santa Fe. The figure is the total assessed minus the $300 exemption.
[c]C: Territorial Council; O: Organizer in 1890; TDC: Member, Territorial Democratic Central Committee; EC: County Executive Committee of El Partido del Pueblo; CP: Club del Pueblo; TD: Delegate, Democratic Territorial Convention; S: Sheriff; Sch: School Superintendent; CC: County Commissioner; T: Treasurer; PJ: Probate Judge; CS: County Surveyor; D: Democrat who never joined El Partido del Pueblo; R: Republican.
[d]ST: Secretary, Territory; DO: District Organizer; EC: Executive Committee; S: Secretary; T: Treasurer; MW: Master Workman, Las Vegas; ND: Delegate to the National Convention; MWT: Master Workman, Territory.
[e]U: Union; I: Independence; P: Populist.
[f]Figure in parentheses is the assessment of López's wife's property.
*Source: La Voz del Pueblo* and *El Independiente.*

# Notes

## 1. Conquered Citizens

1. George Rutledge Gibson, *Journal of a Soldier under Kearny and Doniphan*, ed. Ralph P. Bieber, p. 205.

2. Dwight L. Clarke, *Stephen Watts Kearny, Soldier of the West*, pp. 128–162; Bernard DeVoto, *The Year of Decision, 1846*, pp. 232–240, 248–278; Paul Horgan, *Great River: The Rio Grande in North American History*, pp. 716–736; Howard R. Lamar, *The Far Southwest, 1846–1912: A Territorial History*, pp. 56–82; and Otis A. Singletary, *The Mexican War*, pp. 57–63, give accounts of Kearny's occupation of New Mexico. Memoirs by participants include James William Abert, *Abert's New Mexico Report, 1846–1847*; Gibson, *Journal of a Soldier*; and Phillip St. George Cooke, *The Conquest of New Mexico and California in 1846–1848: An Historical and Personal Narrative*.

3. The Bear Flag Rebellion began on June 6, 1846, when American riflemen under the quasi-direction of Captain John Charles Frémont "arrested" General Mariano Vallejo at his Sonoma home. The "*osos*" committed numerous depredations in the north in the name of revolution. Sloat arrived on July 6 and peacefully "conquered" the south. Sloat, and his successor Stockton, did much to curb the excesses of the Bear Flaggers. See Leonard Pitt, *The Decline of the Californios: A Social History of the Spanish-Speaking Californians, 1846–1890*, pp. 26–42.

4. Frémont, ostensibly on a reconnaissance for the Corps of Topographical Engineers, continually ran afoul of California authorities during the winter of 1845–1846. On March 5, he threw up breastworks at Galiván Peak, but retreated to Sutter's Fort after two days.

5. It was really a seige of General Cos's troops. Cos surrendered on December 9, and was allowed to withdraw south of the Rio Grande upon the promise not to interfere with the restoration of the 1824 Constitution. Since the Texas Revolution is entwined with the Federalist wars of Mexico, the first shots of the hostilities that culminated in Texan independence can be dated from October 2, 1835, when irregulars fired on a Mexican army detachment near Gonzales.

6. The justification that Mexicans had "shed American blood on Ameri-

182 Notes to Pages 5–9

can soil" rested on the Texan claim of the Rio Grande as the boundary with Mexico. See Charles G. Sellers, *James K. Polk, Continentalist, 1843–1846*, pp. 400–409; and Milo M. Quaife, ed., *The Diary of James K. Polk: During His Presidency, 1845–1849*, pp. 384–385, for accounts of Polk's deliberate attempts to provoke war, a war that he had already decided to ask Congress to declare before receipt of the news of Taylor's timely encounter.

7. "Treaty of Guadalupe Hidalgo," Document 60, *Senate Executive Documents*, 30th Congress, 1st Session, Article VII.

8. As with all generalizations there are exceptions to this voluntary-involuntary dichotomy: the French and Spanish of Louisiana and Florida and the British residents of the Oregon territory, for example, were not "voluntary" U.S. residents.

9. Clifford Geertz, *The Interpretation of Cultures*, pp. 12–13. The questions of what culture is, where it exists, and what it does, continue to rage in anthropology and related disciplines. Geertz implies that members of the same culture act in similar ways because they think in similar ways, although he does not imply the degree of uniformity indicated by James F. Downs's definition of culture as a shared mental map or blueprint, or the shared psychological structures proposed by Ward Goodenough. Anthony F. C. Wallace takes the other extreme: "the behavior of people [of the same culture] under various circumstances is predictable, irrespective of knowledge of their motivations, and thus is capable of being predictably related to one's own actions" (*Culture and Personality*, pp. 26–27). In my reading, Wallace is saying that whether individuals of the same culture actually think in the same ways or, in reality, possess unique, idiosyncratic thought processes makes no difference, because they act as if they do—that is, they understand members of their culture better than they understand (and predict the actions of) members of another culture. Since, to my mind, this understanding occurs through shared symbols, just as communication in the same language depends upon a shared knowledge of vocabulary and grammar, I find Geertz's concept of "socially established structures of meaning" to be most useful. It does not, as I use it, imply any degree of uniformity, or lack of uniformity, in the personalities or cognition patterns of individuals.

10. Myth, in this context, does not imply that a story or belief is false, but that it is believed by the community—it is a "significant symbol," a "socially established structure of meaning" known by all.

11. The term was coined by New York newspaperman John L. O'Sullivan: "It is by the right of our manifest destiny to overspread and possess the whole of the Continent which Providence has given us" (quoted in Frederick Merk, *Manifest Destiny and Mission in American History*, p. 32). This term refers to the 1840s and early 1850s, when the U.S. annexed Texas, acquired Oregon, defeated Mexico, and made motions toward acquiring Cuba, all of Mexico, and other Latin American countries as well.

12. The Civil War is the great exception to this burgeoning nationalism, but even it came about from competing ideas about what the nation should be, and the Union fought in the name of preserving national unity. For a discussion of the importance of "movement, migration, and mobility" in forming the national character, see George W. Pierson, "The M-Factor in Ameri-

can History," *American Quarterly* 14 (summer supplement, 1962), 275–279; and Pierson, *The Moving American*.

13. Geertz, *The Interpretation of Culture*, pp. 255–310, presents a comprehensive discussion of politics based on primordial attachments. Geertz defines a primordial attachment as "one that stems from the 'givens'— or more precisely, as culture is inevitably involved in such matters, the assumed 'givens'—of social existence" (p. 259). He identifies six bases for primordial attachments: assumed blood ties, that is, believed common ancestors; race, that is, phenotypical physical features such as skin color; language; region; religion; and custom.

14. Marta Weigle, *Brothers of Light, Brothers of Blood: The Penitentes of the Southwest*, is the best study of the Penitentes.

15. Eric Wolf, *Peasants*, p. 2. See also Wolf, *Peasant Wars of the Twentieth Century*, pp. xi–xv. The definition of peasant, like that of culture, is subject to debate; peasants as a group, furthermore, can be subdivided into any number of categories. I am following Wolf's basic definition by identifying peasants as rural dwellers who are "existentially involved in cultivation and [who] make autonomous decisions regarding the process of cultivation."

16. They functioned autonomously in terms of outsiders, but worked with a high degree of cooperation within the village, especially in such matters as irrigation, land use, and land allocation. See below, chapter 2.

17. Peasants differ from "primitives" in that they are subject to the dictates of a superordinate state, while primitives operate outside the confines of such political structures. Peasants differ from "farmers" in the degree to which they are involved in markets: peasants produce for market only within the context of an assured production for subsistence—to get extra goods not produced on the homestead—while farmers are commited fully to the market—to get maximum return from the most profitable product or products. See Wolf, *Peasant Wars*, pp. xiv–xv, or *Peasants*, pp. 3–6.

18. Eric Hobsbawm, *The Age of Revolution: 1789–1848*, pp. 149–150.

19. Hobsbawm, "Peasants and Politics," *Peasant Studies Newsletter*, summary by T. J. Byers and C. A. Curwen, 1 (July, 1972), 110.

20. Richard N. Adams, *Energy and Structure: A Theory of Social Power*, offers an examination of the relationship between a society's power and its control of the "amount and varieties of the environment," the number and variety of social relationships, and the amount of energy harnessed per capita per year.

21. See Geertz, *The Interpretation of Culture*, pp. 234–341.

22. Fredrik Barth, ed., *Ethnic Groups and Boundaries: The Social Organization of Cultural Difference*. Barth asserts that "a drastic reduction of cultural differences between ethnic groups does not correlate . . . with a reduction in the organizational relevance of ethnic identities, or a breakdown in boundary-maintenance processes" (pp. 32–33).

23. John Higham, *Strangers in the Land: Patterns of American Nativism, 1860–1925*, 2nd ed., pp. 21–23.

24. Ibid., pp. 123–130 and 242–250. See Michael Novak, *The Rise of the Unmeltable Ethnics*, for the perspective from the second generation; of inter-

est also is Charles A. Valentine's analysis of a speech by Daniel P. Moynihan in *Culture and Poverty*, pp. 41–42.

25. Higham, *Strangers in the Land*, pp. 5–11.

26. Otero's father was a *rico* who had been delegate-in-Congress; his mother, a Charleston, South Carolina, belle whom his father met while in Washington.

27. Ted Robert Gurr, *Why Men Rebel*, p. 3.

28. See, for example, Hannah Arendt, *On Revolution*; Crane Brinton, *The Anatomy of Revolution*; Robert R. Palmer, *The Age of Democratic Revolution: A Political History of Europe and America, 1760–1800*; and Carl Leiden and Karl M. Schmitt, *The Politics of Violence: Revolution in the Modern World*. Scholarship about political violence is rooted in John Locke's "right to revolution" aspect of democratic theory, and it is, therefore, natural that attention should focus on national revolutions. Marxist theory, the other major approach to revolution in Western thought, also tends to focus on national revolutions, but because of its emphasis on class conflict and the people, the Marxist approach has led to examinations of "smaller" revolts.

29. See, for example, Hobsbawm, *Social Bandits and Primitive Rebels*, and *Bandits*; George Rudé, *The Crowd in History, 1730–1848*; Paul Friedrich, *Agrarian Revolt in a Mexican Village*. The riots of the 1960s in the U.S. spurred a number of studies that start from violence rather than politics but approach the same general problem of popular discontent. See, for example, *Report of the National Advisory Commission on Civil Disorders*; Hugh Davis Graham and Ted Robert Gurr, eds., *Violence in America: Historical and Comparative Perspectives*; Richard Maxwell Brown, *Strain of Violence: Historical Studies of American Violence and Vigilantism*; and W. Eugene Hollon, *Frontier Violence: Another Look*.

30. "Primitive" or "peasant" rebellions tend to be conservative—looking backward to a Golden Age, or seeking to restore things to their proper balance, not to end injustice but to end "too much"—and small in scope. Because of peasants' limited framework for action, Hobsbawm doubts "whether there can be national peasant movements," although peasant uprisings can become part of broader-based, more ambitious movements. See Hobsbawm, "Peasants and Politics," and *Social Bandits and Primitive Rebels*, pp. 24–25. The Plan de San Diego of 1915 envisioned separating from the United States and thus augered something beyond a peasant revolution. See below, chapters 3 and 10.

31. Fredrick Jackson Turner's "The Significance of the Frontier in American History," delivered at the American Historical Association meeting in 1893, was the first articulation of the "frontier hypothesis" in developed form to explain the uniqueness of the United States. See Frederick Jackson Turner, *The Frontier in American History*, pp. 1–38.

## 2. The Northern Outposts

1. Approximately 750,000–800,000 square miles were lost (including portions of what are now Colorado, Utah, and Nevada), compared to the 761,604 square miles of the present nation of Mexico.

2. Cleve Hallenbeck, *Land of the Conquistadores*; Warren A. Beck, *New*

*Mexico: A History of Four Centuries*; Lynn I. Perrigo, *The American Southwest: Its Peoples and Cultures*; and Horgan, *Great River*, provide accounts of earlier Spanish colonization. See also Warren Beck and Ynez D. Haase, *Historical Atlas of New Mexico*.

3. Jesuit missionary Father Eugenio Francisco Kino began settlement in what is now Arizona near the end of the seventeenth century, but, as Arizona's population remained sparse, I have chosen to omit that state (or territory) from this study.

4. Lamar, *The Far Southwest, 1846–1912*, p. 92. Lamar was referring to New Mexico, Arizona, and Far West Texas, but the image applies to the larger area. Lamar also uses the term "feudal frontier" for the Hispanic settlements.

5. Estimating the population of Spanish descent in New Mexico is an exercise in imprecision; obviously, counting by surname alone omits many people who are culturally *mexicano*. George I. Sánchez, *Forgotten People: A Study of New Mexicans*, p. 30, estimates the Hispanic population in New Mexico in 1938 to be 52 percent. Jack E. Holmes, *Politics in New Mexico*, p. 10, asserts that the percentage dropped below 50 percent during the 1940s. But, given the difficulty in enumeration in remote areas, the *mexicano* population of the state may never have dropped below 50 percent.

6. "Treaty of Guadalupe Hidalgo," Article IX.

7. In addition to Hellenbeck, *Land of the Conquistadores*; Beck, *New Mexico*; Perrigo, *American Southwest*; and Horgan, *Great River*; see also Hubert Howe Bancroft, *History of Arizona and New Mexico, 1530–1888*, and D. W. Meinig, *Southwest: Three People in Geographical Change, 1600–1970*.

8. Meinig, *Southwest*, p. 27.

9. Perrigo, *American Southwest*, pp. 74–75, gives a succinct description. Other works dealing with New Mexican land grants include Herbert O. Brayer, *Pueblo Indian Land Grants of the "Rio Abajo," New Mexico*; Brayer, *William Blackmore: A Case Study in the Economic Development of the West*; Thomas Donaldson, "The Public Domain," *House Miscellaneous Documents*, 45th, 47th Congress, 2nd Session, Document 19; Victor Westphall, *The Public Domain in New Mexico, 1854–1891*; Richard Wells Bradfute, *The Court of Private Land Claims*; and Roxanne Amanda Dunbar, "Land Tenure in Northern New Mexico: An Historical Perspective" (Ph.D. diss., University of California at Los Angeles, 1974). The Crown also recognized the rights of Pueblo Indians to land and sanctioned these rights by grant. See also Appendix C, I–III.

10. Debt peonage developed after the reconquest to take the place of the *encomienda*, a grant that gave the grantee title to both land and the labor of the land's residents.

11. Two histories of the public domain are Harold H. Dunham, *Government Handout*, and Roy M. Robbins, *Our Landed Heritage: The Public Domain, 1776–1936*. The system of surveying and homesteading of western lands began with the Ordinance of 1785 and the Ordinance of 1787.

12. Hallenbeck, *Land of the Conquistadores*, pp. 298–299.

13. Harvey Fergusson, *Rio Grande*, pp. 79–82.

14. Hallenbeck, *Land of the Conquistadores*, pp. 303–314; and Max L. Moorhead, *New Mexico's Royal Road*, pp. 49–53.

15. Both Moorhead and Hallenbeck stress that Anglo merchants used

the existing network, and that many continued south to Chihuahua and Durango from Santa Fe. Prior to independence, New Mexican governors had to channel trade to the merchants in the interior and worked to discourage foreign economic blandishments. See also Marc Simmons, *Spanish Government in New Mexico*, pp. 3, 8, 53–55.

16. Daniel Tyler, "Anglo-American Penetration of the Southwest: The View From New Mexico," *Southwestern Historical Quarterly* 75 (January, 1972), 325–388, examines New Mexican reactions to, and restrictions on, *los extranjeros* on whom the province depended for revenue. Tyler also attempts to revise Governor Armijo's reputation.

17. Simmons, *Spanish Government*; Lansing Bloom, "New Mexico under Mexican Administration, 1821–1846," *Old Santa Fe* 1–2 (July, 1913–April, 1915); Ralph E. Twitchell, *The Leading Facts of New Mexico History*, Vol. 2, pp. 7–15. Under Spanish administration, the *cabildo* (city council) of Santa Fe advised the governor; under Mexico, the *asemblea* (assembly) consisted of representatives from throughout New Mexico. In neither case did they enjoy real power. A *juez de paz* was a justice of the peace, with a jurisdiction roughly equivalent to a precinct; an alcalde had police and judicial powers over an area roughly equivalent to a county; and a prefect was a higher official who governed a district.

18. Arie W. Poldervaart, *Black-Robed Justice*, Chap. 2, "Under the Dreaded Stick," describes the Mexican judicial system in New Mexico; Josiah Gregg, *Commerce of the Prairies*, Vol. 1, pp. 119–126, gives an Anglo's impressions.

19. Gregg, *Commerce of the Prairies*, Vol. 1, pp. 65–69, provides a vivid account of the Revolt of 1837.

20. Lamar, *Far Southwest*, pp. 57–58, 63–66.

21. Ibid., p. 70; see also Theodore Grivas, *Military Governments in California, With a Chapter on Their Prior Use in Louisiana, Florida and New Mexico*; Loomis Morton Ganaway, *New Mexico and the Sectional Controversy*; and Robert W. Larson, *New Mexico's Quest for Statehood*, pp. 59–61. Lamar argues that Kearny did not show the sensitivity that Polk intended. Instead of retaining "so far as possible, the existing native government," Kearny delivered the newly created government "into the hands of the 'American Party' of Taos and the Santa Fe merchants" (p. 65). In any event, the U.S. displayed greater sensitivity toward the new acquisition in 1846, at conquest, than it did four years later.

22. Lamar, *Far Southwest*, p. 85. The probate judges were elected, and, as *mexicanos* controlled the electorate, the broader the powers of the probate courts, the greater the power wielded by the native population.

23. *The New Mexico Blue Book, or State Official Register*, comp. Antonio Lucero, pp. 10–59. See Appendix A for a list of territorial offices. The *mexicano* county-level officeholders were thwarted to some extent by the Anglo ploy of creating new "American" counties around the rim of Spanish settlement.

24. German Jews formed another powerful merchant faction. Alien by religion, language, and nationality, the Jews reaped a high degree of loyalty and profit, most probably because their old-world attitudes blended well with those of the New Mexican people. See William J. Parrish, *The Charles*

*Ilfeld Company: A Study of the Rise and Decline of Mercantile Capitalism in New Mexico*, and Parrish, "The German Jew and the Commercial Revolution in Territorial New Mexico, 1850–1900," *New Mexico Historical Review* 35 (January, April, 1960), 1–29, 129–150.

25. Parrish, *Charles Ilfeld Company*.

26. Some powerful native New Mexicans were officers of banks, railroad corporations, and mining companies. They probably gained these positions because of their political influence rather than because of the capital they invested or their technical expertise. Even most "American" *ricos* clung to ranching-mercantile enterprises, although whether this was due to their inclinations or their exclusion by the Anglo business community is hard to determine.

27. Governor Edmund G. Ross to John O'Grady, March 26, 1887, Letters Sent, Ross Papers, Governors' Papers, New Mexico State Records Center and Archives, Santa Fe.

28. Ibid.

29. New Mexican political relationships were, and are, very complex, and politicians had to work constantly to maintain their base of support. Holmes, *Politics in New Mexico*, pp. 20–49, takes pains to emphasize this complexity and to attack the "Procrustean synthesis" of anthropologists and sociologists that depicts an almost feudal *patrón-peón* relationship. My reading of the correspondence of territorial politicians supports this view; successful politicians had to work as hard, and pay as much attention to detail, as did the great eighteenth-century English politician, Lord Newcastle. See also Victor Westphall, *Thomas Benton Catron and His Era*.

30. Its population—far in excess of the minimum for statehood—and the controversy between slave states and free states combined to have California admitted as a state as one of the provisions of the Compromise of 1850.

31. General sources for early California include C. Alan Hutchinson, *Frontier Settlement in Mexican California: The Híjar-Padres Colony and Its Origins, 1769–1835*; Hubert Howe Bancroft, *History of California*, Vols. I–IV; Bancroft, *California Pastoral*; Irving Burdine Richman, *California under Spain and Mexico, 1535–1847*; Pitt, *Decline of the Californios*; John Walton Caughey, *California: A Remarkable State's History*; John W. Caughey and Laree Caughey, *California Heritage: An Anthology of History and Literature*; W. H. Hutchinson, *California: Two Centuries of Man, Land, and Growth in the Golden State*; Perrigo, *The American Southwest*; Robert Glass Cleland, *The Irvine Ranch of Orange County, 1810–1950*; Daniel J. Garr, "A Rare and Desolate Land: Population and Race in Hispanic California," *Western Historical Quarterly* 6 (April, 1975), 133–148.

32. Pitt, *Decline of the Californios*, pp. 11–14.

33. Hutchinson, *Frontier Settlement*, pp. 55–56 and 394; Caughey, *California*, pp. 79–80; Perrigo, *The American Southwest*, pp. 61–62. Hutchinson puts it most succinctly: California was "in effect an overseas colony of Mexico after the closing of overland communication in 1781" (p. 394).

34. Hutchinson, *Frontier Settlement*, pp. 1–70; Pitt, *Decline of the Californios*, p. 2; Perrigo, *The American Southwest*, pp. 61–62; Caughey, *California*, p. 94. The *Otter*, captained by Ebenezer Dorr, was the first U.S. ship

to put in at a California port, at Monterey in 1796. California's attractiveness and vulnerability did not escape the notice of the seafaring traders: American William Shaler wrote, in 1808, that the Spaniards "have done everything that could be done to render California an object worthy of the great maritime powers" (Hutchinson, *Frontier Settlement*, p. 67).

35. Pitt, *Decline of the Californios*, p. 8. See also Richman, *California under Spain and Mexico*, pp. 228–264.

36. Pitt, *Decline of the Californios*, p. 9.

37. William Henry Ellison, *A Self-Governing Dominion: California, 1849–1860*, pp. 102–136.

38. Robert Glass Cleland, *The Cattle on a Thousand Hills: Southern California, 1850–1880*; Pitt, *Decline of the Californios*, pp. 102, 249–250. Many contemporaries and many historians have little good to say about the Land Law of 1851. William Heath Davis observed that "The depredations of the squatters continued and of others also, who by one means or another had obtained possession; or the owners were so involved in efforts to defend themselves that they became dispirited, crushed, poor and miserable" (quoted in J. E. Reynolds's introduction to Charles Howard Shinn, *Graphic Description of Pacific Coast Outlaws*, p. 15). Cleland observes that the land act "adversely affected the whole economic structure of the state, penalized legitimate landowners, often to the point of ruin, played into the hands of speculators, discouraged settlement and immigration, retarded agricultural progress, and, by creating a resentful and disaffected landless element, served to produce a large measure of social instability" (p. 49).

39. Pitt, *Decline of the Californios*, p. 4.

40. Pitt, *Decline of the Californios*, p. 6. See also Bancroft, *California Pastoral*, pp. 270–273; and Hutchinson, *Frontier Settlement*, the central theme of which is the story of an attempted Mexican colony in California which was defeated by the native *californios*.

41. Pitt, *Decline of the Californios*, p. 7.

42. Hutchinson, *California: Two Centuries*, pp. 69–70.

43. Pitt, *Decline of the Californios*, p. 19.

44. In addition to the works already cited, examinations of Anglo American infiltration and conquest of California can be found in DeVoto, *The Year of Decision*; Singletary, *The Mexican War*; Dale L. Morgan, *Jedediah Smith and the Opening of the West*; John A. Hawgood, *America's Western Frontiers: The Exploration and Settlement of the Trans-Mississippi West*. Hawgood's "The Pattern of Yankee Infiltration in Mexican Alta California, 1821–1846," *Pacific Historical Review* 27 (Feb., 1958), 27–37, examines the role of Thomas O. Larkin and argues that he was not a "fifth columnist." Pitt argues for the importance of the difference in behavior between the maritime Yankees and the overland migrants who began arriving in 1841 as a major reason for *californio* hardening of attitudes toward Anglos (*Decline of the Californios*, pp. 24–25).

45. Pitt, *Decline of the Californios*, p. 34.

46. See John W. Caughey, *Gold Is the Cornerstone*, especially pp. 194–201, for racial hostility and the Foreign Miners' Tax; Rodman W. Paul, *California Gold: The Beginning of Mining in the Far West*; Joseph Henry Jackson, *Anybody's Gold: The Story of California's Mining Towns*; Charles Howard

Shinn, *Mining Camps: A Study in Frontier Government*. See also Leonard Pitt, "The Beginnings of Nativism in California," *Pacific Historical Review* 30 (February, 1961), 23–38.

47. General sources for Texas include Hubert Howe Bancroft, *History of the Northern Mexican States and Texas*; H. E. Bolton, *Texas in the Middle Eighteenth Century*; Carlos E. Casteñada, *Our Catholic Heritage in Texas*; Odie B. Faulk, *A Successful Failure*; David M. Vigness, *The Revolutionary Decades, 1810–1836*; Oakah L. Jones, Jr., *Los Paisanos: Spanish Settlers on the Northern Frontier of New Spain*; D. W. Meinig, *Imperial Texas: An Interpretive Essay in Cultural Geography*; Félix D. Almaráz, Jr., *Tragic Cavalier: Governor Manuel Salcedo of Texas, 1808–1813*.

48. See Eugene C. Barker, *The Life of Stephen F. Austin, Founder of Texas, 1793–1836: A Chapter in the Westward Movement of the Anglo-American People*; and Barker, *Mexico and Texas, 1821–1835*.

49. Barker, *Mexico and Texas*, pp. 12–21; Casteñada, *Our Catholic Heritage*, Vol. VI, pp. 197–198; and Vigness, *The Revolutionary Decades*.

50. Samuel H. Lowrie, *Culture Conflict in Texas, 1821–1835*; Seymour V. Conner, *Adventure in Glory*.

51. Perrigo, *The American Southwest*, p. 133.

52. Joseph Milton Nance, *After San Jacinto: The Texas-Mexican Frontier, 1836–1841*; Nance, *Attack and Counterattack: The Texas-Mexican Frontier, 1842*.

53. Américo Paredes, "Texas' Third Man: The Texas Mexican," *Race* 3 (May, 1963), 49–58; Milton Lindheim, *The Republic of the Rio Grande: Texans in Mexico, 1839–40*, pp. 15–16; Juan Seguín, *Personal Memoirs of Juan A. Seguín, from the Year 1834 to the Retreat of General Woll from the City of San Antonio, 1842*.

54. Lawrence Francis Hill, *José de Escandón and the Founding of Nuevo Santander: A Study in Spanish Colonization*; Jones, *Los Paisanos*, pp. 65–78; Casteñada, *Our Catholic Heritage*, Vol. III, pp. 130–196.

55. Américo Paredes, *"With His Pistol In His Hand": A Border Ballad and Its Hero*, pp. 7–15. We also have this description: "Along the Rio Grande lands were laid off with narrow fronts and each colonist was entitled to his portion or headright, varying in quantity according to the service rendered; and around each town, four leagues were held in common for all, including newcomers and poor people not entitled to or unable to purchase land" (John L. Haynes, October 1, 1859, in "Difficulties on the Southwestern Frontier," *House Executive Documents*, 36th Congress, 1st Session, Document 52, p. 25). Oakah Jones asserts that "class structures and distinctions were very hazy" (*Los Paisanos*, p. 20) and that "the smaller rancho, or stock farm, however, was the predominant rural establishment in Nuevo Santander" (p. 71–72).

## 3. The Border

1. James Reed, *The Border Ballads*, p. 10.

2. Sources for Nuevo Santander include Lawrence Francis Hill, *José de Escandón and the Founding of Nuevo Santander*; Jones, *Los Paisanos*, pp. 65–78; Casteñada, *Our Catholic Heritage*, Vol. III, pp. 130–196; Américo Pa-

redes, *A Texas-Mexican Cancionero; Folksongs of the Lower Border*; Paredes, "With His Pistol in His Hand"; David M. Vigness, "The Lower Rio Grande Valley, 1836–1846" (M.A. thesis, University of Texas at Austin, 1948); Vigness, "The Republic of the Rio Grande: An Example of Separatism in Northern Mexico" (Ph.D. diss., University of Texas at Austin, 1951).

3. The Treaty of Guadalupe Hidalgo was signed and ratified in 1848, but the boundary survey—by a joint U.S.-Mexican commission—had not been completed by the fall of 1852 when an outcry against U.S. Commissioner John Bartlett's "generosity" in allowing the line to be drawn north of El Paso brought the survey to a halt. The issue was resolved in 1854 with the ratification of the Gadsden Purchase, by which the U.S. purchased an additional thirty thousand square miles for ten million dollars.

4. Perrigo, *The American Southwest*, p. 133.

5. See Noel M. Loomis, *The Texas–Santa Fe Pioneers*. For a participant's account see George Wilkins Kendall, *Narrative of the Texas Santa Fé Expedition Comprising a Description of a Tour through Texas and across the Great Southwestern Prairies, the Comanche and Caygua Huntinggrounds with an Account of the Sufferings from Want of Food, Losses from Hostile Indians, and Their March, as Prisoners, to the City of Mexico*. Residents of Antonchico, New Mexico, where the expedition was captured, still remember the incident and will show one the buildings where the Texans were held prior to the march to Mexico.

6. A saying usually attributed to New Mexico's last Mexican governor, Manuel Armijo.

7. John Milton Nance's *After San Jacinto* and *Attack and Counterattack* treat the border conflict in great detail.

8. Nance, *After San Jacinto*, pp. 142–251.

9. Ibid., pp. 252 and 254.

10. Ibid., pp. 45, 114, and 260.

11. Ibid., pp. 109–112, 188–189.

12. Nance, *Attack and Counterattack*, pp. 9–54, 297–334.

13. See, for example, Thomas W. Bell, *A Narrative of the Capture and Subsequent Sufferings of the Mier Prisoners in Mexico, Captured in the Cause of Texas, Dec. 26th, 1842 and Liberated Sept. 16th, 1844*; or Thomas J. Green, *Journal of the Texican Expedition against Mier*. Seventeen prisoners were chosen by lot and summarily executed and the remainder marched to Mexico City where, after a year, 120 survivors of the party of 750 were released. J. Frank Dobie has been quoted as saying that the experiences of Texans as prisoners of Mexicans are the most movingly and dramatically recorded themes of Texas life. It is well to remember, however, that in most cases, the Texans were captured while raiding on foreign soil.

14. Paredes, *A Texas-Mexican Cancionero*, pp. 22–23.

15. Charles W. Goldfinch, *Juan N. Cortina, 1824–1892: A Re-Appraisal*, p. 40; Paredes, "With His Pistol in His Hand", pp. 132–133.

16. Walter Prescott Webb, *The Texas Rangers: A Century of Frontier Defense*, pp. 175–176.

17. Paredes, "With His Pistol in His Hand", p. 134.

18. Ibid., pp. 23–32.

19. John J. Linn, *Reminiscences of Fifty Years in Texas*, pp. 352–354; Carey McWilliams, *North from Mexico: The Spanish-Speaking People of the United States*, p. 106; David J. Weber, ed., *Foreigners in Their Native Land: Historical Roots of the Mexican Americans*, p. 153. Anglo freighters were angered at *mexicano* freighters because the latter were.cheaper and faster.

20. Sources for the Cortina War include "Difficulties on the Southwestern Frontier," *House Executive Documents*, 36th Congress, 1st Session, Document 52; "Troubles on the Texas Frontier," *House Executive Documents*, 36th Congress, 1st Session, Document 81; Goldfinch, *Juan N. Cortina*; José T. Canales, *Juan N. Cortina, Bandit or Patriot?*; McWilliams, *North from Mexico*, pp. 106–108; Rodolfo F. Acuña, *Occupied America: The Chicanos Struggle toward Liberation*, pp. 46–50; Webb, *The Texas Rangers*, pp. 175–193; Paul Jacobs and Saul Landau with Eve Pell, *To Serve the Devil*, Vol. 1, *Natives and Slaves*, pp. 233–237; and Michael G. Webster, "Juan N. Cortina: *Defensor de la Raza*," paper delivered before the Texas State Historical Association, March 6, 1973, Austin, Texas. Copy in author's possession.

21. Webster, "Juan N. Cortina," p. 8.

22. Ibid., p. 9; Goldfinch, *Juan N. Cortina*, pp. 17–24. The primary reason for this request was to have all suits pending in local, state, and federal courts in Texas transferred to the courts of the new territory.

23. "Difficulties on the Southwestern Frontier," p. 21.

24. "The Late Attack on Brownsville," special to the New Orleans *Picayune*, October 10, 1859, in ibid., p. 39.

25. Ibid., p. 21.

26. Ibid., p. 39. Cortina's actions inspired his compatriots and frightened Anglos. Consider this report by one Israel B. Bigelow, dated Oct. 23, 1859: "Cortina is not alone in this enterprise—some desperados, with a similar party, last week broke open the jails at Victoria and San Carlos and liberated over one hundred prisoners, who joined them, and who are now en route for Matamoras, murdering and robbing at their pleasure" (ibid., p. 48).

27. Proclamation signed Juan Nepomuceno Cortina, Rancho del Carmen, County of Cameron, September 30, 1859, in ibid., pp. 70–72.

28. Ibid.

29. Proclamation signed Juan Nepomuceno Cortina, Rancho del Carmen, County of Cameron, November 23, 1859, in ibid., pp. 79–82.

30. Ibid.

31. Paredes, *"With His Pistol in His Hand,"* p. 33. The heroes of Border *corridos* (ballads) meet Hobsbawm's primary criterion for social bandits: "As individuals, they are not so much political or social rebels, let alone revolutionaries, as peasants who refuse to submit" (*Bandits*, p. 19). See also Paredes, *A Texas-Mexican Cancionero*, and Paredes, "José Mosqueda and the Folklorization of Actual Events," *Aztlán* 4 (Spring, 1973), 1–29.

32. I have relied on Paredes, *"With His Pistol in His Hand,"* for the account of Gregorio Cortez.

33. Paredes reconstructed this scene from transcripts of the trial.

34. Beeville *Bee*, August 15, 1913, quoted in Paredes, *"With His Pistol in His Hand,"* p. 102.

35. Ibid., p. 125.

36. Paredes, *A Texas-Mexican Cancionero*, pp. 21–45, 57–59, 62–64.

37. St. Clair Griffen Reed, *A History of the Texas Railroads and of Transportation Conditions under Spain and Mexico and the Republic and the State*, pp. 330–333.

38. The best account of the congress is José E. Limón, "El Primero Congreso Mexicanista de 1911: A Precursor to Contemporary Chicanismo," *Aztlán* 5 (Spring and Fall, 1974), 85–106.

39. Sources for *los sediciosos* include "Investigation of Mexican Affairs," *Senate Documents*, 66th Congress, 2nd Session, Document 285, pp. 1214–1324; Paredes, "With His Pistol in His Hand," pp. 132–133; Paredes, *A Texas-Mexican Cancionero*, pp. 32–34; Michael C. Meyer, "The Mexican-German Conspiracy of 1915," *The Americas* 23 (July, 1966), 76–89; Allen Gerlach, "Conditions along the Border, 1915: The Plan de San Diego," *New Mexico Historical Review* 43 (July, 1968), 195–212; James A. Sandos, "The Plan of San Diego: War and Diplomacy on the Texas Border, 1915–1916," *Arizona and the West* 14 (Spring, 1972), 5–24; Webb, *The Texas Rangers*, pp. 477–486; Juan Gómez-Q., "Plan de San Diego Reviewed," in *Chicano: The Evolution of a People*, ed. Robert A. Calvert, Renato Rosaldo, and G. L. Seligmann, Jr., pp. 123–127; and Charles H. Harris III and Louis R. Sadler, "The Plan of San Diego and the Mexican–United States War Crisis of 1916: A Reexamination," *Hispanic American Historical Review* 53 (August, 1978), 381–408.

40. Gómez-Q., "Plan de San Diego," p. 126.

41. Ibid.

42. Ibid.

43. Harris and Sadler, "The Plan of San Diego," p. 385.

44. Ibid., pp. 386–388.

45. Ibid., pp. 389–390, 392–400. Harris and Sadler see the plan as having three phases: the first from January to June, 1915, marked by quiet organization, although U.S. authorities knew of the first plan; the second, from July to October, 1915, marked by a number of raids by *los sediciosos* and retaliation by U.S. authorities; and the third, from March to July, 1916, in which an invasion with some regular Mexican troops was scheduled but was aborted because the U.S. knew too much about it.

46. Webb, *Texas Rangers*, pp. 87, 478. Webb says of this episode that it was "one of which many members of the force have been heartily ashamed." Consider also the following sentence: "The mystery was deepened when the Americans learned that some of their own Mexicans, people who had lived in close harmony with them for years, were joining the raiders" (p. 482). The possessive quality of the sentence and the apparent bewilderment is very like the South's plaintive "but our nigras are happy."

47. Gómez-Q., "Plan de San Diego," p. 126.

48. Pershing was chasing Pancho Villa, unsuccessfully, after his raid on Columbus, New Mexico. According to Paredes, this raid in U.S. territory made Villa a hero to all Mexicans. See *A Texas-Mexican Cancionero*, p. 39.

49. Harris and Sadler use Mexican sources, particularly military telegrams, to present an impressive case for Carranza's role with *los sediciosos*.

50. Harris and Sadler, "The Plan of San Diego," p. 106.

51. A phrase used by Pablo de la Guerra of California in 1856 and by Juan N. Seguín of Texas in 1858 to describe their situations.

## 4. Social Bandits
## and Community Upheavals

1. Kenneth E. Boulding, *The Image; Knowledge in Life and Society*, puts this idea most directly: ". . . behavior depends on the image." Boulding defines image as "subjective knowledge," that which an individual believes to be true. The "socially established structures of meaning" of a people provide them their images with which they respond to and behave in their world. See also Robert F. Berkhoffer, Jr., *A Behavioral Approach to Historical Analysis*.

2. Hobsbawm, *Bandits*, pp. 13–33. The *Water Margin Novel* is set in the thirteenth century and is an eclectic work that was probably written in much its present form in the late fourteenth or fifteenth century. It has been translated into English by Pearl S. Buck, with the title *All Men Are Brothers*.

3. Sources for Tiburcio Vásquez include Bancroft, *California Pastoral*, pp. 651–654, 678–682; Joseph Henry Jackson, *Bad Company: The Story of California's Legendary and Actual Stage-Robbers, Bandits, Highwaymen and Others . . .*, pp. 297–325; Pitt, *Decline of the Californios*, pp. 254–262; Rubén E. López, "The Legend of Tiburcio Vásquez," *Pacific Historian* 15 (Summer, 1971), 20–30; Ernest May, "Tiburcio Vásquez," *Historical Society of Southern California Quarterly* 29 (1947), 123–134.

4. Pitt, *Decline of the Californios*, pp. 69–82, 104–119, 107–180, 256–262; Jackson, *Bad Company*; Bancroft, *California Pastoral*, pp. 642–684; Bancroft, *Popular Tribunals*, Vol. II. J. E. Reynolds, in his introduction to Shinn's *Graphic Description of Pacific Coast Outlaws*, estimates the number of "major" *californio* bandits during this period at well over one hundred, and argues that they were different from other Western outlaws because they were native to the land of their outlawry and could gain sanctuary in the homes of their more peaceful compatriots, "who nevertheless practiced a nativism engendered by resentment toward the *gringo*" (pp. 16–17)—a major characteristic of social bandits.

5. The Truman interview is reproduced in Weber, ed., *Foreigners in Their Native Land*, pp. 227–228. Eugene T. Sawyer, whose coverage of Vásquez was reprinted as *The Life and Career of Tiburcio Vásquez*, and George A. Beers, *Vásquez; or The Hunted Bandit of the San Joaquín*, are the extant accounts of the two *Chronicle* correspondents.

6. See, for example, Anne B. Fisher, *The Salinas: Upside-Down River*, pp. 178–180. Jackson, in *Bad Company*, cites Robert Louis Stevenson's reference to him as "Vásquez, the bandit" in *The Old Pacific Capital* as evidence of his notoriety—Stevenson expected his readers to know who he meant by this brief identification (pp. 299–300).

7. Weber, *Foreigners in Their Native Land*, pp. 227–228.

8. May, "Tiburcio Vásquez," pp. 133–134.

9. Pitt, *Decline of the Californios*, p. 81.

10. Sources for Joaquín Murieta include John Rollin Ridge [Yellow

Bird], The Life and Adventures of Joaquín Murieta, the Celebrated California Bandit; Walter Noble Burns, The Robin Hood of El Dorado: The Saga of Joaquín Murieta; Jackson, Anybody's Gold, pp. 110–120; Jackson, Bad Company, pp. 3–40; Pitt, Decline of the Californios, pp. 69–82; Bancroft, California Pastoral, pp. 245–249; 655–670; excerpt from Richard G. Mitchell, "Joaquín Murieta: A Study of Social Conditions in Early California," (M.A. thesis, University of California at Berkeley, 1927), pp. 39–69, in Furia y Muerte: Los Bandidos Chicanos, ed. Pedro Castillo and Albert Camarillo, pp. 37–51.

11. Caughey, Gold is the Cornerstone, pp. 194–201.

12. Pitt, Decline of the Californios, p. 79.

13. Ibid., pp. 80–82. Bancroft, California Pastoral, calls Harry Love "a Law-abiding desperado": "Harry greatly enjoyed slaying human beings, but he did not like so well to be hanged for it; so he asked the legislature at Sacramento if he might not go out and kill Joaquín" (p. 660).

14. See Paredes, "With His Pistol in His Hand"; Paredes, A Texas-Mexican Cancionero; and Paredes, "José Mosqueda and the Folkorization of Actual Events," Aztlán 4 (Spring, 1973), 1–29.

15. Interviews with Don H. H. Mondragón, La Loma, N.M., February 18, 1972; Don Manuel Lucero, Tecolotito, N.M., February 15, 1972; Don Phil Márquez, Antonchico, N.M., February 15, 18, 1972; Don Miguel Gonzales, La Loma, N.M., February 15, 18, 1972; Doña Pedro Lucero, Antonchico, February 18, 1972. See also Manuel C. de Baca, Vicente Silva and His Forty Thieves.

16. Ibid. In New Mexico, mucho hombre is used more frequently than muy hombre, at least by those whom I interviewed. They also frequently linked "mean man, bad man, brave man" in their accounts and descriptions.

17. One New Mexico historian, who shall remain nameless, refers to Elfego Baca as "that fat fraud." Be that as it may, he is now among the ranks of mexicano heroes, and his exploits are recounted in V. B. Beckett, Baca's Battle; Elfego Baca's Epic Gunfight at 'Frisco Plaza, N.M., 1884, As Reported at the Time, Together with Baca's Own Final Account of the Battle; Fergusson, Rio Grande, pp. 250–256; Kyle S. Crichton, Law and Order Limited: The Rousing Life of Elfego Baca of New Mexico; and Jack Schaefer, Heroes without Glory: Some Goodmen of the Old West, pp. 287–323.

18. Hobsbawm, Bandits, p. 14.

19. Ibid., p. 20.

20. Sources for the "race war" include Pitt, Decline of the Californios, pp. 148–166; Bancroft, Popular Tribunals, Vol. 1, pp. 490–498.

21. Pitt, Decline of the Californios, p. 162.

22. Ibid., p. 154. The period was marked by vigilante activity and frequent rumors of invasions from Mexico or indigenous "revolutions."

23. Ibid., p. 154–155.

24. This was true in New Mexico as well. To New Mexicans, the Civil War was just another attempted Texas invasion, and after the war the expansion of Texas ranching into New Mexico gave the southeastern corner of the territory (and the state) the name "Little Texas"—the counties of which had instituted the "all-white primary" by the twentieth century. See below, Chapter 6.

25. Sources for the Flores War include Bancroft, *California Pastoral*, pp. 675–676; Bancroft, *Popular Tribunals*, Vol. II, pp. 498–505; Cleland, *Cattle on a Thousand Hills*, pp. 91–92; and Pitt, *Decline of the Californios*, pp. 167–180.

26. Pitt, *Decline of the Californios*, p. 167.

27. Pitt makes this point very persuasively. See Ibid., pp. 167–168.

28. Ibid., p. 120.

29. Ibid., pp. 174–175. See also Bancroft, *Popular Tribunals*, Vol. II, for accounts of a *californio* vigilante movement at San Luis Obispo as early as 1851 (pp. 485–486). In *California Pastoral*, Bancroft describes the reaction to a rumored bandit attack on San Diego in 1858 in which nothing happened, but the furor "aptly illustrates the anarchical conditions of affairs in certain portions of the state at that time" (pp. 677–678).

30. See Webb, *The Texas Rangers*, pp. 345–367; C. L. Sonnichsen, *Ten Texas Feuds*, pp. 108–156; or James B. Gillett, *Six Years with the Texas Rangers, 1875–1881*, ed. M. M. Quaife, pp. 136–150, for accounts of the Salt War. See below, Chap. 6, for an account of the Horrell War.

31. Quoted in Pitt, *Decline of the Californios*, p. 82.

32. See Hobsbawm, *Bandits*, pp. 17–19.

## 5. The Maxwell Land Grant:
## A Setting for
## Long-Term Skirmishing

1. Basic sources for the Maxwell Land Grant include Bureau of Land Management, Santa Fe, *Papers Relating to Land Grants in the Office of the Surveyor General of New Mexico* (microfilm publication of the University of New Mexico Library, Albuquerque, 1955–1957; hereafter cited as BLM) Reel 14; Maxwell Land Grant Collection, Special Collections Division, University of New Mexico Library, Albuquerque; *United States v. the Maxwell Land Grant Company, and others, United States Reports*, Vol. 121; William A. Keleher, *Maxwell Land Grant: A New Mexico Item*; Jim B. Pearson, *The Maxwell Land Grant*.

2. Petition of Guadalupe Miranda and Charles Beaubien, BLM, Reel 14. Mexico organized New Mexico as a department in 1836—see Bancroft, *History of Arizona and New Mexico*, p. 311.

3. Pearson, *Maxwell Land Grant*, pp. 3–5; Lawrence R. Murphy, "The Beaubien and Miranda Grant: 1841–1846," *New Mexico Historical Review* 42 (January, 1967), 27–47; Murphy, "Charles H. Beaubien," in *The Mountain Men and the Fur Trade of the Far West: Biographical Sketches of the Subject*, ed. Leroy R. Hafen, Vol. 6, pp. 23–35. Murphy, "Beaubien and Miranda Grant," p. 32 and fn. 26, speculates that the petitioners gave Armijo a hidden one-quarter interest in the grant; Tyler, "Anglo-American Penetration of the Southwest," pp. 325–338, argues that Armijo granted the land for defense purposes: "Though Armijo appeared to show favoritism to wealthy foreigners . . . these grantees promised financial support which the central government had refused to give" (p. 337).

4. Statement of Cornelio Vigil, February 22, 1843, BLM, Reel 14. Some old-timers testified that the boundaries had never been ridden, as sworn to

by Vigil, and by 1869 even people who claimed to have accompanied Vigil admitted that the mounds (cornerstones) no longer existed. Testimony of Jesus Silva, September 19 and October 13, 1877; and testimony of William Brownell, June 12, 1878, BLM, Reel 14.

5. Testimony of Pablo Lucero, et al., March 14, 1844; statement of Charles Beaubien to the Governor of New Mexico, April 15, 1844, BLM, Reel 14; Murphy, "Beaubien and Miranda Grant," pp. 32–34; Sánchez, *Forgotten People*, pp. 49–51.

6. Decision of the Assembly, April 18, 1844, BLM, Reel 14; Murphy, "Beaubien and Miranda Grant," gives the best account of these machinations.

7. Testimony of Jesus Silva, September 19, 1877, BLM, Reel 14.

8. Testimony of William Brownell, June 12, 1878, BLM, Reel 14.

9. Testimony of Christopher Carson, July 28, 1857, BLM, Reel 14.

10. Good sources for exploration include David J. Weber, *The Taos Trappers: The Fur Trade in the Far Southwest, 1540–1846*; Robert Glass Cleland, *This Reckless Breed of Men: The Trappers and Fur Traders of the Southwest*; and William H. Goetzmann, *Exploration and Empire: The Explorer and the Scientist in the Winning of the American West*. See also Charles A. Kenner, *A History of New Mexican–Plains Indian Relations*; and the Martínez-Beaubien debates in BLM, Reel 14.

11. Maxwell Land Grant Settlers Book, Maxwell Land Grant Collection; Meinig, *Southwest*, pp. 27–35; Pearson, *Maxwell Land Grant*, p. 60. The first attempt at an enumeration of residents on the grant was for the *Ninth U.S. Census* (1870). Approximately 1,900 persons lived on the New Mexican portion and some 600 on the 265,000 acres in Colorado (Congress established Colorado's southern boundary in 1861). Utes and Jizarilla Apaches roamed the region at will until 1876, and Maxwell served as Indian agent.

12. F. Stanley [Stanley Crocciola], *The Grant That Maxwell Bought*, pp. 19–37; Pearson, *Maxwell Land Grant*, pp. 9–11; Keleher, *Maxwell Land Grant*, p. 29; and Murphy, "Beaubien and Miranda Grant," pp. 33–36, agree that Maxwell lived on the grant by 1849, but cannot determine when he first settled. Maxwell probably expended time and money trying to colonize the grant before taking up residence on the Rayado in late 1848 or early 1849.

13. Stanley, *Grant That Maxwell Bought*, pp. 19–37; Pearson, *Maxwell Land Grant*, pp. 11–22.

14. Pearson, *Maxwell Land Grant*, pp. 6–7; Murphy, "Beaubien and Miranda Grant," p. 32.

15. Opinion of Surveyor-General William Henry Pelham, Sept. 17, 1857, BLM, Reel 14.

16. "An Act Confirming Certain Private Land Claims in the Territories of New Mexico and Colorado," June 21, 1860 (Claim No. 15), *Statutes at Large, Treaties and Proclamations of the United States of America*, Vol. 12, p. 71.

17. Pearson, *Maxwell Land Grant*, p. 9.

18. Ibid., pp. 12–14.

19. Stanley, *Grant That Maxwell Bought*, pp. 21–37; Keleher, *Maxwell Land Grant*, pp. 25–38; Pearson, *Maxwell Land Grant*, pp. 44–49.

20. Testimony of William Brownell, June 12, 1878; Testimony of Phillip Mould, June 12, 1878; Testimony of William Mercer, June 29, 1878, BLM, Reel 14.

21. Ibid.; Pearson, *Maxwell Land Grant*, pp. 40–54; George Washington Coe, *Frontier Fighter: An Autobiography of George W. Coe Who Fought and Rode with Billy the Kid, as Related to Nan Hillary Harrison*; Agnes Morley Cleveland, *Satan's Paradise, from Lucian Maxwell to Fred Lambert*. According to some miners, Maxwell was not above duplicity. Phillip Mould testified that in 1866, Maxwell suggested that he prospect Ute Creek and offered to grubstake him. Mould said that he avoided Ute Creek as he did not want to "get in trouble with the grant." Maxwell said, swore Mould, that there would be no trouble as "he [Maxwell] had no right or title to Ute Creek whatever," that in fact his western boundary was "no further west than the mouth of Cimarron Canyon" (Affidavit of Phillip Mould, BLM, Reel 14). The affidavits must be handled critically, however, as they were taken after Maxwell's death on behalf of challengers to the company.

22. Testimony of William Brownell, June 12, 1878, BLM, Reel 14.

23. Pearson, *Maxwell Land Grant*, pp. 20–22.

24. Ibid., pp. 52–53.

25. Secretary of the Interior J. D. Cox to the Commissioner of the General Land Office, December 31, 1869, BLM, Reel 14.

26. Secretary of the Interior Columbus Delano to Messers. Barton, Laroque, and McFarland, July 27, 1871, BLM, Reel 14. Delano disagreed with his predecessor but thought that he had to uphold his policy; he referred the "parties to Congressional or such other relief as they may be able to obtain." Some persuasive territorial officials, including the governor, the surveyor general, and the chief justice, convinced the English investors to go ahead; they became the front men for the company in the territory. In addition, J. P. Benjamin, chairman of the Senate committee that had recommended confirmation in 1860, contended that the grant had been confirmed according to Vigil's description and that the title was sound because "it constituted the highest title known to the law of the United States . . . inasmuch as it emanated from the Legislative and Executive Departments together (the law having been approved by the President)." See Opinion of the Honorable J. P. Benjamin, Chairman of the Senate of the United States on Private Land Claims in Favor of the Title of the Maxwell Land Grant and Railway Company, to Their Property in New Mexico and Colorado, Confirmed as Claim No. 15, January 18, 1871, BLM, Reel 14.

27. Commissioner of the General Land Office Willis Drummond to New Mexico Surveyor-General James K. Proudfit, January 28, 1874, BLM, Reel 14. Drummond ordered that "as the claimants have withdrawn their whole deposit [for surveying] and refused to comply with the terms of the decision [by Secretary Cox to choose the site where they wanted their twenty-two square leagues surveyed] you will regard and treat the lands claimed by them as public lands, and extend the public surveys over the same."

28. Pearson, *Maxwell Land Grant*, p. 62.

29. Ibid., pp. 63–65.

30. Ibid., p. 65.

31. *Santa Fe Weekly New Mexican*, January 25, 1875.

32. "The Territory of Elkins," *New York Weekly Sun*, December 22, 1875; "City and Country," Cimarron *News and Press* (copy, n.d., probably November 13, 1875); Rev. M. Mathieson to Mrs. M. E. McPherson, October 4, 1875, all in U.S. Department of the Interior, *Appointment Papers: Territory of New Mexico, 1850–1907* (National Archives Microfilm Publication, Microcopy No. 750; hereafter cited as Int. Dept., *Appt. Papers*), Reel 1.

33. Maxwell Land Grant Settlers Book, Maxwell Land Grant Collection. The company census gives dates of first settlement and length of occupancy for each site listed.

34. Elkins and Catron had been influential in effecting the sale to the English speculators, and they retained active roles. Elkins served as company attorney and became president of the corporate branch in the U.S. in 1873.

35. Testimony taken during McMains's trial and depositions filed on his behalf, Int. Dept., *Appt. Papers*, Reel 1; U.S. Department of Justice, *Appointment Papers: Territory of New Mexico, 1851–1912* (Record Group 60, National Archives, Washington, D.C., hereafter cited as Justice Dept, *Appt. Papers*). McMains was found guilty "in the fifth degree" and fined $300. Judge H. L. Waldo set aside the verdict because it did not specify of what McMains was guilty; he was never retried.

36. Pearson, *Maxwell Land Grant*, pp. 55–71.

37. For example, at a sheriff's tax sale in 1876, an agent for the Ring purchased company land for $16,479.46, and the company had to pay $20,461.85 to regain the property. The company complained that the Ring was trying to condemn company land as public domain, settle a colony of Mormons there, and incite the Pueblo Indians to revolt.

38. Testimony of Frank Springer, August 30, 1877, Int. Dept., *Appt. Papers*, Reel 1.

39. "City and Country," Cimarron *News and Press*, in Int. Dept., *Appt. Papers*, Reel 1.

40. F. Stanley, *The Private War of Ike Stockton*, pp. 47–80; Coe, *Frontier Fighter*, pp. 6–12.

41. Testimony of Frank Springer, August 30, 1877, Int. Dept., *Appt. Papers*, Reel 1.

42. Ibid.

43. Although not entirely. Jesús Arellano was elected an officer of the Squatters' Club in 1873. According to the Settlers Book, Arellano was a modest farmer, even by *mexicano* standards.

44. Testimony of John L. Taylor, August 6, 1877, Int. Dept., *Appt. Papers*, Reel 1.

45. Sánchez, *Forgotten People*, pp. 3–11, 43–52, eloquently describes life for *los hombres pobres* in northern New Mexico, and the Settlers Book supports his picture.

46. Commissioner of the General Land Office J. A. Williamson to New Mexico Surveyor-General Henry M. Atkinson, June 28, 1877, BLM, Reel 14.

47. Pearson, *Maxwell Land Grant*, p. 76.

48. Ibid., p. 79.

49. Subsidiary companies included the Maxwell Cattle Company, the Raton Coal and Coke Company, and the Springer Cement Company. Sale or lease, in some fashion, dated back to Lucian Maxwell; many settlers signed leases in 1879 only to repudiate them later, but these leases added to the precedent of company ownership.

50. Race prejudice probably played as important a part as distance in the desire for a new county: Frank Springer called Colfax one of the only two "American" counties in the territory. Testimony of Frank Springer, August 30, 1877, Int. Dept., *Appt. Papers*, Reel 1.

51. See *Ninth U.S. Census, Tenth U.S. Census, Eleventh U.S. Census.* Enumeration in New Mexico was notoriously imprecise, and there were undoubtedly more residents than the returns indicate. Charting population increases in Colorado is made difficult because the 1880 enumerators did not tabulate by precinct. However, comparing places of nativity in Las Animas County, Colorado, in 1870 and 1880 indicates *mexicano* migration north was still significant. The number increased more than 30 percent between 1870 and 1880.

52. The company does not list employees, and it is doubtful whether residents who had purchased or leased from the company are included.

53. See Map 5 for areas of concentrated settlement.

54. Length of tenure is incomplete, and that given is suspect: the enumerator relied on oral statements either from the settler or a neighbor, and it was in the company's interest to minimize length of occupancy.

55. *Springer Banner*, March 27, 1890. Quoted in Pearson, *Maxwell Land Grant*, p. 132.

56. Castle Rock Park is six or seven miles south and west of Vermejo Park.

57. M. P. Pels, "Report to the Board of Trustees," August, 1890, Maxwell Land Grant Collection.

58. Thomas Donaldson, "The Public Domain," *House Miscellaneous Documents*, 45th, 47th Congress, 2nd Session, vol. xix, Document No. 45, p. 170.

## 6. Violence on the Maxwell and War in Lincoln County: Two Examples of Skirmishing Resistance

1. Pearson, *Maxwell Land Grant*, pp. 88–89; Keleher, *Maxwell Land Grant*, pp. 84–85.

2. Pearson, *Maxwell Land Grant*, pp. 88–90; Keleher, *Maxwell Land Grant*, pp. 81–82. The Squatters' Club of 1881 included one mexicano, Manuel Salazar. Unlike Jesús Arellano, Salazar was a *político* who served as district attorney.

3. Pearson, *Maxwell Land Grant*, pp. 89–91; *United States v. The Maxwell Land Grant Company, et al.*, 121 *United States Supreme Court Reports*, 325. One of the bases for the charge of fraud was the fact that one of the surveyors was John Elkins, brother of Santa Fe Ring kingpin Stephen Elkins, de-

spite Commissioner Williamson's admonition to pick someone "who has no connection or business transactions referrable to the interests of the owners" (Commissioner of the General Land Office J. A. Williamson to New Mexico Surveyor-General Henry M. Atkinson, June 28, 1877, BLM, Reel 14).

4. See, for example, the transcript of the trial of *The Maxwell Land-Grant Company* v. *George Hixenbaugh*, commenced September 26, 1884, in the First District Court, Territory of New Mexico, County of Colfax, in Justice Dept., *Appt. Papers*.

5. Pels, "Report to the Board of Trustees," August, 1890, The Maxwell Land Grant Collection, contained in company attorney Frank Springer's summary of the history and progress of all litigation, including the omnibus suit. The suit was not settled until October 15, 1892. See also Keleher, *Maxwell Land Grant*, pp. 121–125.

6. Secretary of the Territory and Acting Governor Samuel Losch to Secretary of the Interior L. C. Q. Lamar, March 19, 1885; Losch to President Grover Cleveland, March 23, 1885; all in Justice Dept., *Appt. Papers*. James Masterson was a brother of the fabled "Bat" Masterson.

7. Maxwell Land Grant Settlers Book, enumerator's comments; letters of Thomas Boggs to T. A. Schomberg and Harry Whigham, November 23 to December 19, 1887, Maxwell Land Grant Collection.

8. *United States* v. *The Maxwell Land Grant Company, et al.*, 121 *United States Supreme Court Reports*, 325; Pearson, *Maxwell Land Grant*, pp. 94–111.

9. Pels, "Report to the Board of Trustees," August 1885, Maxwell Land Grant Collection.

10. Pearson, *Maxwell Land Grant*, pp. 112–113. McMains kept up the fight for years. See, for example, O. P. McMains to Thomas Richey, September 25, 1892, Boas Long Collection, New Mexico State Record Center and Archives, Santa Fe. The anti-grant forces had help in Santa Fe as Governor Edmund G. Ross and Surveyor General George Julian attacked the "land rings." Julian publicized the New Mexico situation in "Land-Stealing in New Mexico," *North American Review* 145 (July, 1887), 15–30, contending, among other things, that Cox's twenty-two-square-league limitation was still valid.

11. Pels to the Maxwell Land Grant Committee, July 18, 1887, Maxwell Land Grant Collection.

12. Ibid.; and Pearson, *Maxwell Land Grant*, pp. 112–115.

13. Pels to President Grover Cleveland, August 31, 1887, Maxwell Land Grant Collection.

14. Pearson, *Maxwell Land Grant*, p. 117.

15. The company also suffered from a new legal attack. The Interstate Land Company lodged a claim for a portion of the estate, basing its case on an alleged grant received by a London physician in 1832 while he was living in Saltillo, Mexico. The suit reached the Supreme Court, where that body ruled against the plaintiffs.

16. Pels, "Report to the Board of Trustees," August, 1888, Maxwell Land Grant Collection. Pels deployed a force of men under Zeneas Curtis to protect company property and offered a $1,000 reward for information leading to the capture of anyone guilty of the malicious killing of livestock.

17. Pearson, *Maxwell Land Grant*, pp. 123–125.

18. Ibid., pp. 125–127; Maxwell Land Grant Settlers Book, enumerator's comments; and Thomas Boggs to T. A. Schomberg, November 23, 1887, Maxwell Land Grant Collection.

19. L. S. Preston to Pels, August 1, 1887, Maxwell Land Grant Collection; Pearson, *Maxwell Land Grant*, pp. 131–132.

20. Pels, "Report to the Board of Trustees," August, 1890, Maxwell Land Grant Collection; Pearson, *Maxwell Land Grant*, p. 132.

21. Ibid.

22. The verb "force" is from the deputies' account of the incident. See ibid., p. 134.

23. Pearson, *Maxwell Land Grant*, pp. 133–136.

24. Ibid.; Pels, "Report to the Board of Trustees," April, 1891, Maxwell Land Grant Collection.

25. Pels to J. P. Lower and Sons (Denver), May 22, 1891, Maxwell Land Grant Collection.

26. Pels, "Report to the Board of Trustees," August, 1890; April, 1891; September, 1891, Maxwell Land Grant Collection. See below, Chapters 7–9 for a discussion of the San Miguel County disturbances.

27. Maxwell Land Grant Settlers Book, Maxwell Land Grant Collection. For example, Francisco Chaves, to whose house the bloodhounds led the posse, farmed forty acres, ran no livestock, and had improvements valued at only $50 by the company; Juan Antonio Valdez, regarded by the company as its bitterest foe on the Vermejo, had forty acres fenced and ran twenty-eight head of cattle.

28. Pels, "Report to the Board of Trustees," August, 1890, Maxwell Land Grant Collection.

29. This estimation was found on a sheet of scrap paper with the heading "Shryroch and Holdsworth" and was probably written in 1888. R. B. Holdsworth was a lawyer from Trinidad, Colorado, who worked for the company. The remainder of the notes, covering four sheets in all, refer to other settlers on the grant, their holdings and improvements, and, in some cases, their attitudes. Maxwell Land Grant Collection.

Santistevan's suit went to the New Mexico Supreme Court, where he lost on January 3, 1893, and was given three months to vacate the grant. See *Maxwell Land Grant Company v. Jacinto Santistevan, Report of Cases Determined in the Supreme Court of the Territory of New Mexico from January 3, 1893, to August 24, 1895*, pp. 1–5.

30. Pearson, *Maxwell Land Grant*, pp. 141–143.

31. This was a fairly widespread concern among Anglos in New Mexico and is reminiscent of the fears of Anglos in California two decades earlier. See New Mexico Chief Justice Elisha V. Long to U.S. Attorney General A. H. Garland, August 18, 1888, Justice Dept., *Appt. Papers*. Long wrote that it was feared that "the reserve forces on the Mora and Sangre de Cristo grants" would join the anti-grant men on the Maxwell.

32. See, for example, Lamar, *Far Southwest*, pp. 115–162; William A. Keleher, *Violence in Lincoln County, 1869–1881*; Frederick W. Nolan, *The Life and Death of John Henry Tunstall: The Letters, Diaries and Adventures*

*of an Itinerant Englishman;* or Maurice G. Fulton, *History of the Lincoln County War,* ed. Robert N. Mullin.

33. The *comancheros* traded with the Comanches, usually for livestock stolen in Texas. To Texans, this was an evil commerce, and the fact that its practitioners were *mexicanos* did nothing to lessen the Texans' "Remember-the-Alamo" racial attitudes. To New Mexicans, this was just another manifestation of their continuing search for trading opportunities (see Chapter 2), although the fact that Anglo Texans suffered probably did little to discourage them. See J. Evetts Haley, "The Comanchero Trade," *Southwestern Historical Quarterly* 38 (January, 1935), 151–203; or Meinig, *Southwest,* p. 33.

34. Meinig, *Southwest,* pp. 32–35; William A. Keleher, *The Fabulous Frontier: Twelve New Mexico Items,* pp. 29–55; Ninth *U.S. Census* gave Lincoln County a population of 1,686, of which 1,493 had been born in New Mexico; Tenth *U.S. Census* gave the figures as 2,303 and 1,515 respectively. Placitas had been settled in 1849 and Fort Stanton established in 1855.

35. Aurora Hunt, *Major-General James Henry Carleton, 1814–1873: Western Frontier Dragoon;* Chris Emmett, *Fort Union and the Winning of the Southwest,* pp. 256–304.

36. U.S. Department of the Interior, *Indian Appropriations, Records of the Bureau of Indian Affairs,* Record Group 75, National Archives, Washington, D.C. (hereafter cited as N.A.), Vols. 19, 22; U.S. Department of War, *Register of Contracts, 1871–1876,* Record Group 92, N.A.

37. Keleher, *Violence in Lincoln County,* pp. 51–53, 57; "Petition to the Commissioner of Indian Affairs," January 11, 1869; L. G. Murphy to Colonel Campbell, May 4, 1871; "Report of Major Price to the Department of Missouri," December 19, 1873; F. C. Godfrey to Hon. S. (?) P. Christienay, September 6, 1878; E. A. Hoyt to the Secretary of the Interior, December 28, 1878; and J. Isaacs and J. A. Coe to President Rutherford B. Hayes, June 22, 1878, all in Int. Dept., *Appt. Papers,* Reels 1, 12, and 13. Between his discharge in 1866 and 1869, Murphy served as sutler at Fort Stanton.

38. Keleher, *Fabulous Frontier,* pp. 56–66; Nolan, *John Henry Tunstall,* pp. 233–234.

39. Gilberto Espinosa, Tibo J. Chaves, and Carter M. Ward, *El Rio Abajo,* p. 174; Lamar, *Far Southwest,* pp. 112–116.

40. Phillip J. Rasch, "The Horrell War," *New Mexico Historical Review* 31 (July, 1956), 223–231; Fulton, *Lincoln County War,* pp. 19–31.

41. Keleher, *Violence in Lincoln County,* p. 13. See also Rasch, "The Horrell War"; Nolan, *John Henry Tunstall,* p. 188; and Keleher, *Violence in Lincoln County,* pp. 13–15.

42. Rasch, "The Horrell War," p. 229.

43. Ibid.

44. *Santa Fe New Mexican,* January 27, 1874, quoted in Oliver La Farge, *Santa Fe: The Autobiography of a Town,* pp. 87–88.

45. Keleher, *Violence in Lincoln County,* p. 14.

46. Nolan, *John Henry Tunstall,* p. 188. Patrón's father, Isidro, was one of the four killed when the Horrells raided a *mexicano* wedding.

47. Frank Warner Angel to Secretary of the Interior Carl Schurz, October

3, 1878, "Supplemental and Final Report as to the Charges Against S. B. Axtell," Int. Dept., *Appt. Papers*, Reel 1; Governor Lew Wallace, telegram to the Hon. C. Schurz, October 5, 1878, Int. Dept., *Appt. Papers*, Reel 3; Keleher, *Violence in Lincoln County*; Nolan, *John Henry Tunstall*. Motives for alliances were complex; many small ranchers on the Pecos fought on the Murphy-Dolan side because the firm had helped them fight Chisum's attempt to drive them from the range in 1877.

48. The Lincoln County violence was the last in a long line of problems for Axtell that included the first Colfax County War and charges that he was secretly preparing New Mexico for an invasion by Mormons from Utah. For Wallace and Patrón's action, see Lew Wallace, "Report to the Legislative Assembly, 1879"; Juan B. Patrón to Governor Wallace, January 10, 1880, a statement of the "services of his command," Lew Wallace Papers, New Mexico State Records Center and Archives, Santa Fe. According to Patrón, thirty-nine men served with his command, of which only seven were *americanos*.

49. Copy in A. A. McSween and B. H. Ellis to President Rutherford B. Hayes, April 26, 1878, Int. Dept., *Appt. Papers*, Reel 1. The meeting took place on April 24.

50. "Report of the Governor of New Mexico," in "Report of the Secretary of the Interior," *House Executive Documents*, 50th Congress, 2nd Session, Vol. 12, Document 1; Charles L. Sonnichsen, *Tularosa: The Last Frontier of the West*, p. 7.

51. A. A. Breece to Governor Ross, June 22, 1885, Governor Edmund G. Ross Papers, New Mexico State Records Center and Archives, Santa Fe (hereafter cited as Ross Papers).

52. Ibid.

53. H. Milne to Governor Ross, June 25, 1885, Ross Papers.

54. J. A. Alcock to Governor Ross, June 25, 1885, Ross Papers.

55. Walter Prescott Webb, *The Great Plains*, pp. 227–241.

56. John Y. Hewitt to Governor Ross, June 23, 1885, Ross Papers. For contemporary cattlemen's points of view, see Charles Eddy, "The Livestock Industry of New Mexico," n.d.; letters of Eddy to Governor Ross, September 25, 1885; and J. C. Lea to Governor Ross, July 8, 1885, in Ross Papers.

57. Quoted in the *Santa Fe New Mexican*, May 18, 1906, a staunchly Republican newspaper that accompanied the piece with the pointed comment that the editor could not understand why "Spanish" Democrats did not switch to the Republican Party.

58. Acting Commissioner of the General Land Office William Walker to Governor Ross, August 14, 1885, Ross Papers. Reprinted as part of a broadside in both Spanish and English. Walker is quoting Ross's letter back to him.

59. Governor Ross to E. Carlisle, February 9, 1886, Ross Papers.

60. Governor Ross to Don Jesús Luna, April 8, 1886, Ross Papers.

## 7. Trouble in San Miguel County

1. District Attorney Miguel Salazar to Governor L. B. Prince, August 3, 1890, Governor L. Bradford Prince Papers, Governors' Papers, New Mexico State Records Center and Archives, Santa Fe (hereafter cited as Prince Pa-

pers); O. D. Barrett, "Report to General (Benjamin) Butler," July 26, 1890, U.S., Department of the Interior, *Territorial Papers: Territory of New Mexico, 1851–1912* (N.A. Microfilm Publication, Microcopy No. 364; hereafter cited as *Terr. of N.M.*), Reel 8.

The *Las Vegas Daily Optic* identified Frank Quarrell as "a young Englishman who came to this country a few years back to try ranching" (May 20, 1889), and reported that William W. Rawlins was renouncing his English citizenship despite his troubles with Las Gorras Blancas (May 26, 1890). There is some confusion as to whether Rawlins and Quarrell were partners. Special Agent R. B. Rice to Surveyor-General George Julian, May 24, 1889, BLM, Reel 15, identifies the property as owned by a partnership, and the San Miguel County Assessment Rolls for 1890 (New Mexico State Records Center and Archives, Santa Fe) identify Rawlins and Quarrell as joint owners.

2. The term White Cap was applied to many vigilante groups in the late nineteenth century. Richard Maxwell Brown, "Historical Patterns of Violence in America," in *Violence in America*, ed. Graham and Gurr, contends that white-cappism was a spontaneous movement for the moral regulation of poor whites and ne'er-do-wells of the rural American countryside (p. 65). Governor Prince thought that Las Gorras Blancas had accepted and translated an English label: "What its real name is, we do not know, but the people of Las Vegas soon called the members 'White Caps,' and judging from the signature to their 'platform' . . . they have accepted that title." Draft of "Report to the Secretary of the Interior John W. Noble," n.d., Prince Papers.

3. "San Miguel Del Bado Grant (decree)," BLM, Reel 15; Donaldson, "The Public Domain," pp. 554–561; Olen E. Leonard, *The Role of the Land Grant in the Social Organization and Social Processes of a Spanish-American Village in New Mexico*, p. 168. See also Map 7 and Appendix C.

4. See Appendix C.

5. "Las Vegas Grant (decree)," BLM, Reel 15; Moorhead, *New Mexico's Royal Road*, pp. 104–105; Perrigo, *The American Southwest*, p. 164.

6. Parrish, *Charles Ilfeld Company*, is the best account of economic development in San Miguel County. Ilfeld, a Prussian Jew, came to New Mexico in the 1860s and settled at Las Vegas in 1867. Las Vegas was on the stage route to Santa Fe, was near Fort Union, and served as a "gathering point for wool, hides and metals from the Mesilla and Pecos valleys and from Grant County" (p. 20).

7. Governor Prince to Secretary of the Interior John W. Noble, August 11, 1890, Prince Papers; Secretary Noble to the Commissioner of the General Land Office, December 5, 1891, BLM, Reel 15.

8. Ibid.

9. Frank C. Ogden, John K. Martin, and J. B. Allen to Terence V. Powderly, National Grand Master Workman, August 8, 1890, Prince Papers.

10. Robert H. Weibe, *The Search for Order, 1877–1920*, pp. 66–69, gives a convenient synopsis of the Knights of Labor. For more detail, see Norman J. Ware, *The Labor Movement in the United States: 1860–1895*; or Terence V. Powderly, *The Path I Trod*, ed. Harry J. Carman, Henry David, and Paul N. Gutherie.

11. Quoted in Governor Prince to Secretary Noble, August 8, 1890, Prince Papers.

12. Ibïd.

13. Thomas B. Catron to Stephen B. Elkins, April 18, 1890, Thomas B. Catron Collection, University of New Mexico Archives, Albuquerque (hereafter cited as Catron Collection). Long's opinion infuriated Catron, the most successful land grant lawyer in New Mexico. Catron called it bad law and charged that Long had illegally altered the dates in the trial record in order to have his opinion included in the official transcript. Catron was especially afraid that the principle of community grants might be extended to other grants throughout the area.

14. Governor Prince to Secretary Noble, August 11, 1890, Prince Papers.

15. Ogden et al. to Powderly, August 8, 1890, Prince Papers.

16. J. B. Snouffer to Governor Prince, September 7, 1890, Prince Papers.

17. José Y. Luhan to Governor Prince, July 25, 1890; O. D. Barrett, "Report to General Butler," July 26, 1890; C. J. Mills to Governor Prince, July 19 and 22, 1890; all in Prince Papers. See also Robert W. Larson, "The White Caps of New Mexico: A Study of Ethnic Militancy in the Southwest," *Pacific Historical Review* 44 (May, 1975), 171–185; and Andrew Bancroft Schlesinger, "Las Gorras Blancas, 1889–1891," *Journal of Mexican-American History* 1 (Spring, 1971), 87–143.

18. Clerk of the Court Miguel A. Otero, Jr., to Governor Prince, August 9, 1890, Prince Papers.

19. District Attorney Salazar and Probate Judge Manuel C. de Baca expressed themselves clearly and vehemently in letters to Prince (Salazar to Prince, July 23, 1890, and January 12, 1891; de Baca to Prince, October 10, 1891, all in Prince Papers). County Assessor Eugenio Romero did not write Prince, but he had been, and was to be, the victim of attacks. Sheriff Lorenzo López served all indictments placed in his hands and published a long letter in the *Optic* (August 16, 1890) defending his actions. He had been attacked several times, finally yielding to the raiders' demands, and he became a leader of the new party produced by the turmoil (see below, Chapter 8). Long's relationship with Robert Johnson is revealed in a series of letters collected in the Boas Long Collection. They reveal a business relationship and friendship of at least two years' standing before the beginning of the trial.

20. *Las Vegas Daily Optic*, October 23, 1889. The paper is quoting Long with approval.

21. Ibid., November 2, 1889.

22. Ibid., November 9 and 12, 1889.

23. Ibid., November 25, 1889.

24. Ibid.

25. Clerk of the Court Otero to Governor Prince, August 9, 1890, and Ogden et al. to Powderly, August 8, 1890, Prince Papers.

26. Sheriff Lorenzo López, telegram to Governor Prince, December 11, 1889, Prince Papers.

27. *Optic*, December 16, 1889. Long probably set bail so low because the county could not afford to house so many prisoners until spring, because jailing the accused would have been a hardship for their families, and because the strength of popular support for the fence cutters told Long, the Democratic politician, that harsh treatment was imprudent.

28. Ibid., August 31, 1889.

29. Ibid., November 21 and 25, 1889. The paper stressed the desire for farmers: "We don't want cattle ranchers."

30. Ibid., March 11, 1890. The paper initially estimated the group distributing the platforms at over 300 horsemen. The next day (March 12, 1890) it revised the estimate to 122, but emphasized that all were armed with rifles.

31. See Appendix D for "Nuestra Platforma."

32. Salazar to Governor Prince, July 23, 1890, Prince Papers.

33. *Optic*, March 7, 1890; O. D. Barrett, "Report to General Butler," June 26, 1890, Prince Papers.

34. Ibid.

35. *Optic*, May 20, 1890; summary of *Territory v. Romaldo Fernández*, *Terr. of N.M.*, Reel 8; Barrett, "Report to General Butler"; Salazar to Prince, July 23, 1890, Prince Papers; E. V. Long to E. A. Fiske, August 27, 1890, Boas Long Collection.

36. See Appendix E for a list of White Cap attacks.

37. General Benjamin Butler to Secretary Noble, July 9, 1890, [John] Barney to U.S. Senator J. H. Plumb [Kansas], August 3, 1890, *Terr. of N.M.*, Reel 8; Noble to Prince, May 19, 1890, Prince Papers.

38. *Optic*, August 1, 1890.

39. *Albuquerque Democrat*, clipping, n.d., *Terr. of N.M.*, Reel 8. Territorial Republicans thought the time right for statehood and had hammered out a state constitution in 1889. Prince had journeyed to Washington to lobby for an enabling act. Unfortunately for statehood advocates, the constitution was rejected by the electorate in 1890. See Robert W. Larson, *New Mexico's Quest for Statehood*, pp. 147–168.

40. Prince had spent April and May in Washington. Upon his return to New Mexico, he was stricken by "nervous prostration." Noble, reacting to the reports about the White Caps, wrote Prince on July 28, 1890, "[I] assure you that the country is somewhat aroused about the condition of affairs . . . you will be expected to exert your full force to the suppression of these matters in order to meet the expectations of the Executive." Prince Papers.

41. Prince to Noble, August 11, 1890, Prince Papers. Prince also issued a proclamation calling on "all good citizens to aid the civil authorities in the discovery of the perpetrators of these crimes." August 1, 1890, *Terr. of N.M.*, Reel 8.

42. Félix Martínez, for example, delivered the following speech: "The people are to rise in their might and squelch the land-grabber as well as the fence cutter. The fence cutting which has begun with the plea of giving the people their rights has, in the heat of passion, been permitted to go too far. The fence cutters in their lawlessness must be suppressed, but the land thief in his evil doing must be put down, and put down to stay." *Optic*, August 18, 1890.

43. Prince to Noble, August 20, 1890, Prince Papers.

44. Ibid.; Prince to Noble, August 11, 1890; Noble to Prince, August 19, 1890, Prince Papers.

45. Bennet Milton Rich, *The Presidents and Civil Disorder*; Weibe, *Search for Order*; "Report of the U.S. Attorney General," *House Executive Documents*, 54th Congress, 2nd Session, Vol. 23, Document 9, pp. 154–160.

46. New Mexico Chief Justice James O'Brien to Prince, August 22, 1890, Prince Papers.

## 8. Las Gorras Blancas:
## A Secret Gathering
## of Fence Cutters

1. Although *mexicanos* were not the only threatened group who destroyed fences, the idea of taking direct action against the obvious cause of problems and the mode of organization used to do so were authentic products of *mexicano* culture.

2. For histories of the Western cattle industry, including the introduction of barbed wire and the loss of the public domain, see Lewis Atherton, *The Cattle Kings*; E. E. Dale, *The Range Cattle Industry*, 2nd ed.; Gene Gressley, *Bankers and Cattlemen*; Ernest Staples Osgood, *The Day of the Cattlemen*; James Orin Oliphant, *On the Cattle Ranges of Oregon*; and Webb, *The Great Plains*.

3. "San Miguel del Bado Grant," BLM, Reel 15; Leonard, *Role of the Land Grant*, pp. 167–172; Map 7; and Appendix C.

4. "San Miguel del Bado Grant," BLM, Reel 15.

5. Ibid. An *acequia* is an irrigation ditch. Usually a community dammed a river or stream above the village and constructed an *acequia madre*—main ditch—from which the network of *acequias* to the fields ran.

6. Documents relating to New Mexico land grants are most conveniently found in the BLM microfilm publication of the University of New Mexico Library. Donaldson, "The Public Domain," provides a detailed summary of the situation in New Mexico before the White Cap outbreaks. For a comprehensive analysis of land tenure in northern New Mexico from Oñate to the twentieth century, see Dunbar, "Land Tenure in Northern New Mexico."

7. Beck and Haase, *Historical Atlas of New Mexico*, Maps 2–5.

8. Milton C. Nahm, *Las Vegas and Uncle Joe*, p. 44.

9. One area that could produce a surplus was on the Antonchico Grant just below Antonchico. The *acequia madre* serving the communities from El Llano to Bado de Juan Pais measures twelve miles, waters about 2,100 acres, and is still in use.

10. Sources on the nature of *mexicano* life in the nineteenth century include Leonard, *Role of the Land Grant*; Susan Shelby McGoffin, *Down the Santa Fe Trail*, rev. ed., ed. Stella M. Drumm; Sánchez, *Forgotten People*; Meinig, *Southwest*; Horgan, *Great River*; Gregg, *Commerce on the Prairies*; and interviews in Las Vegas and on the Antonchico Grant.

11. Interview with Tony Márquez, Las Vegas, February 14, 1972. Don Márquez was born and raised at La Loma (formerly El Llano) on the Antonchico Grant, and characterized the attitudes of his relatives.

12. Fabiola C. de Baca, *We Fed Them Cactus*, gives a good description of the life of a ranchero in San Miguel County during the nineteenth century.

13. J. Evetts Haley, "The Comanchero Trade"; Meinig, *Southwest*, p. 33.

14. Quoted in Leonard, *Role of the Land Grant*, p. 185.

15. Leonard points out that El Cerrito, the principal village of his study, was one of these rarities.

16. Holmes, *Politics in New Mexico*, pp. 21–31.

17. Interview with Juan Pena, Las Vegas, February 14, 1972.

18. The Antonchico and Las Vegas Grants were settled by migrants from the San Miguel del Bado Grant. The patterns of settlement are often reflected by place names. For example, the village of San Ignacio, eighteen miles northwest of Las Vegas, was first called Tecoloteños or "natives of Tecolote." T. M. Pearce, ed., *New Mexico Place Names*, pp. 163–164.

19. Conflicts were usually over the use of common resources. El Cerrito's single faction gained its ascendancy by defeating another in a feud that grew out of encroachment on "traditional" grazing areas on the common land. The twelve-mile *acequia madre* between El Llano and Bado de Juan Pais, an example of intervillage cooperation, also created conflicts at times when a village thought that it was not receiving its fair share of water. This tendency toward conflict was also reflected in the chapters of Las Gorras Blancas, who fought each other on occasion in disagreements over which fences to cut. See further discussion of the themes of conflict and cooperation later in Chapter 8.

20. Interview with H. H. Mondragón, La Loma, February 18, 1972. Don Mondragón used the phrase that the people "wanted only to live" repeatedly. He went to great pains to explain why the Antonchico Grant had been reduced to one-third its original size, stressing among other things that many people thought that they had "too much land," that leaders of the grant were stealing from the people, and that politicians throughout the territory (and state) had conspired against them. Yet, at the same time that he listed these factors that imply a passivity on the part of most grant residents, he described incident after incident of violent resistance.

21. One such law, passed by the territorial legislature in 1887 and vetoed by Governor Ross, was entitled "An Act Regulating Practices in Cases of Torts . . ." Its purpose was to aid land grant speculators by, in Ross's words, "revolutionizing the rules of evidence." The bill placed the burden of proof on the defendant so that a speculator had only to claim a tract and then sit back, confident that the occupant(s) would have neither the knowledge nor the funds necessary to challenge the claim. Ross's veto concluded that "this Bill is a cunningly devised scheme of robbery and directed mainly to the eviction of the occupants of this class of land grants for the benefit of doubtful claimants." Ross, "Special Message," February 28, 1887, *Terr. of N.M.*, Reel 8.

22. It is arguable that collusion to defraud was the norm rather than the exception in New Mexico during the territorial years. A striking example of the habits of federal officials is the case of Pueblo Indian Agent Pedro Sánchez and Santa Fe Land Registrar Max Frost. The two obtained nineteen fraudulent homestead entries near Sweetwater in Colfax County, patented in Sánchez's name. As one observer commented: "It must have taken more hands and heads than one to have so thoroughly and handsomely bunched these Homesteads, and to have put them in such solid shape!" Special Agent Paris Folsum to Commissioner of Indian Affairs J. D. C. Atkins, May 18, 1885,

Int. Dept., *Appt. Papers*, Reel 10. Westphall, *The Public Domain in New Mexico*, is the basic study of land policy and problems in New Mexico Territory.

23. This was true throughout the territory. Many powerful New Mexican families, like the Lunas and the Oteros of the Rio Abajo, did not attain their eminence until the Anglos provided markets and business opportunities. See Espinosa, Chaves, and Ward, *Rio Abajo*. In San Miguel County, almost all the *ricos*—Romero, López, Manzanares—fenced acreage on the grants. Even future advocates of the people like Félix Martínez were guilty of fencing and were visited by the White Caps. See clipping of dispatch to the Chicago *Inter-Ocean*, n.d., *Terr. of N.M.*, Reel 8.

24. *Eleventh Census of the United States*.

25. Governor Prince to Secretary of the Interior John W. Noble, August 11, 1890, Prince Papers.

26. O. D. Barrett, "Report to General Butler," July 26, 1890, *Terr. of N.M.*, Reel 8.

27. Barrett to Butler, July 21, 1890, *Terr. of N.M.*, Reel 8.

28. James O'Brien to Governor Prince, July 30, 1890, Prince Papers.

29. Benjamin H. Reed, *Illustrated History of New Mexico*, pp. 760–761, 767.

30. Miguel Salazar to Governor Prince, July 23, 1890, Prince Papers.

31. Numbers involved in fence cutting incidents ranged from one to more than two hundred. Very few villages in San Miguel County exceeded four hundred in total population (or one hundred total votes cast in any election). Newspaper accounts and letters frequently describe seeing the White Caps ride, and all accounts emphasize two points: the large number of participants and the fact that they came from several villages. One interviewee described witnessing the White Caps ride by his house when he was a boy of fourteen. The column passed two-by-two, and he claimed that while men were still passing his house, the leaders had reached the Pecos River, a distance of not less than three-quarters of a mile. Even allowing for memory's blurring by time, that is an impressive number of men. Other interviewees recounted similar descriptions. Interviews with Don Eduardo Montaño, Don and Doña Antonio Ruiz, Antonchico, February 18, 1972; and Don Francisco Sena, Las Vegas, February 11, 1972.

32. Don Sena described the use of homemade whistles as signaling devices, and others agreed. Don Román Ortega of Antonchico also stated that whistles were used to scare informers: hearing a whistle blow in the darkness outside his house was usually enough to still an informer's tongue; if not, bullets would follow. Interview with Don Román Ortega, February 18, 1972.

33. Ogden et al. to Powderly, August 8, 1890, Prince Papers. They date Herrera's commission in 1888 and call it a renewal. Herrera responded to allegations like the above in a letter printed in the *Optic* on April 9, 1890. He admitted that he had left Las Vegas in 1866, but would say no more about the matter as he didn't want to hurt the reputation of an innocent lady. He also denied any connection with the White Caps, although he did acknowledge his connection with the Knights and his support of community rights on the Las Vegas Grant. Robert W. Larson has interviewed several of Herrera's de-

scendants and while they could offer little precise information about the White Cap agitation, they reaffirmed these general assertions. See Larson, "The White Caps of New Mexico."

34. See below, Chapter 9.

35. Interviews with Don H. H. Mondragón, Don Miguel Gonzales, Don George Jarramillo, Don Manual Lucero, and Doña Pedro Lucero, Antonchico Grant, February 15 and 18, 1972. This close correlation between the Knights and the White Caps probably did not hold true to the same extent in other parts of the county, especially in Las Vegas.

36. For a history of the Knights of Labor, see Ware, *The Labor Movement in the United States*; Powderly, *The Path I Trod*; and Weibe, *Search for Order*.

37. Larson, "The White Caps of New Mexico," argues that the "organization of the White Caps was due to the initiative of one man, Juan José Herrera" (p. 175) and concludes: "He acted as a vital link, having apparently been exposed to the rising discontent of Anglo working class people while living away from New Mexico and introducing many of their tactics for bringing about change upon his return" (p. 185). While I agree with Larson that Herrera "acted as a vital link," I disagree with his argument that linkage was between *los pobres* and Anglo labor tactics. With the possible exception of the platform and the wage demands, the tactics were the same as those used by *mexicanos* both before and after the White Cap disturbances, both in New Mexico and elsewhere in the Southwest. Herrera was a "vital link" because he used the Knights to link disaffected communities in common action against a common enemy using well-understood, time-honored tactics. Herrera provided coordination, not innovation, and the distinction is important. For to see Herrera as an innovator is to imply that *mexicanos* were passive and unable to defend themselves, a characterization that runs counter to my understanding of *mexicano* history in the nineteenth century.

38. See Lamar, *Far Southwest*, p. 84.

39. The stipulation about defense in the San Miguel Grant decree indicates the awareness of the problem. The first settlers in the Las Vegas area received a grant in 1823, but Indian attacks drove them from their holdings. See "The Las Vegas Grant," BLM, Reel 15; and Pearce, ed., *New Mexico Place Names*, pp. 12–13 and 85–86. See also Perrigo, *The American Southwest*, pp. 152–153 and 231–234.

40. Leonard, *Role of the Land Grant*, pp. 134–135. Don Mondragón also spoke of family feuds that persist into the present.

41. Recounted to me by Don Miguel Gonzales, grandson of the El Llano *mayordomo* and himself the *mayordomo* of the same portion of the *acequia*, now called La Loma.

42. F. LeDuc to Governor Prince, July 22, 1890, Prince Papers.

43. This seems likely because of the variation between membership of the Knights and of Las Gorras Blancas. Charles Siringo, a Pinkerton detective employed by the territory to investigate the Ancheta shooting in 1891 (see below, Chapter 9), thought that the White Caps were involved and joined the Knights to make contact. He reported that although he had gained the confidence of some White Caps, particularly Nicanor Herrera, through the Knights, the two organizations were not identical (Siringo to Governor

Prince, April 3, 1891, Prince Papers). There was a very close overlap in membership in Siringo's analysis, and his reports also indicate the ethnic identification of the New Mexican Knights: "They are very cautious about taking in new American members" (Siringo to Mr. B. [Bartlett], n.d., Prince Papers).

44. A hypothesis proposed by Tony Márquez of Las Vegas and given further credence by additional interviews. For example, the leader of Las Gorras Blancas at El Llano was Manuel Gonzales, the *mayordomo* of the *acequia*, while the leader in Antonchico, two miles up river, was Nicolás Ortega, remembered as a bad, mean man. The El Llano and Antonchico White Caps disagreed as to whether to cut the fence of Candelario Rael, which stood between the two communities, and faced each other with leveled rifles. Interviews with the grandsons of the two leaders, Miguel Gonzales and Román Ortega, February 18, 1872. The latter said that his grandfather won and that the fence was not cut. But Don Eduardo Martínez wrote Governor Prince that Don Rael's fence had been cut. Don Eduardo Martínez to Governor Prince, July 9, 1890, Prince Papers.

## 9. El Partido del Pueblo Unido

1. O. D. Barrett to General Benjamin Butler, July 21, 1890, *Terr. of N.M.*, Reel 8.

2. See Appendix G.

3. Herrera could have been no younger than his teens in 1866, when he was accused of adultery, making forty his minimum age in 1890. Miguel A. Otero, Jr., said that he was too old to lead the White Caps in 1895. See Miguel A. Otero, Jr., *My Life on the Frontier*, Vol. 2, p. 267.

4. From a campaign biography in *La Voz del Pueblo* (Las Vegas), October 24, 1892. See also Appendix G.

5. Thomas B. Catron to Stephen B. Elkins, August 15, 1892, Catron Papers.

6. *La Voz*, October 24, 1892; Otero, *My Life*, Vol. 2, p. 224.

7. *Optic*, October 22, 1890.

8. Ibid.

9. Ibid., November 5, 1890.

10. See election returns in Appendix F, Tables F-1–F-4. See also Robert J. Rosenbaum, "*Mexicano* versus *Americano*: A Study of Hispanic-American Resistance to Anglo-American Control in New Mexico Territory, 1870–1900" (Ph.D. diss., University of Texas at Austin, 1972), pp. 229–248, for a discussion of the 1890 returns.

11. *La Voz*, March 7 and 14 and July 4, 1891.

12. "Report of the U.S. Attorney General," *House Executive Documents*, 58th Congress, 3rd Session, Document 9, Vol. 32, pp. 95–109. See also Bradfute, *Court of Private Land Claims*.

13. *La Voz*, July 4, 1891.

14. Ibid., April 25, 1891.

15. Ibid., July 11, 1891.

16. S. A. Clark to Governor Prince, May 30, 1892, Prince Papers. Clark wrote: "One of my neighbors is obliged to pay $65 per year to the man that

cut his fence down last year, with the understanding that he is not to cut it up again."

17. Ibid. According to Clark: "The Mexicans boast of cutting fences and burning houses and if we say anything of taking it to court they tell us that the Jury (sic) do not take Americans' testimony and the Mexicans do not testify against each other."

18. The Society of Gentlemen of Law and Order and Mutual Protection.

19. For an example of the confusion in the minds of Anglos, see a telegram and supporting letter from Governor W. T. Thornton to Secretary of the Interior Hoke Smith (September 29 and October 1, 1894) requesting U.S. troops to remain at Fort Marcy in Santa Fe to aid local authorities. Thornton implied that the burning of the capitol building, the murder of Santa Fe County Sheriff Francisco Chaves, the attempted assassination of territorial Senator Ancheta, the Vicente Silva gang, and every other example of the era of "unprecedented crime" that had occurred under his predecessor's administration were the products of a secret organization of *mexicanos*. *Terr. of N.M.*, Reel 8.

20. *La Voz*, March 28, 1891.

21. Ibid.

22. Ibid., October 3, 1891. Armijo wrote: "I say frankly that the perfidy and ill-breeding with which one of those members [of the Law and Order Society] has treated me, had led me to believe that there is no equality or good intentions in the organization," and he concluded that the People's Party "is the party that brings well-being and happiness to the people."

23. The newspaper *Estandarte* of Springer (Colfax County) reported that Eugenio Romero, *jefe* of "*las gorras negras*," was in the county trying to organize a chapter of the Law and Order Society. Reprinted in *La Voz*, April 2, 1892. See also *La Voz*, September 19, 1891, and August 13, 1892. Herrera owned *El Defensor* for about a year (June, 1891, to May, 1892), and he often wrote for the paper, although Pedro G. de Lama was the editor. Herrera maintained his residence in San Miguel County, however.

24. The full sentence, translated, reads: "It is necessary that we are all united, all as brothers, all as members of the same family." *La Voz*, May 16, 1891.

25. Robert W. Larson, *New Mexico Populism: A Study of Radical Protest in a Western Territory*, pp. 34–47, dates the formation of the party from 1888, when it served as a front for the Republican Party (p. 43). As the turmoil of 1890 created realignments, and as it switched its territorial support to the Democrats, it ought more properly be dated from 1890. Larson calls it "the first genuine People's Party in the territory" (p. 47). That may be true, but that does not mean it was part of the National People's Party. The San Miguel party, like the Knights of Labor, became increasingly an ethnically oriented, native New Mexican organization. *La Voz* might print Populist boilerplate, but Anglo Populists were increasingly excluded from the party, particularly because they wanted community grant land declared public domain and opened for settlement.

26. *La Voz*, November 25, 1893.

27. Ibid., December 16, 1893.

28. "With the arrogance of a king." See *La Voz*, November 21 and 28 and December 5, 1891.

29. Ibid., June 4 and 11, 1892. The Borregos led an organization known as the Button Gang. The assassination of Chaves was mentioned repeatedly during the campaign of 1892. The trial of the Borregos lasted until 1897, with Catron fighting very hard for acquittal. Catron's enthusiasm led him to excesses—even by his standards—and disbarment proceedings were brought against him that very nearly succeeded.

30. *La Voz*, October 1, 8, 15, 22, and 29 and November 5, 1892.

31. See Appendix F, Tables F-5 and F-6; and Rosenbaum, "*Mexicano versus Americano*," pp. 282–293.

32. *La Voz*, September 16 and 30, 1893.

33. Ibid., October 14, 1893.

34. Ibid., June 2 and 9, 1894.

35. "Fatal Encounter"; "Bloody Tragedy."

36. Patricio Maes had been hanged from the bridge over the Gallinas River by his fellow gang members, as they suspected him of being on the verge of turning informer. His murder inaugurated the gradual unveiling of Silva's operations. See de Baca, *Vicente Silva*, pp. 16–18. See also *La Voz*, October 29, 1892.

37. *La Voz* and *El Independiente*, July 28, 1894.

38. The Pullman Strike had occurred shortly before, and railroad workers in New Mexico, especially at Raton, had launched violent attacks against the Santa Fe Railroad. Troops had been dispatched from Fort Marcy to quell the disturbances. See "Report of the U.S. Attorney General" (1896), *House Executive Documents*, Document 9, pp. 154–166; U.S. Adjutant-General's Office, *Returns from U.S. Military Posts, 1800–1916* (N.A. Microfilm Publication, Microcopy No. 617), Reel 747, Returns from Fort Marcy; *La Voz* and *El Independiente*, July 28, 1892.

39. "Between the american and mexican." *La Voz* and *El Independiente*, July 28 and August 4, 1894.

40. Ibid.; *Optic*, July 27, 1894.

41. *La Voz* and *El Independiente*, August 4, 1894.

42. *El Independiente*, August 11, 1894.

43. Ibid., August 11, 18, and 25, 1894.

44. Ibid., and *La Voz*, September 8 and 15, 1894.

45. Ibid.

46. See Rosenbaum, "*Mexicano versus Americano*," pp. 310–318.

47. *La Voz*, April 13, 1895.

48. *El Independiente*, December 29, 1894; *La Voz*, September 7, 1895.

49. *La Voz*, April 28, 1894; "Report of the U.S. Attorney General" (1905), pp. 95–109; Leonard, *Role of the Land Grant*, pp. 104–106.

50. Secretary of the Interior Noble to Commissioner of the General Land Office, December 5, 1891, BLM, Reel 15.

51. "An Act to Provide for the Management of the Las Vegas Grant, and for Other Purposes." C. B. No. 101, approved March 12, 1903, *Acts of the Legislative Assembly of New Mexico: Thirty-Fifth Session*, Chapter 47, pp. 72–74. In an interview, Donaldo Martínez, then district attorney of San Miguel

County, said that the board of trustees consisted of three Anglos and two Hispanos. The Hispanos were Eugenio Romero and Lorenzo Delgado, whom
Martínez called "*bandidos.*" Martínez also used the phrase "house lots and
garden plots." Interview, February 11, 1972.

52. *La Voz*, October 27, 1894.

53. Interviews with Don and Doña Antonio Ruiz, Don Eduardo Montaño, Antonchico, February 15, 1972; Don Pedro Gallegos, Delia, February
18, 1972; Doña Pedro Lucero and Don George Jarramillo, Antonchico, February 18, 1972; Don H. H. Mondragón, La Loma, February 18, 1972.

54. Interviews with Don Manuel Lucero, Tecolotito, February 15, 1972;
Don H. H. Mondragón, La Loma, February 18, 1972.

## 10. The Sacred Right
## of Self-Preservation

1. Gurr, *Why Men Rebel*, pp. 155–192.

2. By assimilating individuals, I mean those who try to "pass," not
those who are working toward their group's integration, which would be
adaptive self-preservation according to my terminology. My intergroup/
intragroup polarity is not foolproof: according to it, Indians would not fight
for self-preservation, although I believe that they did (and do).

3. *La Voz*, May 16, 1891.

4. Ibid., January 31, 1891.

5. Ibid., September 16, 1893.

6. Ibid., May 16, 1891.

7. See Lawrence C. Goodwyn, *Democratic Promise: The Populist Moment in America*, for a national perspective of the Populists and Larson, *New
Mexico Populism*, for a territorial history. I do not agree with Larson's equating El Partido del Pueblo with the Populists, but the two movements did re-
inforce each other to some degree in the country.

8. The schism was dramatically evidenced in 1894 when T. B. Mills,
one of the Anglos active in El Partido at its formation, received only 105
votes in the county as the Populist candidate for delegate-in-Congress.

9. Most evident in the lower vote totals that they received.

10. "To educate a child is to lose a good shepherd." Espinosa, Chaves,
and Ward, *Rio Abajo*, p. 59.

11. See *La Voz*, October 27, 1894, for the exception and the paper's
explanation.

12. The best work on the Penitentes is Weigle, *Brothers of Light, Brothers of Blood*.

13. See, for example, James D. McBride, "The *Liga Protectora Latina*: A
Mexican-American Benevolent Society in Arizona," *Journal of the West* 14
(October, 1975), 82–90; Weber, ed., *Foreigners in Their Native Land*, pp.
216–217.

14. Pitt, *Decline of the Californios*, pp. 181–194.

15. George L. Wyllys to Governor Ross, August 8, 1886, Ross Papers.
Wyllys reported that the organization was "not as bad as we had feared," and
gave its title as the Association of the Brotherhood for the Protection of the
Rights and Privileges of the People of New Mexico.

16. La Voz, March 26, 1892.

17. Ibid., March 19, 1892.

18. Ibid., March 12 and April 30, 1892.

19. Reprinted in La Voz, April 2, 1892.

20. Weber, Foreigners in Their Native Land, p. 217.

21. Paredes, "With His Pistol in His Hand," pp. 87–94. Cruz died in 1903 and his place was taken by Colonel F. A. Chapa, editor and publisher of El Imparcial of San Antonio, who carried on until the pardon.

22. Juan Gómez-Q., "The First Steps: Chicano Labor Conflict and Organizing, 1900–1920," Aztlán 3 (Spring, 1972), 13–49; Weber, Foreigners in Their Native Land, pp. 218–219.

23. Farewell Address, by the Reverend Pedro Grado, quoted in Weber, Foreigners in Their Native Land, pp. 249–251; italics in original. See also Limón, "El Primero Congreso Mexicanista."

24. See Abraham Hoffman, Unwanted Mexican Americans in the Great Depression: Repatriation Pressures, 1929–1939.

25. Juan Gómez-Q., in "The First Steps," argues that mexicano urbanization began much earlier than is generally held to be the case, and a number of works in progress address the historical roots of urbanization. However, as a generalization that characterizes the major differences between the nineteenth and twentieth centuries, this is still sound.

26. Higham, Strangers in the Land.

27. Robert A. Cuéllar, "A Social and Political History of the Mexican American Population of Texas, 1929–1963," (M.A. thesis, North Texas State University, 1969); McWilliams, North from Mexico; Acuña, Occupied America; Tony Castro, Chicano Power: The Emergence of Mexican America.

28. Cuéllar, "A Social and Political History," pp. 55–61.

29. Ibid., pp. 75–89; Castro, Chicano Power, pp. 148–182, 215–227.

30. I have in mind here the kind of process described by E. P. Thompson, The Making of the English Working Class.

31. "Hispanics: A Major Minority," Austin American-Statesman, February 26, 1979.

32. Terms first developed by Ferdinand Tönnes in the 1880s. A Gemeinschaft is a society into which people are born and to which they belong, therefore, because they are the same "kind" of people. A Gesellschaft is a society in which the bonds are voluntary and based on the rational pursuit of self-interest.

33. PIGS stands for Poles, Irish, Italians, Greeks, Germans, Slavs, Swedes, and so forth. See Novak, The Rise of the Unmeltable Ethnics.

34. These considerations range from things like bilingual education and those Indian reservations that have enjoyed success (to a degree) by Indian terms, to the black nationalists' idea of separate states within the national boundaries.

35. Many groups, in other words, are expressing the same point of view that James Baldwin made about the situation of Afro-Americans in his Notes of a Native Son.

36. See Gurr, Why Men Rebel, pp. 155–231. I have hardly done justice to Gurr's theoretical work with this simplistic explanation.

37. See Hobsbawm, Bandits, pp. 21–23, 51.

38. Hobsbawm, "Peasants and Politics."

39. Gurr, *Why Men Rebel*, p. 11. Turmoil for Gurr is "relatively spontaneous, unorganized political violence with substantial popular participation, including violent political strikes, riots, political clashes, and localized rebellions."

40. Hobsbawm, *Bandits*, p. 16.

41. Ibid., pp. 90–93; Eric Wolf, *Peasant Wars of the Twentieth Century*, pp. 35–37.

42. See John Womack, Jr., *Zapata and the Mexican Revolution*. His description of Zapata being chosen by the elders of Anenecuilco to lead them in a time of crisis (pp. 3–9) points out the difference between banditry and community resistance quite graphically.

43. Hugh Davis Graham, "The Paradox of American Violence: A Historical Appraisal," in *Collective Violence*, ed. James F. Short, Jr., and Marion E. Wolfgang, pp. 201–209.

44. David M. Potter, *People of Plenty: Economic Abundance and the American Character*, presents an interesting study on the role that abundance has played in United States history.

45. The best works about Tijerina are Richard Gardner, *¡Grito! Reies Tijerina and the New Mexico Land Grant War of 1967*; Peter Nabokov, *Tijerina and the Courthouse Raid*; and Patricia Bell Blawis, *Tijerina and the Land Grants: Mexican Americans in Struggle for Their Heritage*.

# Bibliography

## Primary Sources

### Archives

Assessment Rolls, San Miguel County, 1890. New Mexico State Records Center and Archives, Santa Fe.

Bureau of Land Management, Santa Fe. *Papers Relating to Land Grants in the Office of the Surveyor General of New Mexico.* Microfilm Publication of the University of New Mexico Library, Albuquerque, 1955–1957.

Catron, Thomas B., Collection. Special Collections Division, University of New Mexico Library, Albuquerque.

Governors' Papers. New Mexico State Records Center and Archives, Santa Fe. Herbert J. Hagerman, Jr. (Governor, 1906–1907); Miguel A. Otero, Jr. (Governor, 1897–1906); L. Bradford Prince (Governor, 1889–1893); Edmund G. Ross (Governor, 1885–1889); William T. Thornton (Governor, 1893–1897); Lew Wallace (Governor, 1879–1881).

Long, Boas, Collection. New Mexico State Records Center and Archives, Santa Fe.

Maxwell Land Grant Collection. Special Collections Division, University of New Mexico Library, Albuquerque.

Otero, Miguel A., Jr., Papers. Special Collections Division, University of New Mexico, Albuquerque.

Secretaries of the Territory Papers. New Mexico State Records Center and Archives, Santa Fe. Lorian Miller (Secretary, 1893–1897); William G. Ritch (Secretary, 1873–1884).

U.S. Adjutant-General's Office. *Returns from U.S. Military Posts, 1800–1916.* National Archives Microfilm Publication, Microcopy No. 617.

U.S. Department of the Interior. *Appointment Papers: Territory of New Mexico, 1850–1907.* National Archives Microfilm Publication, Microcopy No. 750.

———. *Indian Appropriations, Records of the Bureau of Indian Affairs.* Record Group 75, National Archives, Washington, D.C.

———. *Territorial Papers: Territory of New Mexico, 1851–1912.* National Archives Microfilm Publication, Microcopy No. 364.

U.S. Department of Justice. *Appointment Papers: Territory of New Mexico, 1851–1912.* Record Group 60, National Archives, Washington, D.C.

U.S. Department of State. *Territorial Papers: New Mexico Territory, 1851–1872.* National Archives Microfilm Publication, Microcopy No. T-17.

U.S. Department of War. *Register of Contracts, 1871–1876.* Record Group 92, National Archives, Washington, D.C.

———. *Station Books.* Record Group 92, National Archives, Washington, D.C.

Vigil, Donaciano, Collection. New Mexico State Records Center and Archives, Santa Fe.

### Public Documents

"An Act Confirming Certain Private Land Claims in the Territories of New Mexico and Colorado," June 21, 1860. *Statutes at Large, Treaties and Proclamations of the United States of America,* Vol. 12, edited by George D. Sanger. Boston: Little, Brown and Co., 1893.

"An Act to Provide for the Management of the Las Vegas Grant, and for other Purposes," March 12, 1903. *Acts of the Legislative Assembly of New Mexico: Thirty-Fifth Session.* Santa Fe: New Mexico Printing Co., 1903.

"Difficulties on the Southwestern Frontier." *House Executive Documents,* 36th Congress, 1st Session, Document 52. Washington, D.C.: Thomas H. Ford, Printer, 1860.

Donaldson, Thomas. "The Public Domain." *House Miscellaneous Documents,* 45th, 47th Congress, 2nd Session, Document 19. Washington, D.C.: Government Printing Office, 1884.

"Investigation of Mexican Affairs." *Senate Documents,* 66th Congress, 2nd Session, Document 285. Washington, D.C.: Government Printing Office, 1920.

*Maxwell Land Grant Company v. Jacinto Santistevan. Report of Cases Determined in the Supreme Court of the Territory of New Mexico from January 3, 1893 to August 24, 1895,* Charles H. Gildersleeve, Reporter. Columbia, Missouri: E. W. Stephens, 1897.

*The New Mexico Blue Book, or State Official Register.* Compiled by Antonio Lucero, Secretary of State. Santa Fe: Antonio Lucero, 1915.

"Report of the Governor of New Mexico." In "Report of the Secretary of the Interior." *House Executive Documents,* 50th Congress, 2nd Session, Document 1. Washington, D.C.: Government Printing Office, 1889.

———. *House Executive Documents,* 51st Congress, 2nd Session, Document 1. Washington, D.C.: Government Printing Office, 1891.

———. *House Executive Documents,* 52nd Congress, 1st Session, Document 1. Washington, D.C.: Government Printing Office, 1892.

*Report of the National Advisory Commission on Civil Disorders.* New York: Bantam Books, 1968.

"Report of the U.S. Attorney General." *House Executive Documents,* 54th Congress, 2nd Session, Document 9. Washington, D.C.: Government Printing Office, 1896.

———. *House Executive Documents,* 58th Congress, 3rd Session, Document 9. Washington, D.C.: Government Printing Office, 1905.

"Treaty of Guadalupe Hidalgo." *Senate Executive Documents,* 30th Congress, 1st Session, Document 60. Washington, D.C.: Wendall and Van Benthenson, 1848.

"Troubles on the Texas Frontier." *House Executive Documents*, 36th Congress, 1st Session, Document 81. Washington, D.C.: Thomas H. Ford, Printer, 1860.
United States Bureau of the Census. *Seventh Census of the United States* (1850).
———. *Eighth Census of the United States* (1860).
———. *Ninth Census of the United States* (1870).
———. *Tenth Census of the United States* (1880).
———. *Eleventh Census of the United States* (1890).
———. *Twelfth Census of the United States* (1900).
United States v. the Maxwell Land Grant Company, and others. *United States Supreme Court Reports*, Vol. 121. J. C. Bancroft Davis, Reporter. New York: Banks and Brothers, 1887.

### Interviews
Dwight Durán. Las Vegas, February 11, 13, 14 and 18, 1972.
Pedro Gallegos. Delia (Antonchico Grant), February 18, 1972. Miguel Gonzales, interpreter.
Miguel Gonzales. La Loma (Antonchico Grant), February 15 and 18, 1972.
George Jarramillo. Antonchico (Antonchico Grant), February 18, 1972. Miguel Gonzales, interpreter.
Manuel Lucero. Tecolotito (Antonchico Grant), February 15, 1972. Miguel Gonzales, interpreter.
Doña Pedro Lucero. Antonchico (Antonchico Grant), February 18, 1972. Miguel Gonzales, interpreter.
Phil Márquez. Antonchico (Antonchico Grant), February 15 and 18, 1972.
Tony Márquez. Las Vegas, February 14, 1972.
Donaldo Martínez. Las Vegas, February 11, 1972.
H. H. Mondragón. La Loma (Antonchico Grant), February 18, 1972.
Eduardo Montaño. Antonchico (Antonchico Grant), February 15, 1972. Miguel Gonzales, interpreter.
Eloys Montoya. Las Vegas, February 15 and 18, 1972.
Román Ortega. Antonchico (Antonchico Grant), February 18, 1972. Miguel Gonzales, interpreter.
Juan Pena. Las Vegas, February 14, 1972.
Antonio Ruiz and Doña Ruiz. Antonchico (Antonchico Grant), February 15, 1972. Miguel Gonzales, interpreter.
Camilo Sais. Antonchico (Antonchico Grant), February 18, 1972. Miguel Gonzales, interpreter.
Francisco Sena. Las Vegas, February 11, 1972. Dwight Durán, interpreter.
Cristóbal Trujillo. Las Vegas, February 11 and 12, 1972.

### Newspapers
*Chloride* [N.M.] *Black Range*, 1886–1890.
*El Defensor del Pueblo* (Albuquerque), 1891–1892.
*El Independiente* (Las Vegas), 1894–1895.
*Eureka* (Las Vegas), January, 1880.
*Las Vegas Daily Optic*, 1881, 1886–1894.
*La Voz del Pueblo* (Las Vegas), 1891–1895.

New York Times, 1886–1894.
Santa Fe New Mexican, 1872–1894, 1903.

### Books and Articles

Abert, James William. Abert's New Mexico Report, 1846–1847. Albuquerque: Horn and Wallace, 1962.
Arny, William F. M. Interesting Items Regarding New Mexico: Its Agricultural, Pastoral, and Mineral Resources, People, Climate, Soil, Scenery, Etc. Santa Fe: Manderfield and Tuckerman, 1873.
Avery, A. Handbook and Travelers Guide of New Mexico and Durango, Colorado: For Tourists, Miners, Capitalists, and Emigrants. Denver: C. Price and Co., 1881.
Beckett, V. B. Baca's Battle; Elfego Baca's Epic Gunfight at 'Frisco Plaza, N.M., 1884, As Reported at the Time, Together with Baca's Own Final Account of the Battle. Houston: Stagecoach Press, 1962.
Beers, George A. Vásquez; or The Hunted Bandit of the San Joaquín. New York: R. M. Dewitt, 1875.
Bell, Thomas W. A Narrative of the Capture and Subsequent Sufferings of the Mier Prisoners in Mexico, Captured in the Cause of Texas, Dec. 26, 1842, and Liberated Sept. 16, 1844. DeSoto County, Mississippi: R. Morris and Co., 1845.
Bliss, Charles R. New Mexico. Boston: Frank Wood, Printer, 1879.
Brevoort, Elias. New Mexico: Her National Resources and Attractions, Being a Collection of Facts, Mainly Concerning Her Geography, Climate, Population, Schools, Mines and Minerals, Etc. Santa Fe: Elias Brevoort, 1874.
Clever, Charles P. New Mexico: Her Resources, Her Necessities for Railroad Communication in the Atlantic and Pacific States, Her Great Culture. Washington, D.C.: McGill and Withers, 1868.
Coe, George Washington. Frontier Fighter: An Autobiography of George W. Coe Who Fought and Rode with Billy the Kid, as Related to Nan Hillary Harrison. Boston: Houghton Mifflin Co., 1934.
Coe, Wilbur. Ranch on the Ruidoso: The Story of a Pioneer Family in New Mexico, 1871–1968. New York: Alfred A. Knopf, 1968.
Cooke, Phillip St. George. The Conquest of New Mexico and California in 1846–1848: An Historical and Personal Narrative. New York: Putnam's Sons, 1878.
Cozzens, Samuel Woodworth. The Marvelous Country; or Three Years in Arizona and New Mexico. Boston: Lee and Shepard, 1876.
Curry, George. George Curry, 1861–1947: An Autobiography. Edited by H. B. Hening. Albuquerque: University of New Mexico Press, 1958.
Davis, William H. H. El Gringo; or New Mexico and Her People. New York: Harper and Brothers, 1857.
De Baca, Manuel C. Vicente Silva and His Forty Thieves. Translated by Lane Kauffman. Washington, D.C.: Edward McLena, 1947.
Defouri, James H. Historical Sketch of the Catholic Church in New Mexico. San Francisco: McCormick Brothers, Printers, 1887.
Eickemeyer, Rudolf. Letters from the Southwest. New York: J. J. Little Co., 1894.
Emory, William H. Notes of a Military Reconnaissance. Introduction and

notes by Ross Calvin. Albuquerque: University of New Mexico Press, 1951.

Frost, Max, and Paul F. Walter, eds. *Land of Sunshine: A Handbook of the Resources, Products, Industries and Climate of New Mexico.* Santa Fe: New Mexican Printing Co., 1906.

Garrard, Lewis. *Wah-to-Yah and the Taos Trail.* Norman: University of Oklahoma Press, 1955.

Gibson, George Rutledge. *Journal of a Soldier under Kearny and Doniphan.* Edited by Ralph P. Bieber. Glendale, California: Arthur H. Clark Co., 1935.

Gillett, James B. *Six Years with the Texas Rangers, 1875–1881.* Edited by M. M. Quaife. First published, 1921. New Haven: Yale University Press, 1963.

Green, Thomas J. *Journal of the Texican Expedition against Mier.* New York: Harper and Brothers, 1845.

Gregg, Josiah. *Commerce of the Prairies.* 2 vols. New York: J. B. Lippincott Co., 1962.

Julian, George W. "Land-Stealing in New Mexico." *North American Review* 145 (July, 1887), 15–30.

Kendall, George Wilkins. *Narrative of the Texas Santa Fé Expedition Comprising a Description of a Tour through Texas and across the Great Southwestern Prairies, the Comanche and Caygua Huntinggrounds with an Account of the Sufferings from Want of Food, Losses from Hostile Indians, and Their March, as Prisoners, to the City of Mexico.* First published, 1844. Austin: Steck Co., 1935.

Linn, John J. *Reminiscences of Fifty Years in Texas.* First published, 1883. Austin: Steck Co., 1935.

McColl, George A. *Letters from the Frontiers.* Philadelphia: J. B. Lippincott Co., 1868.

McCutchan, Joseph D. *Mier Expedition Diary: A Texan Prisoner's Account.* Edited by Joseph Milton Nance. Austin: University of Texas Press, 1978.

McGoffin, Susan Shelby. *Down the Santa Fe Trail.* Rev. ed. Edited by Stella M. Drumm. New Haven: Yale University Press, 1962.

Meline, James F. *Two Thousand Miles on Horseback, Santa Fe and Back: A Summer Tour through Kansas, Nebraska, Colorado, and New Mexico, in the Year 1866.* New York: Hurd and Houghton, 1867.

Menual, John. *New Mexico and Its Claims, Briefly Presented by the Commissioner from the Presbytery of Santa Fe to the General Assembly of 1881.* Laguna, New Mexico: Laguna Mission Press, 1881.

Nicholl, Edith M. *Observations of a Ranchwoman in New Mexico.* New York: Macmillan Co., 1898.

Otero, Miguel A., Jr. *My Life on the Frontier.* Vol. 1. New York: Press of the Pioneers, 1934.

———. *My Life on the Frontier.* Vol. 2. Albuquerque: University of New Mexico Press, 1939.

———. *The Real Billy the Kid.* New York: Rufus Rockwell Wilson, 1936.

Powderly, Terence V. *The Path I Trod.* Edited by Harry J. Carman, Henry David, and Paul N. Gutherie. New York: Columbia University Press, 1940.

Ridge, John Rollin [Yellow Bird]. *The Life and Adventures of Joaquín Murieta, the Celebrated California Bandit*. First published, 1854. Norman: University of Oklahoma Press, 1955.

Ryus, William H. *The Old Santa Fe Trail*. Fort Davis, Texas: Frontier Book Co., 1968.

Seguín, Juan. *Personal Memoirs of Juan A. Seguín, from the Year 1834 to the Retreat of General Woll from the City of San Antonio, 1842*. San Antonio: The Ledger Book and Job Office, 1858. Typescript in Barker Library, University of Texas at Austin.

Shinn, Charles Howard. *Graphic Description of Pacific Coast Outlaws*. Los Angeles: Western Lore Press, 1958.

———. *Mining Camps: A Study in Frontier Government*. 1st ed., 1884. New York: Alfred A. Knopf, 1948.

Siringo, Charles A. *A Cowboy Detective: A True Story of Twenty-Two Years with a World-Famous Detective Agency*. Chicago: W. B. Conkey Co., 1912.

## Secondary Sources

### Books

Acuña, Rodolfo F. *Occupied America: The Chicanos Struggle toward Liberation*. San Francisco: Canfield Press, 1972.

———. *Sonoran Strongman: Ignacio Pesqueria and His Times*. Tucson: University of Arizona Press, 1974.

Adams, Richard Newbold. *Energy and Structure: A Theory of Social Power*. Austin: University of Texas Press, 1975.

Almaráz, Félix D., Jr. *Tragic Cavalier: Governor Manuel Salcedo of Texas, 1808–1813*. Austin: University of Texas Press, 1971.

Arendt, Hannah. *On Revolution*. New York: Viking Press, 1963.

Atherton, Lewis. *The Cattle Kings*. Bloomington: Indiana University Press, 1961.

Bancroft, Hubert Howe. *California Pastoral*. San Francisco: The History Co., 1888.

———. *History of Arizona and New Mexico, 1530–1888*. San Francisco: The History Co., 1889.

———. *History of California*. Vols. I–IV. San Francisco: A. L. Bancroft, 1884–1890.

———. *History of the Northern Mexican States and Texas*. San Francisco: A. L. Bancroft and Co., 1884.

———. *Popular Tribunals*. 2 vols. San Francisco: The History Co., 1887.

Barker, Eugene C. *The Life of Stephen F. Austin, Founder of Texas, 1793–1836: A Chapter in the Westward Movement of the Anglo-American People*. Nashville: Cokesbury Press, 1926.

———. *Mexico and Texas, 1821–1835*. Dallas: P. L. Turner Co., 1928.

Barth, Fredrik, ed. *Ethnic Groups and Boundaries: The Social Organization of Cultural Difference*. Boston: Little, Brown and Co., 1970.

Beck, Warren A. *New Mexico: A History of Four Centuries*. Norman: University of Oklahoma Press, 1962.

———, and Ynez D. Haase. *Historical Atlas of New Mexico*. Norman: University of Oklahoma Press, 1969.

Berkhoffer, Robert F., Jr. *A Behavioral Approach to Historical Analysis.* New York: Free Press, 1969.

Blawis, Patricia Bell. *Tijerina and the Land Grants: Mexican Americans in Struggle for Their Heritage.* New York: International Publishers, 1971.

Bolton, H. E. *Texas in the Middle Eighteenth Century.* Berkeley: University of California Press, 1915. Reprint, Austin: University of Texas Press, 1970.

Boulding, Kenneth E. *The Image: Knowledge in Life and Society.* Ann Arbor: Ann Arbor Paperbacks, University of Michigan Press, 1961.

Bradfute, Richard Wells. *The Court of Private Land Claims.* Albuquerque: University of New Mexico Press, 1975.

Brayer, Herbert O. *Pueblo Indian Land Grants of the "Rio Abajo," New Mexico.* Albuquerque: University of New Mexico Press, 1939.

————. *William Blackmore: A Case Study in the Economic Development of the West.* 2 vols. Denver: Bradford-Robinson, 1949.

Brinton, Crane. *The Anatomy of Revolution.* New York: W. W. Norton and Co., 1938.

Brown, Lorin W., Charles L. Briggs, and Marta Weigle. *Hispano Folklife of New Mexico: The Lorin W. Brown Federal Workers' Project Manuscripts.* Albuquerque: University of New Mexico Press, 1978.

Brown, Richard Maxwell. *Strain of Violence: Historical Studies of American Violence and Vigilantism.* New York: Oxford University Press, 1975.

Browning, Harley L., and S. Dale McLemore. *A Statistical Profile of the Spanish-Surname Population of Texas.* Austin: Bureau of Business Research, University of Texas, 1964.

Buck, Pearl S. *All Men Are Brothers.* First published in 1933. New York: Grove Press, 1957.

Burns, Walter Noble. *The Robin Hood of El Dorado: The Saga of Joaquín Murieta.* New York: Coward-McCann, 1932.

Calvin, Ross. *Sky Determines: An Interpretation of the Southwest.* Albuquerque: University of New Mexico Press, 1965.

Canales, José T. *Juan N. Cortina, Bandit or Patriot?* San Antonio: Artes Gráficas, 1951.

Carter, Harvey L. *"Dear Old Kit": The Historical Christopher Carson.* Norman: University of Oklahoma Press, 1968.

Casteñada, Carlos E. *Our Catholic Heritage in Texas.* 6 vols. Austin: Von Boeckmann-Jones Co., 1936–1950.

Castillo, Pedro, and Albert Camarillo, eds. *Furia y muerte: Los bandidos chicanos.* Los Angeles: Aztlán Publications, UCLA, 1973.

Castro, Tony. *Chicano Power: The Emergence of Mexican America.* New York: Saturday Review Press, 1974.

Caughey, John W. *California: A Remarkable State's History.* 3rd ed. Englewood Cliffs, New Jersey: Prentice-Hall, 1970.

————. *Gold is the Cornerstone.* Berkeley: University of California Press, 1948.

————, and Laree Caughey. *California Heritage: An Anthology of History and Literature.* Los Angeles: Ward Ritchie Press, 1962.

Chávez, Fray Angelico. *Origins of New Mexico Families in the Spanish Colonial Period.* Santa Fe: Historical Society of New Mexico, 1954.

Clarke, Dwight L. *Stephen Watts Kearny, Soldier of the West.* Norman: University of Oklahoma Press, 1961.
Cleland, Robert Glass. *The Cattle on a Thousand Hills: Southern California, 1850–1880.* 2nd ed. San Marino, California: Huntington Library, 1951.
———. *The Irvine Ranch of Orange County, 1810–1950.* San Marino, California: Huntington Library, 1952.
———. *This Reckless Breed of Men: The Trappers and Fur Traders of the Southwest.* New York: Alfred A. Knopf, 1950.
Cleveland, Agnes Morley. *Satan's Paradise, from Lucian Maxwell to Fred Lambert.* Boston: Houghton Mifflin Co., 1952.
Coan, Charles F. *A History of New Mexico.* 3 vols. Chicago and New York: American Historical Society, 1925.
Conner, Seymour V. *Adventure in Glory.* Austin: Steck-Vaughn, 1963.
Crichton, Kyle S. *Law and Order Limited: The Rousing Life of Elfego Baca of New Mexico.* Glorietta, New Mexico: Rio Grande Press, 1969.
Dale, E. E. *The Range Cattle Industry.* 2nd ed. Norman: University of Oklahoma Press, 1960.
De Baca, Fabiola C. *We Fed Them Cactus.* Albuquerque: University of New Mexico Press, 1954.
De La Garza, Rudolph O., Z. Anthony Kruszewski, and Tomás A. Arcinega. *Chicanos and Native Americans: The Territorial Minorities.* Englewood Cliffs, New Jersey: Prentice-Hall, 1973.
De Voto, Bernard. *The Year of Decision, 1846.* Boston: Little, Brown and Co., 1943.
Díaz, Albert James. *A Guide to the Microfilm Papers Relating to New Mexico Land Grants.* Albuquerque: University of New Mexico Press, 1960.
Donnelly, Thomas C. *The Government of New Mexico.* Albuquerque: University of New Mexico Press, 1953.
Dunham, Harold H. *Government Handout.* Ann Arbor: Edwards Brothers, 1941.
Dusenberry, William. *Mexican Mesta: Administration of Ranching in Colonial Mexico.* Urbana: University of Illinois Press, 1963.
Edmondson, Munro S. *Los Manitos: A Study of Institutional Values.* New Orleans: Tulane University Press, Middle American Research Institute, 1957.
Ellison, William Henry. *A Self-Governing Dominion: California, 1849–1860.* Berkeley: University of California Press, 1950.
Emmett, Chris. *Fort Union and the Winning of the Southwest.* Norman: University of Oklahoma Press, 1965.
Espinosa, Gilberto, Tibo J. Chaves, and Carter M. Ward. *El Rio Abajo.* Belen, New Mexico: Pampa Print Shop, n.d.
Faulk, Odie B. *A Successful Failure.* Austin: Steck-Vaughn Co., 1965.
Fergusson, Harvey. *Rio Grande.* New York: William Morrow Co., Apollo Editions, 1967.
Fisher, Anne B. *The Salinas: Upside-Down River.* New York: Farrar and Rinehart, 1945.
Forbes, Jack D. *Apache, Navajo and Spaniard.* Norman: University of Oklahoma Press, 1960.

Friedrich, Paul. *Agrarian Revolt in a Mexican Village*. Englewood Cliffs, New Jersey: Prentice-Hall, 1970.

Fulton, Maurice G. *History of the Lincoln County War*. Edited by Robert N. Mullin. Tucson: University of Arizona Press, 1968.

Ganaway, Loomis Morton. *New Mexico and the Sectional Controversy*. Albuquerque: University of New Mexico Press, 1944.

García, F. Chris. *Chicano Politics: Readings*. New York: MSS Information Corporation, 1973.

Gardner, Richard. ¡*Grito! Reies Tijerina and the New Mexico Land Grant War of 1967*. New York: Harper Colophon Books, 1971.

Geertz, Clifford. *The Interpretation of Cultures*. New York: Basic Books, 1973.

Gibson, Arrel M. *The Life and Death of Colonel Albert Jennings Fountain*. Norman: University of Oklahoma Press, 1965.

Goetzmann, William H. *Exploration and Empire: The Explorer and the Scientist in the Winning of the American West*. New York: Alfred A. Knopf, 1967.

Goldfinch, Charles W. *Juan N. Cortina, 1824–1892: A Re-Appraisal*. Brownsville: Bishop's Print Shop, 1950.

Gonzales, Nancie L. *The Spanish-Americans of New Mexico: A Heritage of Pride*. Albuquerque: University of New Mexico Press, 1969.

Goodwyn, Lawrence C. *Democratic Promise: The Populist Moment in America*. New York: Oxford University Press, 1976.

Goss, Helen Rocco. *The California White Cap Murders: An Episode in Vigilantism*. Santa Barbara, California: Lawton and Alfred Kennedy, 1969.

Graham, Hugh Davis, and Ted Robert Gurr, eds. *Violence in America: Historical and Comparative Perspectives*. New York: New American Library, 1969.

Greever, William S. *Arid Domain: The Santa Fe Railway and Its Western Grant*. Stanford: Stanford University Press, 1954.

Gressley, Gene. *Bankers and Cattlemen*. New York: Alfred A. Knopf, 1966.

Grivas, Theodore. *Military Governments in California, with a Chapter on Their Prior Use in Louisiana, Florida and New Mexico*. Glendale, California: Arthur H. Clarke Co., 1963.

Gurr, Ted Robert. *Why Men Rebel*. Princeton: Princeton University Press, 1970.

Hafen, Leroy R., ed. *The Mountain Men and the Fur Trade of the Far West: Biographical Sketches of the Subject*. 10 vols. Glendale, California: Arthur H. Clarke Co., 1965–1972.

Hallenbeck, Cleve. *Land of the Conquistadores*. Caldwell, Idaho: Claxton Printers, 1950.

Hawgood, John A. *America's Western Frontiers: The Exploration and Settlement of the Trans-Mississippi West*. New York: Alfred A. Knopf, 1967.

Herskovits, Melville J. *Cultural Relationism: Perspectives in Cultural Pluralism*. Edited by Frances Herskovits. New York: Vintage Books, 1973.

Higham, John. *Strangers in the Land: Patterns of American Nativism, 1860–1925*. 2nd ed. New York: Atheneum, 1971.

Hill, Lawrence Francis. *José de Escandón and the Founding of Nuevo San-*

tander: *A Study in Spanish Colonization*. Columbus: Ohio State University Press, 1926.

Hobsbawm, Eric. *The Age of Revolution: 1789–1848*. New York: World Publishing Co., 1962.

———. *Bandits*. New York: Dell Publishing Co., 1969.

———. *Social Bandits and Primitive Rebels*. New York: Free Press, 1959.

Hoffman, Abraham. *Unwanted Mexican Americans in the Great Depression: Repatriation Pressures, 1929–1939*. Tucson: University of Arizona Press, 1974.

Hollon, W. Eugene, *Frontier Violence: Another Look*. New York: Oxford University Press, 1974.

Holmes, Jack E. *Politics in New Mexico* Albuquerque: University of New Mexico Press, 1967.

Horgan, Paul. *Great River: The Rio Grande in North American History*. New York: Holt, Rinehart and Winston, 1954.

Hunt, Aurora. *Major-General James Henry Carleton, 1814–1873: Western Frontier Dragoon*. Glendale, California: Arthur H. Clarke, 1958.

Hutchinson, C. Alan. *Frontier Settlement in Mexican California: The Híjar-Padres Colony and Its Origins, 1769–1835*. New Haven: Yale University Press, 1969.

Hutchinson, W. H. *California: Two Centuries of Man, Land, and Growth in the Golden State*. Palo Alto: American West Publishing Co., 1969.

Jackson, Joseph Henry. *Anybody's Gold: The Story of California's Mining Towns*. New York: D. Appleton-Century Co., 1941.

———. *Bad Company: The Story of California's Legendary and Actual Stage-Robbers, Bandits, Highwaymen and Others. . . .* First published, 1939. New York: Harcourt, Brace and Co., 1949.

Jacobs, Paul, and Saul Landau, with Eve Pell. *To Serve the Devil*. Vol. 1, *Natives and Slaves*. New York: Random House, 1971.

Jacoby, Erich H. *Man and Land*. London: Andre Deutch, 1971.

Johnson, Chalmers. *Revolutionary Change*. Boston: Little, Brown and Co., 1966.

Jones, Oakah L., Jr. *Los Paisanos: Spanish Settlers on the Northern Frontier of New Spain*. Norman: University of Oklahoma Press, 1979.

———. *Pueblo Warriors and Spanish Conquest*. Norman: University of Oklahoma Press, 1966.

Keleher, William A. *The Fabulous Frontier: Twelve New Mexico Items*. Rev. ed. Albuquerque: University of New Mexico Press, 1962.

———. *Maxwell Land Grant: A New Mexico Item*. Santa Fe: Rydal Press, 1942.

———. *Violence in Lincoln County, 1869–1881*. Albuquerque: University of New Mexico Press, 1952.

Kenner, Charles A. *A History of New Mexican–Plains Indian Relations*. Norman: University of Oklahoma Press, 1969.

Kilgore, D. E. *A Ranger Legacy: 150 Years of Service to Texas*. Foreword by Colonel Wilson E. Spier. Austin: Madrona Press, 1973.

La Farge, Oliver. *Santa Fe: The Autobiography of a Town*. Norman: University of Oklahoma Press, 1959.

Lamar, Howard R. *The Far Southwest, 1846–1912: A Territorial History.* New Haven: Yale University Press, 1966.

Larson, Robert W. *New Mexico Populism: A Study of Radical Protest in a Western Territory.* Boulder: Colorado Associated University Press, 1974.

———. *New Mexico's Quest for Statehood.* Albuquerque: University of New Mexico Press, 1968.

Lavender, David. *Bent's Fort.* Garden City, New York: Doubleday and Co., 1954.

Leiden, Carl, and Karl M. Schmitt. *The Politics of Violence: Revolution in the Modern World.* Englewood Cliffs, New Jersey: Prentice-Hall, Inc., 1968.

Leonard, Olen C. *The Role of the Land Grant in the Social Organization and Social Processes of a Spanish-American Village in New Mexico.* Albuquerque: Calvin Horn Publishing Co., 1970.

Lindheim, Milton. *The Republic of the Rio Grande: Texans in Mexico, 1839–40.* Waco: W. M. Morrison, 1964.

Loomis, Noel M. *The Texas–Santa Fe Pioneers.* Norman: University of Oklahoma Press, 1958.

Lowrie, Samuel H. *Culture Conflict in Texas, 1821–1835.* New York: Columbia University Press, 1932.

McWilliams, Carey. *North from Mexico: The Spanish-Speaking People of the United States.* First published, 1948. New York: Greenwood Press, 1968.

Madsen, William. *The Mexican-Americans of South Texas.* New York: Holt, Rinehart and Winston, 1964.

Mead, Margaret, ed. *Cultural Patterns and Technical Change.* New York: New American Library, 1955.

Meier, Matt S., and Feliciano Rivera. *The Chicanos: A History of Mexican Americans.* New York: Hill and Wang, 1972.

Meinig, D. W. *Imperial Texas: An Interpretive Essay in Cultural Geography.* Austin: University of Texas Press, 1969.

———. *Southwest: Three People in Geographical Change, 1600–1970.* New York: Oxford University Press, 1971.

Merk, Frederick. *Manifest Destiny and Mission in American History.* New York: Vintage Books, 1963.

Moorhead, Max L. *The Apache Frontier: Jacobo Ugarte and Spanish-Indian Relations in Northern New Spain, 1769–1791.* Norman: University of Oklahoma Press, 1968.

———. *New Mexico's Royal Road.* Norman: University of Oklahoma Press, 1958.

Moquin, Wayne, and Charles Van Doren, eds. *A Documentary History of the Mexican Americans.* Introduction by Feliciano Rivera. New York: Praeger Publishers, 1971.

Morgan, Dale L. *Jedediah Smith and the Opening of the West.* New York: Bobbs-Merrill Co., 1953.

Murphy, Lawrence R. *Frontier Crusader—William F. M. Arny.* Tucson: University of Arizona Press, 1972.

Nabokov, Peter. *Tijerina and the Courthouse Raid.* Albuquerque: University of New Mexico Press, 1967, 1970.

Nahm, Milton C. *Las Vegas and Uncle Joe*. Norman: University of Oklahoma Press, 1964.

Nance, Joseph Milton. *After San Jacinto: The Texas-Mexican Frontier, 1836–1841*. Austin: University of Texas Press, 1963.

———. *Attack and Counterattack: The Texas-Mexican Frontier, 1842*. Austin: University of Texas Press, 1964.

Nolan, Frederick W. *The Life and Death of John Henry Tunstall: The Letters, Diaries and Adventures of an Itinerant Englishman*. Albuquerque: University of New Mexico Press, 1965.

Novak, Michael. *The Rise of the Unmeltable Ethnics*. New York: Macmillan Publishing Co., 1973.

Oliphant, James Orin. *On the Cattle Ranges of Oregon*. Seattle: University of Washington Press, 1968.

Osgood, Ernest Staples. *The Day of the Cattlemen*. Chicago: University of Chicago Press, 1929.

Palmer, Robert R. *The Age of Democratic Revolution: A Political History of Europe and America, 1760–1800*. 2 vols. Princeton: Princeton University Press, 1959, 1964.

Paredes, Américo. *A Texas-Mexican Cancionero: Folksongs of the Lower Border*. Chicago: University of Illinois Press, 1976.

———. *"With His Pistol In His Hand": A Border Ballad and Its Hero*. Austin: University of Texas Press, 1958.

Parrish, William J. *The Charles Ilfeld Company: A Study of the Rise and Decline of Mercantile Capitalism in New Mexico*. Cambridge: Harvard University Press, 1961.

Paul, Rodman W. *California Gold: The Beginning of Mining in the Far West*. Cambridge: Harvard University Press, 1947.

Pearce, T. M., ed. *New Mexico Place Names*. Albuquerque: University of New Mexico Press, 1965.

Pearson, Jim B. *The Maxwell Land Grant*. Norman: University of Oklahoma Press, 1961.

Perrigo, Lynn I. *The American Southwest: Its Peoples and Cultures*. New York: Holt, Rinehart and Winston, 1971.

Pierson, George W. *The Moving American*. New York: Alfred A. Knopf, 1972.

Pitt, Leonard. *The Decline of the Californios: A Social History of the Spanish-Speaking Californians, 1846–1890*. Berkeley: University of California Press, 1970.

Poggie, John J., Jr. *Between Two Cultures: The Life of an American-Mexican*. Tucson: University of Arizona Press, 1973.

Poldervaart, Arie W. *Black-Robed Justice*. Santa Fe: Historical Society of New Mexico, 1948.

Potter, David M. *People of Plenty: Economic Abundance and the American Character*. Chicago: University of Chicago Press, 1954.

Quaife, Milo M., ed. *The Diary of James K. Polk: During His Presidency, 1845–1849*. Chicago: A. C. McClury and Co., 1910.

Read, Benjamin M. *Illustrated History of New Mexico*. Santa Fe: New Mexican Printing Co., 1912.

Reed, James. *The Border Ballads*. London: Athlone Press, 1973.

Reed, St. Clair Griffen. *A History of the Texas Railroads and of Transportation *Conditions under Spain and Mexico and the Republic and the State*. Houston: St. Clair Publishing Co., 1941.

Rendón, Armando B. *Chicano Manifesto: The History and Aspirations of the Second Largest Minority in America*. New York: Collier Books, 1971.

Rich, Bennet Milton. *The Presidents and Civil Disorder*. Menasha, Wisconsin: George Bantu Publishing Co., 1941.

Richman, Irving Burdine. *California under Spain and Mexico, 1535–1847*. Boston: Houghton Mifflin Co., 1911.

Robbins, Roy M. *Our Landed Heritage: The Public Domain, 1776–1936*. Princeton: Princeton University Press, 1942.

Rudé, George. *The Crowd in History, 1730–1848*. New York: John Wiley and Sons, 1964.

Sánchez, George I. *Forgotten People: A Study of New Mexicans*. Albuquerque: Calvin Horn, 1967.

Sawyer, Eugene T. *The Life and Career of Tiburcio Vásquez*. Oakland, California: Biobooks, 1944.

Schaefer, Jack. *Heroes without Glory: Some Goodmen of the Old West*. Boston: Houghton Mifflin Co., 1965.

Scholes, Frances V. *Church and State in New Mexico, 1610–1650*. Albuquerque: University of New Mexico Press, 1937.

Sellers, Charles G. *James K. Polk, Continentalist, 1843–1846*. Princeton: Princeton University Press, 1966.

Short, James F., Jr., and Marion E. Wolfgang, eds. *Collective Violence*. New York: Aldine and Atherton, 1972.

Simmons, Marc. *Little Lion of the Southwest: A Life of Manuel Antonio Chaves*. Chicago: Swallow Press, 1973.

———. *Spanish Government in New Mexico*. Albuquerque: University of New Mexico Press, 1968.

Singletary, Otis A. *The Mexican War*. Chicago: University of Chicago Press, 1960.

Sonnichsen, C. L. *Ten Texas Feuds*. Albuquerque: University of New Mexico Press, 1951.

———. *Tularosa: The Last Frontier of the West*. New York: Devon-Adair, 1960.

Spradley, James P., and David W. McCurdy. *The Cultural Experience: Ethnography in Complex Society*. Chicago: Science Research Associates, 1972.

Stanley, F. [Stanley Crocciola]. *The Grant That Maxwell Bought*. Denver: World Press, 1952.

———. *The Private War of Ike Stockton*. Denver: World Press, 1959.

Steiner, Stan. *La Raza: The Mexican Americans*. New York: Harper Brothers, 1969.

Steward, Julian H., Charles J. Erasmus, Solomon Miller, and Louis C. Farus, eds. *Contemporary Change in Traditional Societies*. Urbana: University of Illinois Press, 1967.

Stratton, Porter. *The Territorial Press of New Mexico, 1834–1912*. Albuquerque: University of New Mexico Press, 1969.

Swadesh, Frances Leon. *Los Primeros Pobladores: Hispanic Americans of the Ute Frontier*. Notre Dame: University of Notre Dame Press, 1974.

Taylor, Morris F. *O. P. McMains and the Maxwell Land Grant Conflict.* Tucson: University of Arizona Press, 1979.

Thompson, E. P. *The Making of the English Working Class.* New York: Vintage Books, 1963.

Turner, Frederick Jackson. *The Frontier in American History.* Foreword by Ray Allen Billington. New York: Holt, Rinehart & Winston, 1962.

Twitchell, Ralph E. *The Leading Facts of New Mexico History.* 5 vols. Cedar Rapids: Torch Press, 1911–1917.

Ulibarrí, Sabine R. *Tierra Amarilla: Stories of New Mexico.* Translated by Thelma Campbell Nason. Albuquerque: University of New Mexico Press, 1971.

Valentine, Charles A. *Culture and Poverty.* Chicago: University of Chicago Press, 1968.

Vigness, David M. *The Revolutionary Decades, 1810–1836.* Austin: Steck-Vaughn Co., 1965.

Wallace, Anthony F. C. *Culture and Personality.* New York: Random House, 1961.

Ware, Norman J. *The Labor Movement in the United States: 1860–1895.* New York: Appleton and Co., 1929.

Waters, Frank. *To Possess the Land.* Chicago: Sage Books, Swallow Press, 1973.

Waters, L. L. *Steel Trails to Santa Fe.* Lawrence: University of Kansas Press, 1950.

Webb, Walter Prescott. *The Great Plains.* New York: Grosset and Dunlap, 1931. Reprint, Austin: University of Texas Press, 1964.

———. *The Texas Rangers: A Century of Frontier Defense.* Cambridge: Houghton Mifflin Co., 1935. Reprint, Austin: University of Texas Press, 1965.

Weber, David J. *The Taos Trappers: The Fur Trade in the Far Southwest, 1540–1846.* Norman: University of Oklahoma Press, 1971.

———, ed. *Foreigners in Their Native Land: Historical Roots of the Mexican Americans.* Albuquerque: University of New Mexico Press, 1973.

Weibe, Robert H. *The Search for Order, 1877–1920.* New York: Hill and Wang, 1967.

Weigle, Marta. *Brothers of Light, Brothers of Blood: The Penitentes of the Southwest.* Albuquerque: University of New Mexico Press, 1976.

Westphall, Victor. *The Public Domain in New Mexico, 1854–1891.* Albuquerque: University of New Mexico Press, 1965.

———. *Thomas Benton Catron and His Era.* Tucson: University of Arizona Press, 1973.

Wolf, Eric. *Peasants.* Englewood Cliffs, New Jersey: Prentice-Hall, 1966.

———. *Peasant Wars of the Twentieth Century.* New York: Harper and Row, 1969.

Womack, John, Jr. *Zapata and the Mexican Revolution.* New York: Vintage Books, 1968.

### Articles

Alvarez, Rodolfo. "The Psycho-Historical and Socioeconomic Development of the Chicano Community in the U.S." *Social Science Quarterly* 53 (March, 1973), 920–942.

Bloom, Lansing. "New Mexico under Mexican Administration, 1821–1846." *Old Santa Fe* 1 (July, 1913–April, 1914), 3–49, 131–175, 235–287, 347–368; and 2 (July, 1914–April, 1915), 3–56, 119–169, 223–277, 351–380.

Carlson, Alvar Ward. "New Mexico's Sheep Industry, 1850–1900." *New Mexico Historical Review* 44 (January, 1969), 25–49.

Garr, Daniel J. "A Rare and Desolate Land: Population and Race in Hispanic California." *Western Historical Quarterly* 6 (April, 1975), 133–148.

Gerlach, Allen. "Conditions along the Border, 1915: The Plan de San Diego." *New Mexico Historical Review* 43 (July, 1968), 195–212.

Gómez-Q., Juan. "The First Steps: Chicano Labor Conflict and Organizing, 1900–1920." *Aztlán* 3 (Spring, 1972), 13–49.

———. "Plan of San Diego Reviewed." In *Chicano: The Evolution of a People*, edited by Robert A. Calvert, Renato Rosaldo, and G. L. Seligmann, Jr., pp. 123–127. Minneapolis: Winston Press, 1973.

———. "Toward a Perspective on Chicano History." *Aztlán* (Fall, 1971), 1–49.

———, and Luis L. Arroyo. "On the State of Chicano History." *Western Historical Quarterly* 7 (April, 1976), 155–185.

Goodrich, James W. "Revolt at Mora, 1847." *New Mexico Historical Review* 47 (January, 1972), 49–60.

Greenleaf, Richard E. "Land and Water, 1700–1821." *New Mexico Historical Review* 47 (April, 1972), 85–112.

Haley, J. Evetts. "The Comanchero Trade." *Southwestern Historical Quarterly* 38 (January, 1935), 151–203.

Harris, Charles H. III, and Louis R. Sadler. "The Plan of San Diego and the Mexican–United States War Crisis of 1916: A Reexamination." *Hispanic American Historical Review* 53 (August, 1978), 381–408.

Hawgood, John A. "The Pattern of Yankee Infiltration in Mexican Alta California, 1821–1846." *Pacific Historical Review* 27 (February, 1958), 27–37.

Hobsbawm, Eric. "Peasants and Politics." *Peasant Studies Newsletter*, summary by T. J. Byers and C. A. Curwen, 1 (July, 1972), 109–114.

Jenkins, Myra Ellen. "The Baltasar Baca 'Grant': History of an Encroachment." *El Palacio* 68 (Spring, 1961), 47–64.

———. "Spanish Land Grants in the Tewa Area." *New Mexico Historical Review* 47 (April, 1972), 113–134.

Johanson, Sigurd. "The Population of New Mexico: Its Composition and Changes." *New Mexico Agricultural Experiment Station Bulletin*, No. 273 (June, 1940).

———. "The Social Organization of Spanish American Villages." *Southwestern Social Science Quarterly* 33 (March, 1942), 151–159.

Knowlton, Clark S. "The Spanish Americans in New Mexico." *Sociology and Social Research* 45 (July, 1961), 448–454.

Kramer, Paul V. "The Spanish Borderlands of Texas and Tamaulipas." *Texana* 10 (Summer, 1972), 260–272.

Lamar, Howard R. "Land Policy in the Spanish Southwest, 1846–1891: A Study in Contrast." *Journal of Economic History* 22 (December, 1962), 498–523.

Larson, Robert W. "The White Caps of New Mexico: A Study of Ethnic Militancy in the Southwest." *Pacific Historical Review*, 44 (May, 1975), 171–185.

Laumbach, Verna. "Las Vegas before 1850." *New Mexico Historical Review* 8 (October, 1933), 241–264.

León-Portilla, Miguel. "The Norteño Variety of Mexican Culture: An Ethnohistorical Approach." In *Plural Society in the Southwest*, edited by Edward Spicer and Raymond H. Thompson, pp. 77–115. New York: Weatherhead Foundation, 1972.

Limón, José E. "El Primero Congreso Mexicanista de 1911: A Precursor to Contemporary Chicanismo." *Aztlán* 5 (Spring and Fall, 1974), 85–106.

López, Rubén E. "The Legend of Tiburcio Vásquez." *Pacific Historian* 15 (Summer, 1971), 20–30.

McBride, James D. "The *Liga Protectora Latina*: A Mexican-American Benevolent Society in Arizona." *Journal of the West* 14 (October, 1975), 82–90.

McLemore, S. Dale. "The Origins of Mexican-American Subordination in Texas." *Social Science Quarterly* 53 (March, 1973), 656–670.

May, Ernest. "Tiburcio Vásquez." *Historical Society of Southern California Quarterly* 29 (1947), 123–134.

Meyer, Michael C. "The Mexican-German Conspiracy of 1915." *The Americas* 23 (July, 1966), 76–89.

Murphy, Lawrence R. "The Beaubien and Miranda Grant: 1841–1846." *New Mexico Historical Review* 42 (January, 1967), 27–47.

O'Malley, Pat. "Social Bandits, Modern Capitalism and the Traditional Peasantry. A Critique of Hobsbawm." *Journal of Peasant Studies* 6 (July, 1979), 489–501.

Paredes, Américo. "José Mosqueda and the Folklorization of Actual Events." *Aztlán* 4 (Spring, 1973), 1–29.

———. "Texas' Third Man: The Texas Mexican." *Race* 3 (May, 1963), 49–58.

Parrish, William J. "The German Jew and the Commercial Revolution in Territorial New Mexico, 1850–1900." *New Mexico Historical Review* 35 (January, April, 1960), 1–29, 129–150.

Pierson, George W. "The M-Factor in American History." *American Quarterly* 14 (Summer Supplement, 1962), 275–279.

Pitt, Leonard. "The Beginnings of Nativism in California." *Pacific Historical Review* 30 (February, 1961), 23–38.

Rasch, Phillip J. "The Horrell War." *New Mexico Historical Review* 31 (July, 1956), 223–231.

———. "The People of the Territory of New Mexico versus the Santa Fe Ring." *New Mexico Historical Review* 47 (April, 1972), 185–202.

———. "The Tularosa Ditch War." *New Mexico Historical Review* 43 (July, 1969), 229–235.

Romano, Octavio I. "The Anthropology and Sociology of the Mexican Americans: The Distortion of Mexican American History." *El Grito* 2 (Fall, 1968), 13–26.

———. "The Historical and Intellectual Presence of Mexican-Americans." *El Grito* 2 (Winter, 1969), 32–46.

Sandos, James A. "The Plan of San Diego: War and Diplomacy on the Texas Border, 1915–1916." *Arizona and the West* 14 (Spring, 1972), 5–24.

Schlesinger, Andrew Bancroft. "*Las Gorras Blancas, 1889–1891.*" *Journal of Mexican-American History* 1 (Spring, 1971), 87–143.

Scholes, Frances V. "Civil Government and Society in New Mexico in the Seventeenth Century." *New Mexico Historical Review* 10 (April, 1935), 71–111.

Simmons, Marc. "Settlement Patterns and Village Plans in Colonial New Mexico." *Journal of the West* 8 (January, 1968), 7–21.

———. "Spanish Irrigation Practices in New Mexico." *New Mexico Historical Review* 47 (April, 1972), 135–150.

Swadesh, Frances L. "The Alianza Movement in New Mexico." In *The Underside of American History*, Vol. 2. Edited by Thomas R. Frazier, pp. 294–316. New York: Harcourt Brace Jovanovich, 1971.

Taylor, Morris F. "A New Look at an Old Case: The Bent Heirs' Claim in the Maxwell Grant." *New Mexico Historical Review* 43 (July, 1969), 213–228.

———. "The Two Land Grants of Gervacio Nolan." *New Mexico Historical Review* 47 (April, 1972), 151–184.

Tyler, Daniel. "Anglo-American Penetration of the Southwest: The View from New Mexico." *Southwestern Historical Quarterly* 75 (January, 1972), 325–388.

Webster, Michael G. "Juan N. Cortina: *Defensor de la Raza.*" Paper delivered before the Texas State Historical Association, March 6, 1973, Austin, Texas. Copy in author's possession.

### Theses and Dissertations

Cuéllar, Robert A. "A Social and Political History of the Mexican American Population of Texas, 1929–1963." M.A. thesis, North Texas State University, 1969.

Dunbar, Roxanne Amanda. "Land Tenure in Northern New Mexico: An Historical Perspective." Ph.D. dissertation, University of California at Los Angeles, 1974.

Rosenbaum, Robert J. "*Mexicano* versus *Americano*: A Study of Hispanic American Resistance to Anglo-American Control in New Mexico Territory, 1870–1900." Ph.D. dissertation, University of Texas at Austin, 1972.

Sunseri, Alvin. "New Mexico in the Aftermath of the Anglo-American Conquest, 1846–1861." Ph.D. dissertation, Louisiana State University, 1973.

Tijerina, Andrew Anthony. "Tejanos and Texas: The Native Mexicans of Texas, 1820–1850." Ph.D. dissertation, University of Texas at Austin, 1977.

Vigness, David M. "The Lower Rio Grande Valley, 1836–1846." M.A. thesis, University of Texas at Austin, 1948.

———. "The Republic of the Rio Grande: An Example of Separatism in Northern Mexico." Ph.D. dissertation, University of Texas at Austin, 1951.

Zeleny, Carolyn. "Relations between Spanish-Americans and the Anglo-Americans in New Mexico: A Study of Conflict and Accommodation in a Dual-Ethnic Relationship." Ph.D. dissertation, Yale University, 1944.

# Index